Professional Team Sports and the Soft Budget Constraint

NEW HORIZONS IN THE ECONOMICS OF SPORT

Series Editors: Wladimir Andreff, *Department of Economics, University of Paris 1 Panthéon Sorbonne, France* and Marc Lavoie, *Department of Economics, University of Ottawa, Canada*

For decades, the economics of sport was regarded as a hobby for a handful of professional economists who were primarily involved in other areas of research. In recent years, however, the significance of the sports economy as a percentage of GDP has expanded dramatically. This has coincided with an equivalent rise in the volume of economic literature devoted to the study of sport.

This series provides a vehicle for deeper analyses of the demand for sport, cost–benefit analysis of sport, sporting governance, the economics of professional sports and leagues, individual sports, trade in the sporting goods industry, media coverage, sponsoring and numerous related issues. It contributes to the further development of sports economics by welcoming new approaches and highlighting original research in both established and newly emerging sporting activities. The series publishes the best theoretical and empirical work from well-established researchers and academics, as well as from talented newcomers in the field.

Titles in the series include:

Professional Team Sports and the Soft Budget Constraint

Edited by

Rasmus K. Storm

Head of Research, Danish Institute for Sports Studies, Denmark and Adjunct Associate Professor, NTNU Business School, Norwegian University of Science and Technology, Trondheim, Norway

Klaus Nielsen

Professor of Institutional Economics, Birkbeck University of London, UK

Zsolt Havran

Senior Assistant Professor, Corvinus University of Budapest, Hungary

NEW HORIZONS IN THE ECONOMICS OF SPORT

 Edward Elgar
PUBLISHING

Cheltenham, UK • Northampton, MA, USA

Published by
Edward Elgar Publishing Limited
The Lypiatts
15 Lansdown Road
Cheltenham
Glos GL50 2JA
UK

Edward Elgar Publishing, Inc.
William Pratt House
9 Dewey Court
Northampton
Massachusetts 01060
USA

A catalogue record for this book
is available from the British Library

Library of Congress Control Number: 2022941082

This book is available electronically in the **Elgar**online
Economics subject collection
http://dx.doi.org/10.4337/9781800375994

ISBN 978 1 80037 598 7 (cased)
ISBN 978 1 80037 599 4 (eBook)

Printed and bound by CPI Group (UK) Ltd, Croydon, CR0 4YY

In memory of János Kornai (1928–2021)

Contents

Figures

Tables

Contributors

Krisztina András, Associate Professor, Corvinus University of Budapest

Krisztina András is an Associate Professor in the Department of Business Economics at Corvinus Business School. She is the Director of the Sport Business Research Centre at the Corvinus University of Budapest and is responsible for the Sports Economics Master's degree programme at Corvinus University. Her primary research topics are professional sports, sport and competitiveness, and the effects of sport's mega events. She is often interviewed on sport management issues. She was the vice-president of the Guardian of Budapest 2024 Olympic Games and is the vice-president of the Sport Management Committee of the Hungarian Society of Sport Science.

Wladimir Andreff, Professor Emeritus, University of Paris

Wladimir Andreff is Professor Emeritus at the University Paris 1 Panthéon Sorbonne, Honorary President of the International Association of Sports Economists and the European Sports Economics Association, Honorary Member of the European Association for Comparative Economic Studies, former President of the French Economic Association (2007–2008), President of the Scientific Council at the Observatory of the sports economy, French Ministry for Sports. He is a member of 12 editorial boards, he is a reviewer in 30 other economic journals, and he has achieved 44 missions for international bodies (UNDP, UNESCO, UNIDO, ILO, EU programmes, Council of Europe) and foreign governments. His scientific publications cover international economics, economics of transition, and sports economics (400+ papers, 29 books).

Bernt Arne Bertheussen, Professor, School of Business and Economics, UiT, The Arctic University of Norway, Tromsø

Bernt Arne Bertheussen does empirical research in business strategy and firm performance. This includes papers on how the institutional environment influences the attractiveness of industries, such as the European football industry.

Nadine Dermit-Richard, University of Rouen

Nadine Dermit-Richard, PhD, is currently senior lecturer at the University of Normandy, Rouen, France. She undertakes research in managerial economics, financial economics and business economics. Her current main project revolves around questions of football regulation.

Aurélien François, University of Rouen

Aurélien François gained a PhD in Sports Management in 2012 at the University of Burgundy, Dijon, France. He is currently a lecturer at the University of Normandy, Rouen, France. His research topics are focused on CSR in sport, public management specifically for sporting facilities and arenas as well as the professional sports leagues regulations.

Zsolt Havran, Senior Assistant Professor, Corvinus University of Budapest

Zsolt Havran is a Senior Assistant Professor at Corvinus University of Budapest in the Department of Business Economics. His research topic is human resource management in professional sport. His research interests include the transfer market of professional football, the valuation of professional players and football markets of the Central and Eastern European region. He is a member of the Sport Business Research Centre in the Corvinus University of Budapest, the European Association for Sport Management, the Central-Eastern-European Chapter of the Academy of International Business and the Hungarian Society of Sport Science.

Tünde Máté, Assistant Professor, Corvinus University of Budapest

Tünde Máté is an Assistant Professor at Corvinus University of Budapest in the Department of Business Economics. Her research topic is the impacts of international sports programmes and the residents of the host city. She is a member of the Sport Business Research Centre in the Corvinus University of Budapest and the Hungarian Society of Sport Science.

Karolina Nessel, Assistant Professor, Jagiellonian University in Kraków

Karolina Nessel is an Assistant Professor at the Institute of Entrepreneurship of Jagiellonian University in Kraków, Poland. Her research interests include sport economics and management, and her current work is focused on career paths and internationalization processes in the sport industry. She is a member of EASM, WASM and IASE.

Christian Gjersing Nielsen, Senior Academic Researcher, Danish Institute for Sports Studies

Christian Gjersing Nielsen works within the disciplines of sport management and sports economics. He has focused on empirical questions and has studied spectator demand in Danish soccer and Danish team handball. Further, the impact of sport events is among his interests. His most recent work has been published in *Regional Studies*, *European Sport Management Quarterly* and *Journal of Sport Science*.

Klaus Nielsen, Professor, Birkbeck – University of London

Klaus Nielsen is a Professor of Institutional Economics at the Department of Management, Birkbeck, University of London, where he is a member of the Birkbeck Sport Business Centre. He teaches research methods, innovation, business in the European Union and economics of sport. His current research areas include varieties of capitalism, innovation, social capital, elite sports and the economics of sports. He has coordinated several research projects on Danish elite sports, sports participation and economic aspects of sport. His work has been published in several books and in leading journals.

Miklós Rosta, Director and Head of Department, Corvinus University, Budapest

Miklós Rosta received his PhD in Economics in 2012. Currently, he is the head of the Department of Comparative and Institutional Economics and Director of the Center of Central Asia Research at Corvinus University of Budapest. His main research interests include issues connected to institutional economics and public management studies. He serves as editor of the Hungarian Economic Review (Közgazdasági Szemle). His publications have appeared in *Public Choice*, *Administration & Society*, *International Studies of Management & Organization*, and *Economy and Society*, and in 2012 he published a monograph titled *Innovation, Adaptation or Imitation: The New Public Management*. In 2019, he received a Bolyai research grant from the Hungarian Academy of Science.

Harry Arne Solberg, Professor, NTNU Business School, Trondheim

Harry Arne Solberg works at the NTNU Business School, Norwegian University of Science and Technology. He undertakes research in the area of sports economics and sport management. This involves issues related to sport and the media, sporting events and team sport economics among others. He has published a significant number of papers in international journals.

Rasmus K. Storm, Head of Research and Adjunct Associate Professor

Rasmus K. Storm, PhD, is Head of Research at the Danish Institute for Sports Studies (Idan) and he is an Adjunct Associate Professor (20%) at NTNU Business School in Trondheim, Norway. He was among the first scholars to introduce the SBC approach in the area of sports economics and management and has been published in a number of the best international sports science and sport management journals.

Stefan Szymanski, Professor, University of Michigan

Stefan Szymanski is the Stephen J. Galetti Collegiate Professor of Sport Management at the University of Michigan. His research interests include sports management and economics, sport history, culture and society, European sport and the internationalization of sport, international sports federations, and the governance of sport. He has published a significant number of papers and books on these subjects in distinguished journals and serves on several editorial boards. He started researching the economics of professional football in the late 1980s and has since come to spend his time researching the economics and business of sport.

Foreword

Miklós Rosta

János Kornai's concept of the soft budget constraint is now one of the basic concepts of economics. We often meet it in the literature without even mentioning the name of János Kornai, assuming that everyone who is a little familiar with economics knows it. The acceptance of the concept in mainstream economics is indicated by the fact that nearly 100 studies using the concept of soft budget constraint appeared in the columns of *Journal of Economic Literature*, *Journal of Economic Perspective*, *Quarterly Journal of Economics*, and *American Economic Review*.[1] In addition to mainstream economics, the soft budget constraint has been fertilizing a number of other areas as well. More and more people are using it recently in the field of sports economics, too. This volume is a good proof that the concept has already been institutionalized in this field of economics. The profession not only uses the concept of the soft budget constraint; there is also a substantive discourse about it within the research community. This volume is a good example of how the soft budget constraint can be applied in an innovative way in the field of sports economics. We find true Kornaist studies in the volume, since the theory-building based on empirical foundations, so characteristic of Kornai, characterizes several chapters. The authors of this volume use case studies presented in detail and analyzed by qualitative methods, as well as data sets processed using quantitative methods – embedded into scientific debates – to elucidate problems in professional football. The volume constitutes a serious contribution to economic knowledge. It is of interest not only to sports economists, but also to those interested in broader economic topics. The soft budget constraint syndrome, i.e., the phenomenon where an organization can rightly assume that another organization will bail it out if bankruptcy approaches, which influences its behavior, is not only a property of the socialist economy but also of the capitalist economic system, also in industries like professional football. Today, many examples indicate that even in capitalist economic systems there can be an expectation in economic organizations that that different organizations — government organizations, international organizations, banks, investment companies, and so on — would throw a lifebelt at them if they get into trouble. There may be a number of reasons why they may be bailed out, but the result in any case is that incentives are distorted. Organizations in need of bailout respond more strongly to the rescue organization's signals than to market signals. This can also have a serious market-distorting effect on professional football. One of the advantages of this volume is that it illuminates this effect with real cases, analyzing empirical data from different regions using different methodologies.

It is an exemplary initiative of the editors to provide a space for collaboration between Western and Central and Eastern European researchers to analyze the effects of the soft budget constraint syndrome within the framework of a comparative study. No doubt these comparative analyses not only make a theoretical contribution to the field of science, but also have a significant practical impact.

In addition, the studies in this volume provide an opportunity to reflect on the role of specialist policy recommendations and regulation in professional team sports and their effectiveness. They include an analysis of UEFA's Financial Fair Play program which is one means of tightening the soft budget constraint in the case of football clubs. There are several important issues in relation to regulation. It is questionable, of course, whether different regulations lead to the same result among professional football clubs of different countries. It is also an issue at what level it is necessary to intervene to tighten the budget constraint: at club level, at league level, or at the European level. The authors of this volume analyze the interactions between different levels of intervention.

The volume not only strengthens the dialogue between researchers working in different regions of Europe, but also fosters common thinking between different research directions in sports economics. Although most of the authors are committed to the usability of the concept of soft budget constraint in the field of sports economics and provide evidence for this with their studies, Stefan Szymanski's study also presents the views of representatives of the profession who doubt the usability of the concept of the soft budget constraint in the field of sports economics. This is an important and unavoidable scientific debate that contributes to a better understanding of how the soft budget constraint can be applied in this area. This is not the first time that the concept of soft budget constraint has generated a meaningful debate in the scientific community, just think of the famous debate between Kornai and Gomulka about the relationship between soft budget constraint and price system in the case of the socialist system (Gomoulka, 1985; Kornai, 1985).

Outstanding scientific results are created through cooperation between different generations of researchers formulating new innovative ideas by supporting each other, arguing with each other, and pursuing a dialogue. This volume is a result of cooperation between experienced researchers who are already armed with international success and young scholars working together to map the significance of the soft budget constraint and publish new research findings. The studies published in the volume prove that Klaus Nielsen, Rasmus K.

Storm, together with Zsolt Havran, a young Hungarian researcher, are working successfully together on the establishment of a scientific school.

In summary, the volume is a significant contribution to the literature on sports economics and the soft budget constraint, simultaneously proving that the concept of János Kornai, first published in 1979, is still fertile for the scientific community. Through their thought-provoking studies, the authors of this volume contribute to the widening application of the concept of soft budget constraint by researchers and practitioners dealing with sports economics. The studies unquestionably demonstrate that the soft budget syndrome is a useful tool for achieving a deeper analysis of professional competitive sports.

NOTE

1.   See: https://www.kornai-janos.hu/Kalligram4_folyoiratok_pp53-54.pdf.

REFERENCES

Gomulka, S. (1985). Kornai's Soft Budget Constraint and the Shortage Phenomenon: A Criticism and Restatement. *Economics of Planning*, 19(1), 1–11.

Kornai, J. (1985). Gomulka on the Soft Budget Constraint: A Reply. *Economics of Planning,* 19(2), 49–55.

Acknowledgements

The editors of this book hereby send a big thank you to Corvinus University of Budapest which kindly hosted a meeting – and paid for the authors' travel and accommodation – in early 2020 where drafts of the included papers were presented and discussed.

We are grateful to János Kornai, who followed the project from its initial beginning, and who the editors had the pleasure to meet during the Budapest seminar to discuss elements of the project. Kornai was very happy to see his work being applied to sport. Sadly, he passed away before this book was published.

As editors we are honored and happy to have worked with a theoretical framework developed by one of the most distinguished scholars in the profession of economics. Further, it has felt like the biggest recommendation of the project to receive such generous support from the very geographical heart of where the SBC framework has been built. It is our hope that the readers of this book can sense this atmosphere surrounding the project in these chapters, and that we have pushed the framework and its application a bit further ahead.

Obituary, János Kornai (1928–2021)

Klaus Nielsen

The Hungarian economist János Kornai, who has died aged 93, was the most influential economist in Eastern Europe in the last fifty years. His original explanation of the structural failure of the planned economies of the communist bloc countries of Eastern Europe in the 1970s and 1980s became common knowledge among Western economists, contributed to the breakdown of communism and influenced the subsequent transition to market economy.

His most influential work was *Economics of Shortage* (1980). The book provided a systematic analysis of how the command economy worked in practice. Kornai identified chronic shortages as its main characteristic, arguing that this was not a result of planners' errors, wrong prices or lazy and obstructive workers but rather of systemic flaws. Shortages arose from the fact that loss-making state-owned enterprises would never be closed down. They had easy access to government subsidies and always survived in spite of persistent losses. Whereas the behaviour of most companies in Western market economies are constrained by the need to balance revenues and outlays this was not the case in the planned economies. The budget constraint of state-owned enterprises was soft whereas it is most often hard in market economies. The soft budget constraint meant that companies hoarded material and financial resources to make sure that they could fulfil the planned production targets knowing that they would be bailed out anyway in case of deficits. The overall outcome in situations with soft budget constraints is chronic shortages, wasted resources and general inefficiency.

The idea of the soft budget constraint has since inspired generations of economists as a means of explaining a range of important phenomena beyond its original application in command economies. It is relevant whenever an economic unit is deemed too big to fall which creates expectations of bailout and accordingly influences management behaviour. The decision making of big banks and professional football clubs among others can be explained by their soft budget constraint.

In 1986, János Kornai took up a professorship at Harvard University for half of each year while staying in Budapast the other half. He was now able to write more openly and his criticism of communism as a political and economic system was sharpened in publications such as *The Socialist System:*

The Political Economy of Communism (1992). When the communist regimes in Eastern Europe collapsed in 1989, he wrote a short book *Road to a Free Economy*, outlining a clear program for a transition to market economy. He maintained that this should be done gradually, and not through mass privatisation and shock therapy. Much hardship could have been prevented if the post-socialist reformers had paid more attention to his advice.

Born in Budapest, János came from a well-to-do Hungarian-Jewish family. His father, Pal Kornhauser, was a business attorney who provided legal advice to German companies in Hungary. His father was murdered in 1944 in the Auschwitz concentration camp. He also lost a brother in the Holocaust and barely survived the German occupation of Budapest himself. He was conscripted into labour service in 1944, from where he escaped.

After the war, he changed his name from to Kornai. He studied philosophy for two years at Pázmány Péter University in Budapest. He became an enthusiastic supporter of communism and worked almost ten years for a communist newspaper until he became disillusioned with the system and entered academia. Kornai gained his knowledge of economics through self-study and went on to gain a degree equivalent to a PhD elsewhere from the Hungarian Academy of Sciences. His doctoral dissertation 'Overcentralization in Economic Administration' which was full of facts about the flaws of the centrally planned economy received much attention when it was defended to a public audience at the time of the short-lived Hungarian uprising against the Stalinist system in 1956.

As an eloquent and visible supporter of the Hungarian revolution, he suffered from the subsequent repression; he was threatened with imprisonment, expelled from academia, denied a passport and had to take up obscure jobs in industry ministries for the following decade. When the repression softened from the end of the 1960s, he was able to write and publish. During the last two decades of the communist regime, he articulated a highly critical understanding of the planning system under the suspicious eye of the communist party. Through clever self-censorship he was able to keep the secret police at arm's length without compromising his main ideas, and he even influenced attempts to reform the economic system.

A kind, humble and courageous man and a mentor for many younger scholars in Hungary and beyond, he was never awarded the Nobel Prize although he was rumoured to be close and certainly deserved it. This may partly be due to his criticism of general equilibrium theory, the crown jewel of mainstream economic theory, which was systematically articulated in in his book *Anti-Equilibrium* (1971). Unlike most of the profession, his approach to understanding economics was inductive, building theories from observations of real economic problems, rather than the deductive application of the general assumptions of mainstream economics which he did not find suitable in the context of the socialist reality. Kornai introduced a new way of understanding this reality based on real economic problems such as the information asymmetry, bargaining, conventions and routines inherent in the socialist command economy.

In 2002, he left Harvard University and returned to Hungary. He was emeritus professor at both Harvard University and Corvinus University of Budapest. He remained active even in the last years of his life. He continued writing influential papers about transition and reform in his nineties. He was one of Hungary's earliest and most vociferous critics of the regime of Victor Orbán.

He had advised the Chinese government in its early stages of economic reform in the 1980s but became a strong critic of the autocratic regime of Xi Jinping. He regretted his role which he saw as contributing to the creation of a Frankenstein. Influenced by his experience of Nazism and communism at close hand his views were fundamentally shaped by his belief in the primacy of freedom, human rights and democracy above economic growth and material welfare.

Source: Guardian News & Media 2022

1. Introduction: new research pathways in the soft budget constraint approach

Rasmus K. Storm, Klaus Nielsen and Zsolt Havran

WHY A BOOK ON THE SBC APPROACH?

The influence of the soft budget constraint (SBC) approach is significant in the social sciences, in particular economics (Mitchell, 2000). Developed by the late Hungarian economist János Kornai (1986, 1992), the approach has become institutionalized as a powerful tool for examining the problems of socialist and post-socialist economies (Kornai, 2001), especially the phenomenon of shortage (Kornai, 1980a, 1980b). A multitude of phenomena in capitalist societies, such as financial instability (e.g. Maskin & Xu, 2001) and the banking crisis (e.g. Jannik & Theocharis, 2016), have also been studied using the SBC approach.

This book aims to expand on existing research by developing the potential of the application of the SBC approach in the area of sports economics and management. Still relatively few such studies exist, although the body of literature is growing, showing the potential of Kornai's ideas.

PRIOR APPLICATIONS OF THE SBC APPROACH IN SPORTS ECONOMICS AND MANAGEMENT

The first references to Kornai and SBC in the sports economics and management literature appeared around 2005 with Andreff and Storm & Nielsen among the first to introduce and apply the approach more extensively (for a more thorough review, see the chapter by Andreff in this volume). Andreff (2007, 2015) and Storm & Nielsen (2012) outline the theoretical foundation for the application of the SBC approach to professional team sport leagues in Europe, where emotional attachments and prestige can prompt bailouts from sponsors, creditors, and even public authorities, thus distorting the normal capitalist connection between profits and survival.

Andreff (2015) uses the approach to analyze the managerial problems associated with running professional sports clubs facing SBCs. Storm & Nielsen (2015) argue that the approach has also relevance in the American context where a kind of inverse softness exists with support present ex ante instead of ex post, resulting in a kind of inverse softness. Franck (2014) sees the problems of the financially unstable European football[1] business as caused by the prevalence of soft budget constraints and argues that the problems can be solved through the implementation of the UEFA financial fair play (FFP) program, which hardens the budget constraints of the clubs. In line with Franck (2018), Pieper (2017) argues that FFP has already had a positive impact on the professional clubs' financial conditions.

The SBC approach is not endorsed by everybody in the field. For instance, Szymanski (2015) is critical of the relevance of the SBC approach in relation to European professional football and sees no need for hardening of budget constraints as proposed by some of the SBC advocates. Rather, the FFP break-even rule, which is central to the idea of hardening, is seen as a threat to competitive balance and as a means to protect the success of big clubs, thus freezing the existing league hierarchies (Peeters & Szymanski, 2014).

SUBSTANCE AND STRUCTURE OF THE BOOK

This volume is based on the belief that the SBC framework can advance our understanding of crucial aspects of professional team sports. The contributions provide novel insight from empirical studies and theoretical reflections following Kornai's insights. This involves discussion of the potential and weaknesses of the approach in order to push the research frontier forward.

This book aims to develop the approach through theoretical enrichment as well as new empirical evidence. The framework is deployed in new contexts (more nations, more clubs). Further, through the analysis of problems such as financial (mis)management, competitive (im)balance and regulatory issues regarding professional leagues, new evidence will be revealed to the benefit of researchers and managers alike. The chapters in this volume are a testimony to this.

At hand is a comprehensive volume with contributions by established scholars in the field as well as chapters written by young, talented researchers who have taken up the ambition of using the SBC approach on professional team sports. As the field of research is still in its initial stages of development, it is the hope that this book will inspire broader and deeper research in the area.

In the residual part of this chapter, we briefly introduce central aspects of the SBC framework, while in parallel introducing each of the book chapters to put them into the context of the theories' central terms, aspects, and substance. In this way, the reader will be able to follow how the various chapters use and develop the framework while also specifying its application to sport management and economics.

THE SBC FRAMEWORK: THE BASICS

What is a soft budget constraint? In short, the SBC concept describes a situation where an organization, for example a public enterprise or a private company, is bailed out from financial distress or collapse (Kornai, Maskin, & Roland, 2003). Instead of facing a hard budget constraint (HBC) – where '…proceeds from sales and costs of input are a question of live and death …' to the organization (Kornai, 1980b, p. 303) – the bailout instils a softness in the budget constraint of the organization, thus keeping it alive.

According to the original understanding of the term, an HBC is (as is the case with an SBC) an environmental condition exercising a '(…) form of economic coercion (…)' restricting its potential survival when faced with financial difficulties and generally making it obey market competition in all potential dimensions (ibid.).

Originally, Kornai developed the SBC concept in order to understand shortage (Kornai, 1980b, 1980a). He saw the existence of soft budget constraints as a catalyst of inefficiency that prevailed in almost all sectors of society (except the space and the military industry) behind the Iron Curtain (Kornai, 1986). Borrowing the idea of the budget constraint from microeconomic theory, he helped to shed light on the core problems of planned economies.

Kornai outlines five conditions of hardness (Kornai et al., 2003; Maskin, 1999): H1: exogenous prices (where the organization is a price taker of inputs and outputs); H2: hard taxes (where the organization cannot obtain exemptions from tax rules or legislation); H3: hard subsidies (where direct or indirect public subsidies are not provided for the organization); H4: no credit (where no credit from other organizations – for example other firms or banks – can be obtained to help the organization); and H5: no external investment (for running the organization (except for its foundation)). Storm & Nielsen (2015) add another condition of hardness – H6: no soft accounting practices – where no 'creative' accounting can be applied to help the distressed organization from collapsing.

If all six H-conditions of hardness prevail, an ideal-type situation of 'perfect' hardness exercises a strict coercion on behavior. This situation is seldom found in practice but establishes a theoretical (bi)pole of analytical understanding. In contrast, 'perfect softness' can be said to characterize a situation where efficiency and sound financial operations are not a matter of 'life and death' (Kornai, 1980b, p. 308) of the organization, where the growth of the organization has no link to its financial performance, or when the firm keeps surviving '(…) even when investment entails grave losses (…)' (Kornai,

1979, p. 807). This would usually be the case if all conditions of hardness are softened to various degrees but often only one or a few of the H-conditions of hardness needs to be softened to secure the survival of a given organization in spite of losses.

According to the SBC theory, hardening the budget constraints of organizations is important because, under conditions of softness, ex ante expectations of ex post rescue in case of financial distress develop within organizations. One of Kornai's (2014) main observations was that when ex ante expectations of ex post support are institutionalized in organizations – i.e. when they face soft environmental conditions – managerial inefficiency becomes the order of the day. In this situation, management staff focus on pleasing the (vertical) supporter organization that is assisting the organization financially instead of optimizing production procedures, sales, or management processes that are critical for survival and profit-making under HBCs (Kornai, 1986; Maskin, 1999). The soft budget constraint facing an organization has impacts on behavioral patterns of the organization, and if such conditions prevail, widespread hoarding of resources (in football, mainly players), overspending, and inefficient use of such resources develop.

In short, if the creative destruction of capitalist societies (whose firms (normally) are facing relatively hard budget constraints) is prevented by successive bailouts or supporting initiatives, shortages start to develop because little holds companies back from hoarding resources, and negotiation and bargaining takes precedence over market incentives and efficient allocation of resources (Kornai, 1992). In sum, perpetually failing organizations survive despite their substantial and successive losses, resulting in a significant overall loss to societal prosperity and wealth (Kornai, 2006).

THE CHALLENGE OF SBC: INTRODUCING CHAPTERS 2–3

In European professional football there is much evidence of SBCs with many instances of persistent financial problems but also rescues, bailouts, and a high survival rate among the clubs (Storm & Nielsen, 2015). In the book's two first chapters, these characteristics are identified and dealt with in order to give a better understanding of their characteristics and to reflect on what can be done to deal with the problems.

One of the answers to the problem of overspending and financial mismanagement is regulation. Several ideas have sufficed with UEFA's Financial Fair Play program (FFP) as the most prominent and recent one. In Chapter 2 ('Soft Budget Constraints and Institutional Logics in European Football'), the authors take this idea further by suggesting an organization that is external to the football business itself and modeled after the World Anti-Doping Agency.

Their suggestion is based on a thorough examination of European professional football using not only the SBC approach but combining it with institutional theory. They argue that two long-lasting paradoxical financial practices in European football are much better understood this way. One of these practices is the tendency of clubs to continue to overspend even when revenues are increasing. The other practice is that clubs rarely go bankrupt despite experiencing ongoing deficits.

The authors argue that two often competing but sometimes complementary institutional logics are underpinning the soft overspending and bailout practices: a dominant sporting logic and a weaker economic logic. Consequently, the two intertwined SBC practices constitute a self-destructive financial logic of European football. The vicious circle continues because clubs and leagues operate in ways that are individually rational, but collectively irrational. Finally, the authors discuss reasons why clubs have been allowed to operate under SBCs and also comment on challenges that can make it difficult to establish an efficient regulation system that can harden the budget constraints in European football.

The difficulties of hardening budget constraints are also the centre of attention in Chapter 3 ('Hardening the Soft Budget Constraint in Professional Team Sports: Why Is It So Hard?'). Digging deeper into the theoretical literature on SBCs, Wladimir Andreff detects that its determinants have been analyzed as being macroeconomic (nationwide in socialist and transition economies), then microeconomic (softness of a firm's budget), and finally meso-economic (at industry level such as the banking business). It is argued that hardening SBCs implies measures taken at macro-national, meso-industrial, and micro-entrepreneurial levels.

The contribution explores in forensic detail how the SBC in professional team sports could be hardened, and why it is so difficult to implement this in practice. At the club level, the measures include handling fans' pressures, tight financial management, transparent accounting (no slush funds, bungs, etc.), and improving the quality of club governance. At the meso level, i.e. the league, measures to harden the SBC pertain to a tight enforcement of league rules – in particular, regarding bailing out benefactors, clubs' external auditing, financial supervision by the league, including at the international (ex: UEFA FFP) level, and a change in the league's bargaining TV rights revenues and their redistribution. At the macro level the following is at stake: lax finance (subsidies, tax exemptions) by regional and national governments and financial institutions, tax arrears, social contribution arrears, mutual payment arrears, de facto exemption of sports clubs from bankruptcy law enforcement, and the enforcement of the (international) EU competition (anti-trust) law. The chapter concludes by suggesting some practical recipes and recommended policy measures for hardening the budget constraint.

VARIATION AND DYNAMICS OF BUDGET CONSTRAINTS IN EUROPEAN FOOTBALL: INTRODUCING CHAPTERS 4–6

While there is evidence pointing to the existence of SBCs in European professional football, there are also variations to how soft – or how hard – the environmental conditions are formed in the European leagues and even within each of the leagues.

Looked at from the point of view of the H-conditions of hardness, one might talk about a continuum ranging from (perfect) hard, over almost hard to soft, and extremely soft, depending on the context the club in question faces. Along this continuum, more and more of the H-conditions of hardness are softened. However, it is not clear from the SBC literature how one is to operationalize this continuum more specifically besides it being a theoretical heuristic tool to understand specific cases. The variations and different dynamics regarding the institutionalization of SBCs is the theme of Chapters 4–6, all of which consider the dynamics of budget constraints in order to understand how they differ within leagues or across different nations.

Chapter 4 ('Budget Constraints in French Professional Football: Contrasting Situations') addresses the question related to French football. It aims to develop an empirically based typology for different degrees of softness – taking into consideration the specific context of professional team sports with the dual objectives of the organizations, i.e. sporting as well as financial performance. The authors hypothesize that the character of budget constraints imposed on clubs is not uniform and that in French professional football, although some clubs operate within an SBC, others are subject to a much harder budget constraint. While much of the previous research has analyzed the leagues as a whole, this chapter broadens the perspective and analyzes the French professional football league at the level of each of the participating clubs, with the aim of identifying different levels of budget constraints. It shows that only a few large clubs, owned by moguls with a patron's behavior, evolve within the framework of the SBC. These are the big European deficit-generating clubs often cited as examples in the literature on this issue. However, it also demonstrates that a lot of the clubs face harder forms of budget constraints. The contribution thus adds to existing research by nuancing the approach and the understanding of the dynamics and existence of budget constraints in professional team sports clubs.

Much of the existing research on SBC in European football has – paradoxically as it may seem – examined Western European leagues even though the theory originally was developed to understand a phenomenon institutionalized in Eastern European nations. In Chapter 5 ('Heterogeneity of Budget

Constraints in Hungarian and Polish Football'), the authors dig deeper into two Eastern European nations to look at how budget constraints manifest themselves in those contexts. The authors argue that 30 years after the change of political and economic regimes in Hungary and Poland, the transition of the sport systems in both countries is not yet complete. The sport organizations, despite their growing commercialization and professionalization, are still, to a varying degree dependent on ad hoc state aid. Similar to the situation in Western European football, the expectations of managers that their organizations will get rescued ex post by an external agent in case of a financial distress impact their decisions and behaviors ex ante and lead to the SBC syndrome.

More specifically, the SBC phenomenon starts as a mental issue, and the softness of the budget limit may be estimated by the probability of rescue as perceived by managers. The chapter undertakes an empirical evaluation of the heterogeneity of the budget softness perceived by top managers of football clubs in Hungary and Poland. A survey is conducted among football clubs of the top two divisions in both countries, and its results are analyzed with segmentation and profiling techniques. In general, the clubs evaluate the probability of their bankruptcy in a case of sudden and serious financial problems as low, and among external rescue options, most hope is placed in the owner.

Chapter 6 ('The Soft Budget Constraint Syndrome in Hungarian Professional Football from a Central and Eastern European Perspective') also aims to expand the research on SBC in professional football through an analysis of the characteristics of the operation of professional football in Central and Eastern Europe (CEE). To reveal the specificities of CEE football, the chapter is based on a thorough analysis of sporting and financial performance, revenue, spectators, and social media interest in nine nations (Bulgaria, Croatia, Czech Republic, Hungary, Poland, Romania, Serbia, Slovakia, and Slovenia) revealing significant differences in the structure and role of public funding. The analysis shows that Hungarian football provides a striking example, being characterized by the combination of huge financial contributions and minimal sporting success. The special features of Hungarian football are outlined in order to understand how SBC obstructs the development of football.

IS THE SBC FRAMEWORK NEEDED? AND ARE THERE LIMITS TO SOFTNESS?: INTRODUCING CHAPTERS 7–8

Connected to the question of variations in the softness (and hardness) of budget constraints – examined in the chapters introduced above – are the equally important questions of, first, whether there are fundamental flaws to the theoretical approach that misinterpret the situation and give a misleading understanding of how professional team sports function, and, second, whether there are limits to how much the environment can soften the budget constraint of professional team sports clubs. In other words, are there limit(ation)s to the application of the framework in the context of professional team sports, and what are the limits to softness in professional team sports clubs. Whereas the first question questions the usefulness of the approach, the second question is about further development of the SBC framework.

The first question is considered in Chapter 7 ('Is there Evidence of Softness in the Budget Constraint in Football? Some Evidence from English Clubs'). In this chapter the author argues that there is not enough evidence to show the relevance of the theory. In other words, even though it is recognized that the SBC theory offers interesting insights into the mechanisms and problems of socialist and post-socialist economies, it is argued that it has not much to offer sports economics and management research.

The chapter assumes that it follows from the SBC theory that even if the club fails, the employees of the clubs will retain their jobs. If this is not the case, club failure does not have the behavioral consequences assumed in the SBC theory. It is argued that an empirical test is needed to test whether evidence of SBCs in European football can be found. Using data from English football on member-ship of the boards of directors and the club manager (head coach), the author shows that there is in fact a high probability of dismissal (higher for directors than for managers), which seems to undermine the theory. Instead, he suggests another approach not based on a failure of governance but on the riskiness inher-ent in the system of promotion and relegation. In the chapter, this theory is tested against the data and is shown to fit. Based on this, the challenge to advocates of the soft budget constraint theory is to develop convincing empirical tests to confirm the SBC hypothesis. It is argued that, for the moment, the soft budget constraint theory is seen as no more than an untested assertion.

Regarding the second question, it can – from a theoretical point of view – be hypothesized that there is a potential limit to how much environmental supporter organizations can assist a given organization. In the case of repeated financial problems faced by – say – a football club, the question is for how long supporter-organizations will be willing to – or are capable of – pouring money in or softening other dimensions of the budget constraint. Kornai argues that because of sunk costs associated with the dynamic commitment problem, it is likely that new rescue operations can be repeated for a long time. Especially in a command economy, the state is a powerful supporter with significant resources at hand and with the power to exercise control over many of the H-conditions of hardness. For example, by softening taxation rules and practices and provision of soft loans and subsidies, state authorities can support troubled organizations for a very long time. However, in capitalist economies, supporter organizations include private creditors, and, in the case of professional football, sponsors or fan trusts with limited resources and with limited or no control over conditions such as taxation or pricing.

The final Chapter 8 ('Limits of Softness in Professional Team Sport Clubs') aims to understand these limits. Following an overview of bailouts in European professional football, the authors investigate the limits to the 'too big to fail' phenomenon that characterizes many of the rescue mechanisms present among the big European team sports clubs by means of two case studies: the financial collapse of Glasgow Rangers (no explanation necessary) and Gudme Oure Gudbjerg (GOG) – a very successful Danish team handball club – respectively.

The authors show how clubs may experience the boundaries of environmental softness – even though the same clubs have experienced significant environmental softness prior to the collapse. The chapter examines whether there are potential institutional settings where the probability of rescue is significantly lower than what would usually be expected, considering the importance and significance of the clubs to the local community and larger fan base. The case studies show how structural external shocks but also accumulated debt, combined with soft accounting and other forms of prior softness, in the end hardened the environmental conditions for the clubs examined. It is concluded that it is often tax liabilities that trigger insolvency proceedings, and the tax authorities often decline an agreement to write off debt in the few cases where clubs are liquidated. Pressure from fans/supporters/local communities often contributes to pushing a club into bankruptcy. New owners may come to the rescue. However, overspending – sometimes fueled by fraudulent behavior – and collapse of the owners' other businesses may push the clubs over the edge.

Chapter 8 addresses the issues raised in the preceding chapter by outlining how softness influences decision making even against the self-interests of managers. It also qualifies the situations in which the theory applies by specifying the limits to SBC in capitalist economies.

By ending the volume with significant criticism of the relevance of the SBC framework when applied to sport management and economics, followed by an attempt to further develop the theory by addressing an issue that has not previously been much analyzed, we have outlined some of the future research pathways in the soft budget constraint approach. It is the editors' hope that, in the future, more researchers will aim to apply the approach to new contexts as well as further deepening the theoretical strengths of the approach in a dialogue with the critics of the approach. Continuous discussion about relevance, correctness, and validity is essential to push the research frontier ahead. We hereby invite interested scholars to take part in this endeavor.

NOTES

1.   In this book, which mainly deals with European professional football, we use 'soccer' and 'football' as similar terms.

REFERENCES

Andreff, W. (2007). French Football: A Financial Crisis Rooted in Weak Governance. *Journal of Sports Economics, 8*(6), 652–661.
Andreff, W. (2015). Governance of Professional Team Sport Clubs: Agency Problem and Soft Budget Constraint. In W. Andreff (Ed.), *Disequilibrium Sport Economics: Competitive Imbalance and Budget Constraints* (pp. 175–223). Cheltenham, UK and Northampton, MA: Edward Elgar.
Franck, E. (2014). Financial Fair Play in Europen Club Football: What Is It All About? *International Journal of Sport Finance, 9*(3), 193–217. https://doi.org/10.2139/ssrn .2284615].
Franck, E. (2018). European Club Football after 'Five Treatments' with Financial Fair Play – Time For An Assessment. *International Journal of Financial Studies, 6*(97). https://doi.org/10.3390/ijfs6040097.
Jannik, J., & Theocharis, G. (2016). *Soft Budget Constraints, European Central Banking and the Financial Crisis.* Discussion Papers 2016/7, Free University Berlin, School of Business & Economics. Retrieved from https://www.econstor.eu/ bitstream/10419/130763/1/857758543.pdf.
Kornai, J. (1979). Resource-Constrained versus Demand-Constrained Systems. *Econometrica, 47*(4), 801–819.
Kornai, J. (1980a). *Economics of Shortage: Volume A.* Amsterdam: North-Holland Publishing Company.
Kornai, J. (1980b). *Economics of Shortage: Volume B.* Amsterdam: North-Holland Publishing Company.
Kornai, J. (1986). The Soft Budget Constraint. *Kyklos, 39,* 3–30.
Kornai, J. (1992). *The Socialist System.* Oxford: Oxford University Press.
Kornai, J. (2001). Hardening the Budget Constraint: The Experience of the Post-socialist Countries. *European Economic Review, 45*(9), 1573–1599. https://doi.org/10.1016/ S0014-2921(01)00100-3.
Kornai, J. (2006). *By Force of Thought: Irregular Memoirs of an Intellectual Journey.* Cambridge, MA: The MIT Press.
Kornai, J. (2014). The Soft Budget Constraint: An Introductory Study to Volume IV of the Life's Work Series. *Acta Oeconomica, 64*(S1), 25–79. https://doi.org/10.1111/j .1467-6435.1986.tb01252.x.
Kornai, J., Maskin, E., & Roland, G. (2003). Understanding the Soft Budget Constraint. *Journal of Economic Literature, 41*(4), 1095–1136. https://doi.org/10.1257/ 002205103771799999.
Maskin, E. S. (1999). Recent Theoretical Work on the Soft Budget Constraint. *American Economic Review, 89*(2), 421–425. https://doi.org/10.1257/aer.89.2.421.
Maskin, E. S., & Xu, C. (2001). Soft Budget Constraint Theories: From Centralization to the Market. *Economics of Transition, 9*(1), 1–27. https://doi.org/10.1111/1468 -0351.00065.

Mitchell, J. (2000). Theories of Soft Budget Constraints and the Analysis of Banking Crises. *Economics of Transition*, *8*(1), 59–100. https://doi.org/10.1111/1468-0351 .00036.

Peeters, T., & Szymanski, S. (2014). Financial Fair Play in European Football. *Economic Policy*, *29*(78), 343–390. https://doi.org/10.1111/1468-0327.12031.

Pieper, J. (2017). Financial Fair Play in European Football. In U. Wagner, R. K. Storm, & K. Nielsen (Eds.), *When Sport Meets Business: Capabilities, Challenges, Critiques* (pp. 167–185). London: Sage Publications.

Storm, R. K., & Nielsen, K. (2012). Soft Budget Constraints in Professional Football. *European Sport Management Quarterly*, *12*(2), 183–201. https://doi.org/10.1080/ 16184742.2012.670660.

Storm, R. K., & Nielsen, K. (2015). Soft Budget Constraints in European and US Leagues – Similarities and Differences. In W. Andreff (Ed.), *Disequilibrium Sport Economics: Competitive Imbalance and Budget Constraints* (pp. 151–171). Cheltenham, UK: Edward Elgar. https://doi.org/10.4337/9781783479368.00012.

Szymanski, S. (2015). *Money and Soccer: A Soccernomics Guide*. New York: Nation Books.

2. Soft budget constraints and institutional logics in European football

Bernt Arne Bertheussen and Harry Arne Solberg[1]

INTRODUCTION

The financial problems in European club football have received substantial attention in the literature (Barajas & Rodríguez, 2010, Beech et al., 2010, Haugen & Solberg, 2010, Lago et al., 2006, Scelles et al., 2016, Storm, 2012). However, some improvements have been registered in recent years, and particularly in the top earning leagues (England, Germany, and Spain) (Deloitte, 2018, UEFA, 2017). One reason for the improvements is the financial regulations that have been implemented. In 2011, UEFA introduced Financial Fair Play (FFP) regulations to curb clubs' spending and help clubs compete under the most comparable financial conditions. The purpose was not only to reduce overspending and make the clubs' finances more sustainable, but also to contribute to fairer financial conditions in the sports competition arena (UEFA, 2012). Additionally, several domestic leagues have implemented clubs licensing systems that are based on criteria similar to the FFP regulations. For more details, see for example Kaplan (2015).

Another reason for the improvements has been the strong growth in media revenues, which particularly have benefited the elite league in England, France, Germany, Italy, and Spain, known as the Big Five (UEFA, 2017). This has not been the case in smaller leagues, where clubs earned practically the same in 2017 as five years earlier.

Despite the improvements, the problems are not over, according to UEFA's Benchmark studies. In 2017, 39% of the elite clubs in the top 20 leagues reported financial losses. The French Ligue 1 and the Italian Serie A had negative aggregate operating results every year in the period from 2007/8 to 2016/17. The annual average deficit per club was, respectively, €3.7 million and €5.2 million. Note that the operating result excludes player trading and certain exceptional items. Outside the top 20 leagues, 51% of the clubs reported losses. According to Szymanski (2012), the problems have been more common in smaller leagues than in the big leagues. This involves both elite leagues in the small and medium-size football nations, as well as second-tier leagues in the Big Five. The clubs in the English Championship (second tier) had aggregate financial losses every year in the period from 2007/8 to 2016/17 (Deloitte, 2018). Despite the financial problems, European clubs rarely go bankrupt (Szymanski, 2012, Kuper & Szymanski, 2009). Compared with other commercial industries, surprisingly many football clubs survived with financial stress for a long period (ibid.).

This chapter analyses why the apparently unsustainable soft budgeting practices have become the 'financial rules' of the European football game. Why have the clubs been allowed to operate in such an 'unhealthy' financial manner, i.e., under soft budget constraints (SBCs)? Further, since many football governing bodies have implemented regulations to harden the budget constraints, we also discuss criteria such regulations should be based on to solve the problems.

Most of the previous analyses have focused on the behaviour of clubs, but to a lesser degree on the environment in which the clubs operate. Therefore, this chapter will focus particularly on the institutional environment in which the clubs operate. Accordingly, it provides increased insight into forces underpinning institutionalised SBC practices that can threaten the sustainability of hybrid (dual-purpose) organisations. Such firms are driven by a primary logic related to their main purpose, such as winning football matches, and a secondary logic linked to the funding of these activities (Gammelsæter, 2010). Budgeting practices of hybrid organisations present particular challenges when financial constraints hinder them from achieving their primary objective (Carlsson-Wall, 2016). The limits of sound budgeting practices can then be stretched; in a worst-case scenario, this can threaten the existence of a hybrid organisation (Morrow, 2014).

The next section presents a literature review. The following section explains the legitimacy and sustainability of the seemingly paradoxical budgeting practices in European football by combining SBC theory and institutional theory. It argues that institutional theory represents an innovative contribution to research on SBC theory. In a subsequent section, the paradoxical soft budgeting practices in European club football are described using empirical data. The final sections discuss and conclude the study.

LITERATURE REVIEW: WHY THE PROBLEMS HAVE APPEARED AND CONTINUED

Profit- Versus Win-Maximizing Football Clubs

According to Terrien & Andreff (2019), the literature identifies three objectives of professional sports teams:

1. Profit maximising under sporting constraint
2. Win maximisation under hard budget constraint, and
3. Win maximisation under soft budget constraint.

The main strategic option is between profit and win maximisation. Clubs operating in a win-maximising regime will spend more on talents compared with those in a profit-maximising regime. Furthermore, redistribution of revenues will increase the payroll in a win-maximising regime and reduce the payroll in a profit-maximising regime. Both these arguments will lead to lower profit in the win-maximising case than that in the profit-maximising case. For more details, see for example Sloane (1971), Fort (2000), Dobson & Goddard (2001), and Késenne (2007) for more details. Clubs may alter from win orientation towards profit maximisation from one year to another, and vice versa, according to Terrien et al. (2017). These perspectives, however, do not explain why clubs go beyond the break-even level. Additionally, it is important to have in mind that the nature of the budget constraint also depends on environmental conditions, i.e., the social importance of the team (Storm & Nielsen, 2012), the governance mechanisms within the organisation, the league (Andreff, 2007), or the international federation (Terrien & Andreff, 2019).

After examining insolvency in English professional football, Szymanski (2017) concluded that failure can be identified with idiosyncratic shocks to productivity (the wage–performance relationship) and demand (the performance–revenue relationship). This conclusion is consistent with standard organisation theory models of exiting an industry. A consensus has been agreed upon in sport economics literature that professional teams in North America behave like profit maximisers, while a form of utility maximisation seems to be the objective in European football clubs, where the utility function of club owners includes sporting performance (Fort, 2003, Késenne, 1996, Rottenberg, 1956, Sloane, 1971, 2015). According to Vroman (1997), European club owners are willing to sacrifice some financial return to achieve better sporting results. It would probably be more appropriate, however, to regard these two regimes as polar cases: the behaviour of North American teams is closer to that of profit maximisers, while the behaviour of European clubs is closer to that of win maximisers. However, teams in both continents emphasise both objectives (Gratton & Solberg, 2007).

Haugen & Solberg (2010) showed that clubs operating in a win-maximising regime can end up in prisoners' dilemma situations when trying to pass so-called needle eyes, i.e., by trying to win the league, avoid relegation, acquire promotion, or qualify for financially lucrative tournaments. These forces are strengthened when the prize money increases.

All these analyses assume that clubs maximise sporting performance, given the conditions in which they operate. The key to success is recruiting quality players. Due to the shortage of quality players, the buying clubs often end up in bidding wars orchestrated by agents representing the players or the selling clubs. As a result, many clubs fall into the trap of the winner's curse (Andreff, 2015).

The Soft Budget Constraints Perspective on Clubs' Financial Behaviour

Among the contributions that have used other theoretical perspectives are Andreff (2007), Storm (2012), and Storm & Nielsen (2012) who argued that European clubs operate in a regime with soft budgets. Their ideas were inspired by the Hungarian economist János Kornai (1986). He analysed why companies in the old socialist economies could chronically operate on the edge of insolvency without being forced out of business. The clubs are considered too important to fail; therefore, they receive 'free money' from an owner or creditor, also named sugar daddies, with a negative risk premium or a benefactor to stay liquid and in business (Storm, 2012, Storm & Nielsen, 2012). When clubs find themselves in financial difficulties, they often obtain the necessary additional funding. This can be subsidies from benefactors in the form of equity, loans, or gifts. On the revenue side, flexible pricing of, for example, sponsorship contracts can make budgeting constraints softer. Moreover, internal pricing under actual costs, for example related to stadium rent, can be used to make the cost budgets more flexible. The soft budgeting practice, which is widespread in the European football club, undermines one of the most basic financial coercive drivers for a firm in a market economy, which is the bankruptcy institute. This encourages clubs to take excess risks (Dietl & Franck, 2007).

Such perspectives, however, do not fully explain why football clubs operate in conflict with 'financial recommendations'. Human nature tends to observe the practices of others when making decisions (DiMaggio & Powell, 1983). In some instances, clubs feel coerced to adopt the same budgeting strategies as their competitors though these strategies may cause problems. The many cases where clubs have been saved from bankruptcy in the very last hour may have increased their willingness to take risks. If many clubs are successful with such a strategy, those who choose differently may have to pay the price by losing matches and experiencing reductions in revenues. This mechanism can make it difficult to uphold healthy budgeting practices. In such cases, institutional theory can contribute to a more comprehensive understanding of the forces at work.

THE INSTITUTIONAL THEORY PERSPECTIVE ON CLUBS' BUDGETING BEHAVIOUR

The institutional theory provides a lens through which we can investigate forces that support legitimacy of organisational practices (DiMaggio & Powell, 1983). This includes forces embedded within culture, social settings, regulations, tradition, and history, in addition to economic incentives. Simultaneously, firm resources are important (Thornton et al., 2012). Legitimacy refers to the adoption of (e.g., budgeting) practices considered to be appropriate by key stakeholders (DiMaggio & Powell, 1983). These include club fans, sponsors, media, and owners. The basic idea of institutional theories is that organisations operate under social bindings that greatly affect their actions and social structures (Thornton et al., 2012). Instead of making decisions based on economic rationality, organisations engage in behaviours aimed at maximising their legitimacy.

Institutional theories further argue that organisations within a field become increasingly alike by adopting similar (e.g., budgeting) practices, structures, and rhetoric over time (DiMaggio & Powell, 1983). Thornton et al. (2012) defined an institution as a culture-specific practice that includes norms, cognition, recipes, and meaning systems that guide human behaviour. According to them, an organisational field is a group of organisations that constitute a recognised area in the institutional life at an aggregate level. This study explores the role of institutional logics and isomorphic drivers to understand seemingly identical budgeting practices across European football leagues.

Institutional Logics Driving Football Clubs' Budgeting Behaviour

The term institutional logic was first introduced by Alford and Friedland (1985) to describe contradictory practices and convictions built into modern Western social institutions. A central assumption is that appropriate behaviour within the individual logics is governed by norms that guide the actions of the actors (Selznick, 1957). Thornton & Ocasio (1999: 804) defined institutional logic as 'the socially constructed and historical patterns of material practices, assumptions, values, beliefs, and rules by which individuals produce and reproduce their material subsistence, organize time and space, and provide meaning to their social reality'.

A collective identity can be developed among members of a social group based on their perception of having something in common internally within the group. The identity comprises cognitive, normative, and emotional contracts among the actors. When collective identities become institutionalised, a distinctive institutional logic develops: 'Institutional logics are the organizing principles that shape the behaviour of field participants' (Reay & Hinings, 2009: 631). A key assumption is that appropriate behaviour in a given institution complies with norms that prescribe the manner in which the institution's actors should act (Selznick, 1957). Over time, institutional logics will be developed and reinforced due to formal structures and normative constructions being reflected in each other. Such a logic constitutes an important theoretical structure because this logic can explain a sense of 'common purpose and unity' within an organisational field. Accordingly, different organisational fields are characterised by their own dominant institutional logic even if two or more logics simultaneously exist within a given field (Scott, 2008, Thornton & Ocasio, 1999).

The theoretical term of institutional logic has gained new relevance in connection with the study on hybrid organisations. Hybridisation can be described as a process in which separate organisational types or principles (e.g., a sport organisation and a commercial organisation) are mixed or merged into a new organisational type, i.e., a hybrid (Johansen et al., 2015). New reforms, such as the increased commercialisation of modern football, will typically bring new values that will affect practices and normative belief systems. This can lay the foundation for the development of parallel institutional logics within the same hybrid football organisation. Research has indicated that neither minor nor major changes in institutional settings lead to 'old' logics being replaced by 'new' logics. Instead, the logics live side by side, partly competitive and partly complementary.

This study argues that a hybrid top football club is primarily run by two sorts of logics: a sporting logic and a financial logic. As European football clubs are win-maximisers (Sloane, 1971, 2015), the sporting logic is dominant within this organisational field. However, in line with increased commercialisation, the activities of top football clubs across Europe are increasingly influenced by a financial logic (Gammelsæter, 2010). Basically, the financial logic of a football club is like that of any other firm in a market-based economy. Producers operating in a profit-maximising regime have to manage its finances according to hard budget constraints (Storm & Nielsen, 2012). If an economic rational owner is unhappy with the return on her investment, she will sell her stake and reinvest the money in other assets with a better expected return on risk. The many accounts with red figures (losses) illustrate that this has not been the case in European football. Many owners have not left the sinking ships.

Isomorphic Pressure on Football Clubs to Adapt the Same Budgeting Practices

DiMaggio & Powell (1983) claimed that organisations compete for resources (e.g., player talents) and customers (e.g., fans, sponsors, and wealthy owners). In addition, they compete for political power and institutional legitimacy. In these processes, three forces drive organisations into isomorphic directions and force them to become increasingly more similar in terms of organisational strategies, structures and practices. These forces are coercive, normative, and mimetic pressures.

Coercive pressure originates from laws (e.g., bankruptcy laws and regulations such as Financial Fair Play regulations (FFP)), accreditations (e.g., access to UEFA's Champions League competition), and broader cultural expectations (e.g., from supporters and the media). Coercive drivers involve those in powerful positions, which pressurise other organisations within the field. Coercive isomorphism in European football is driven by formal and informal pressures exerted by a club of powerful entities such as the national and European football associations and by cultural expectations from supporters and the media.

Normative pressures are associated with professional values that can be created through socialisation at work, formal education, networking, and certification processes. Normative pressures involve integrating new rules and legitimate practices within an organisation.

Mimetic pressure relates to how organisations respond to uncertainties that may be associated with their own goals or requirements from their environment. When things are uncertain, clubs can be tempted to adopt the behaviour of each other. Accordingly, mimetic pressure occurs when an organization imitates the actions of successful competitors; that is when an 'organization consciously models itself after another that it believes to represent a high level of success and achievement in the public eye' (Hanson, 2001: 649).

Normative and mimetic drivers are often internally linked to the organisational field, whereas coercive isomorphism is frequently related to the organisation's environment. Empirically, distinguishing the effects of each pressure is difficult since these are separate processes that may work simultaneously and affect the characteristics of an organisation in different ways (DiMaggio & Powell, 1983).

PARADOXICAL BUDGETING PRACTICES IN EUROPEAN FOOTBALL

This section provides empirical evidence based on secondary data of two seemingly paradoxical financial practices in European football. The study further argues that each practice is a separate, though intertwined, dimension of clubs' SBC behaviour. Moreover, it is argued that both practices are underpinned by a dominant sporting logic and a subordinate financial logic.

The Overspending Practice

The entries in Table 2.1 and 2.2 show that revenues in the Big Five have increased substantially, mainly due to the strong growth in media revenues, which have become the major source of revenue.

Table 2.1   Average revenues per club, European leagues (€ million)

	2012	2018	% change
Big Five leagues			
England	139	293	111%
France	58	95	64%
Germany	108	186	72%
Italy	86	125	45%
Spain	93	169	82%
Medium-size leagues			
Belgium	16	22	38%
Netherlands	24	33	38%
Turkey	31	42	35%
Smaller leagues			
Denmark	13	14	8%
Greece	10	9	-10%
Norway	11	9	-18%
Sweden	8	9	13%

Source: UEFA Club Licensing Benchmarking reports 2012 and 2018 (UEFA, 2012, 2019).

These leagues have also enjoyed a strong growth in media revenues from external markets, with the English Premier League (EPL) in the driving seat. By 2019, 40% of its media revenues came from external markets, a proportion that is likely to further increase in the coming years.[2] Technical innovations in the media industry have generated a massive growth in the transmission capacity. Accordingly, the clubs at the top of the popularity ladder find it easier to access fans also outside their core markets. Media revenues have been more moderate in the medium- and smaller-size leagues (Solberg, 2017).

The most successful clubs have earned substantial revenues from UEFA tournaments (UEFA, 2017). In 2016, Spanish elite clubs received €323m from UEFA, which accounted for 16% of their total income. The corresponding figures were €312m (10%) in England, €207m (12%) in Germany, €196m (20%) in Italy, and €159m (15%) in France. The annual growth rate for commercial products and sponsorships has increased beyond 20% in the last five years (2011–2016) for the biggest clubs in Europe and is somewhat lower for the smaller clubs (UEFA, 2017: 47–69).

Table 2.2 shows the number of clubs with profit and losses every other year in the period from 2010 to 2018. The number of clubs with losses has declined in the big leagues, while the results were mixed in the medium-size and smaller leagues.

It is important to have in mind the difference between operating result and profit/losses, where the latter also includes trade of players and financial revenues and cost. In general, the clubs at the top of the financial ladder spend more on buying players out of contracts than they receive from selling players, a pattern which is opposite of the clubs further down the financial ladder. For several years, the English Premier League has had the highest revenues. In 2016, 16 EPL clubs had positive operating results, while four clubs had operating deficits. The same year, 11 clubs had positive profit, while nine clubs had negative profit, i.e., losses. In Belgium, only two clubs had positive operating results the same year, whereas 14 clubs had negative results. Here, nine clubs had positive profit, while seven had negative profit. In Denmark, only three clubs had positive operating results, whereas 11 clubs had negative results. Seven Danish clubs had positive profit, and the same number had negative profit.[3]

Table 2.2   *Number of clubs with aggregate profits/losses after tax*

	2010		2012		2014		2016		2018	
	Profit	Loss	Profit	Loss	Profit	Loss	Profit	Loss	Profit	Loss
Big Five leagues										
England	4	16	10	10	15	5	11	9	12	8
France	6	14	10	10	6	14	14	6	6	12
Germany	7	11	12	6	12	6	14	4	13	5
Italy[a]	4	16	9	11	7	12	12	8	6	12
Spain[b]	13	7	12	5	15	5	18	2	18	2
Medium-size leagues										
Belgium	8	8	6	10	7	9	10	6	6	10
Netherlands	8	10	12	6	8	10	12	6	14	4
Turkey	6	6	5	12	2	16	3	15	4	14
Small-size leagues										
Denmark	1	11	4	10	5	7	7	7	8	6
Greece[d]	3	8	1	13	4	11	4	11	5	11
Norway	3	13	10	6	6	10	13	3	8	8
Sweden	8	8	5	11	4	12	14	2	11	5

Notes: [a] One Italian club missing in 2014. [b] Missing results from three clubs in 2012.
[c] Missing results from one club in 2012. [d] Missing results from two clubs in 2012.
Source: UEFA Club Licensing Benchmarking reports 2010, 2012, 2014–2018.

Wage costs are the most important element in the clubs' cost structure and the factor that primarily prevents clubs from gaining profits (Solberg & Haugen, 2010). Thus, the wage and revenue ratio are a 'red-flag' indicator in FFP. In 2014, over 38% of the 680 top clubs in Europe had a wage share of more than 70% of revenues. In 2015, 10 of the 20 Italian Serie A clubs had a wage rate in excess of 75% (Deloitte, 2016). In 2016, 96% of the clubs' revenues contributed to payroll and other operating expenses (ibid.). The remaining revenues should cover transfer costs, non-operating expenses, interest expenses, taxes, and return on invested capital. This, however, has not been the case for many clubs.

Having said that, some improvements have been registered in recent years, as seen from Figure 2.1, which shows that the aggregate profit of European clubs amounted to €140 million in 2018. This was a great improvement compared with the eight preceding years, when the average loss was €771m per year. The loss figures stated are net, i.e., after taxes and financial items (UEFA, 2019). Additionally, the total debt burden decreased in the same period. One reason for this improvement is the FFP regulation and the domestic club licensing systems. Another reason is the growth in media revenues in the Big Five leagues.

Despite this, many clubs in medium-size leagues and smaller leagues still struggle with financial difficulties. In England, the Championship clubs (second level) had aggregate deficits, both in terms of operating results and financial results every year in the period from the 2007/8 season to the 2016/17 season. The average club had a pre-tax loss of £7.3 million and an operating loss of £7.8 million. In 2018, 41% of the clubs in the Big Five leagues had negative profit. In the three medium-size leagues and the four smaller leagues mentioned in Table 2.2, the equivalent percentages were 54% and 48%, respectively.[4] These figures illustrate that the financial problems had not been resolved.

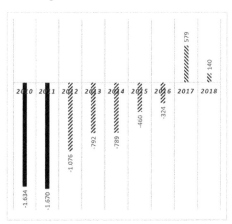

Figure 2.1   *European clubs' bottom line losses before and after the gradual introduction of FFP in 2012*

The Bailout Practice

Despite the financial problems, football clubs rarely go bankrupt (Szymanski, 2012). Compared with other commercial industries, surprisingly clubs survive with financial stress for a long period. In 1923, the English Football League was comprised of 88 clubs divided into four divisions. In the 2007/8 season, 85 (97%) of them were still in full operation. Furthermore, 75 of the 88 clubs (85%) were still in the league, while more than half (54%) were in the same division as in 1923 (Kuper & Szymanski, 2009). In comparison, only 20 of the 100 largest companies in England in 1912 were among the 100 largest in 1995. Moreover, 50 of them had survived, seven were liquidated, six were nationalised, and 37 were merged or acquired by other companies (Szymanski, 2012). From 1986 to 2008, 68 clubs in English football became insolvent and six of them went bankrupt (Beech et al., 2010). Furthermore, none of these six disappeared. Immediately, new clubs were established with new owners in all six cases, and a similar pattern has been found in Italy and Spain (Storm & Nielsen, 2012).

DISCUSSION

Mimetic Pressure to Overspend

The financial resources clubs spend on players and coaches is a significant predictor of their sporting results. Szymanski (2003) and Kuper & Szymanski (2009) revealed that the relation between a club's payroll and its table position in the English Premier League is strong ($r^2 = 0.9$). The rivalry between the sporting logic and financial logic is further reinforced by sporting thresholds that can have major financial consequences (Haugen & Solberg, 2010). The best clubs in the domestic elite leagues aim to qualify for international tournaments. If they succeed, the financial injection can make them dominant in their domestic leagues. Clubs pursuing international successes are tempted through isomorphic pressure to further increase their spending to improve the chances of qualifying. Those unwilling to copy such behaviour risk lagging behind. The worst-case scenario is relegation, which reduces the revenues but without a corresponding reduction in the costs (Beech et al., 2010). The strategy to achieve sporting success is recruiting better players through transfer spending and salaries. This, in turn, leads to a permanent mimetic wage pressure among the clubs.

When players are bought out of their contracts, the selling clubs try to orchestrate bidding wars between potential buyers. In some instances, this can initiate arms' races between buying clubs, particularly when superstars change clubs. The many incidents of the winner's curse are a result of these processes

(Andreff, 2015). The clubs succeed in signing the players, but later realise they have spent too much. Over the years, players' salaries have become the single most expensive cost in European club football, particularly in the Big Five leagues. The players can relocate to the highest-bidding club due to the EU's principle of free movement of labour; however, a club does not possess this freedom to relocate because of the strong connection to the geographic proximity of its followers (Giulianotti & Robertson, 2004).

Clubs try to obtain competitive advantages by paying more in transfer fees and salaries. However, the relative competition is a zero-sum game. If one club improves its table position, this will always be at the expense of another club (Solberg & Haugen, 2010). If the rivals respond to this pay game through mimetic behaviour, the wage levels throughout the league will increase without anyone having achieved a sporting advantage. Thus, a strategy that is rational for the individual club later turns out to be irrational overspending at the industry level (Morrow, 2014). The situations that create such behaviour often have the character of a prisoner's dilemma. Such processes are a fight between a sporting logic and a financial logic, normally with the sporting logic as the winner.

Coercive Pressure to Bail Out

A bailout is the colloquial term for the provision of financial help to a firm (or a country) that otherwise would be on the brink of failure or bankruptcy. Through a bailout, an insolvency process can be avoided. A bailout can be done for profit motives or to avoid systemic risk (Shull, 2012).

In line with any costs, overspending can be financed by equity or debt. In a market-based economy, a private firm must be able to pay off its debt to survive, i.e., behave financially according to HBCs. If the firm is short of money, the creditors can require the court to appoint a liquidator who can sell the firms' assets. Once all the assets have been sold, the firm is dissolved and will no longer exist. Accordingly, the ever-present threat of bankruptcy forces commercial firms to live within their means following HBC (Kornai, 1986).

The institutionalising of the bailout practice has allowed clubs to operate in an 'unhealthy' financial manner according to SBC. Other things being equal, this practice gives clubs a financial competitive advantage over their rivals that do not adopt the same strategy. The bailout practice has added fuel to the never-ending rat race, thereby forcing clubs to spend more money (Frank & Lang, 2014). Empirical data show that many clubs have adopted this strategy and hence made such behaviour normal. A major reason for this is that clubs have been rescued by their financial owners or creditors (Storm & Nielsen, 2012).

If the financial logic of the market comes to an end through a soft bailout process, a club is released of its incentive to keep costs under control. Accordingly, free or inexpensive access to credit reduces or eliminates the need for cost discipline imposed by the bankruptcy institution (Nier & Baumann, 2006). Consequently, a significant coercive corrective pressure will not be adequate, and this may motivate clubs to follow an SBC approach and continue overspending.

Normative Pressure to Bail Out

Popular football clubs own valuable brand names, and many have customers and fans worldwide. In their local societies, they have a significant social and political role as they act as important cultural carriers. Many of them have characteristics of social institutions through the relationship with key interest groups, primarily the supporters. For them, the club is an important identity marker (Brown et al., 2008, Morrow, 2003).

When analysing their budgeting behaviour, one must consider that the decisions are influenced not only by the owners but also by stakeholders who have no formal power per se. Due to strong historical ties, the informal ownership is often retained within the local community. Local fans consider themselves to be the ultimate 'social owners' of their teams (Cocieru et al., 2019, Gerrard, 2000). By standing together, they can influence the policy, e.g., encouraging the owners to put more efforts into recruiting talent. Hardcore fans feel psychologically connected to a club (Guttmann, 1986, Wann et al., 2000). For those with a high level of club identification, the role as a club follower is a central component of their identity. The club's success becomes the fan's success, and the club's failures become the fan's failures. Motives of sociability assume that humans are social beings, a reality reflected in numerous classical theories of human motivation (Alderfer, 1972, Maslow et al., 1970). Indeed, even residents who are moderately interested in football can feel an identity with their local club. For some, the city would not be the same without a club in the elite league. The local media often plays a special role by allowing the stakeholders to communicate their messages.

A club's special social position can represent a significant financial advantage that traditional commercial firms do not possess. This can be valuable in the case of a financial crises. Club owners, lenders, and benefactors may feel obliged to help clubs to avoid a financial collapse (Morrow, 2014). The local community that encircles the club may find it worthwhile to support the club at whatever cost no matter how bad the club has been managed and steered towards a crisis. Particularly, local sponsors may fear being left as a scapegoat if they do not try to save clubs from bankruptcy. This, in turn, creates a normative pressure on local stakeholders to bail out the club.

Internal Bailouts

An important characteristic of sport competitions is the mutual dependency between the competitors that is necessary to create commercially interesting products. This goes back to the ideas in the article 'The Peculiar Economics of Professional Sports' by Walter Neale (Neale, 1964). Since then, several contributions have addressed the challenges of upholding the uncertainty of outcome and competitive balance. See for example Késenne (2007) for more profound analyses.

The dependency between clubs, however, can work in multiple ways. Although the purpose of upholding competitive balance is to prevent the biggest clubs from becoming too dominant, smaller clubs will also benefit in other ways, for example by attracting more spectators when playing at home against the big clubs. In the literature, this is known as the superstar effect (Rosen, 1981). This will also be reflected in the joint sale of sponsorship deals and the sale of media rights. Smaller clubs will therefore benefit from playing in a league with especially popular clubs, and likewise will suffer financially if they disappear, e.g., because of relegation.

This was illustrated some years ago when Glasgow Rangers and Juventus, two of the most popular clubs in Scotland and Italy, respectively, were relegated from their respective elite leagues due to financial irregularities. Rangers and Celtic have historically dominated the Scottish Premier League (SPL), as they have constituted 70% of its turnover, and their home games have produced 55–60% of all SPL spectators (Morrow, 2015). During the 2010 and 2011 season, nine of the top 10 TV SPL matches included at least one of these two teams. Therefore, broadcasting contracts had termination clauses if either Celtic or Rangers were not involved in the SPL (see Morrow, 2015 for more details). When Rangers were relegated in 2012, football finance experts calculated the cost for each club in the SPL to be around £1m a season. During that time, such a reduction could push four of the five SPL clubs that booked a 2011 profit back into the red.[5] The issue has also been illustrated by the debate on whether the two clubs should be allowed to join the English Premier League.[6]

Juventus, historically the most popular Italian club, was relegated to Serie B (second level) as a consequence of the Calciopoli scandal, where several clubs were judged for rigging games by selecting favourable referees. Juventus was stripped of the 2004–2005 Serie A title and was downgraded to last place in the 2005–2006 championship. Other clubs were also judged and punished, but Juventus was the only club that was relegated. Consequently, the club had to sell several players, some of whom were sold to foreign clubs. Due to Juventus' popularity, the case had negative spillover effects on the other teams in Serie A similar to those in Scotland (see Boeri & Severgnini, 2014 for more details). These two examples illustrate that other clubs are vulnerable if especially popular clubs are eliminated from the league.

If the big clubs recruit superstars, which include both domestic and foreign players, this will increase the commercial value of the league as a unit and hence benefit the remaining clubs in the league. Although they may find it more difficult to win matches against the big teams, the growth in the commercial value among media companies and sponsors may outweigh the negative effects.

EU regulations, which allow the free movement of players across borders, strengthen the mobility of football players. Because of that mobility, regulations aiming to reduce the costs need to be harmonised among the leagues. If not, those practising the strictest regulations risk losing players to those with more liberal regulations. Hence, domestic football governing bodies have conflicting interests with one another. Football governing bodies may therefore find themselves in situations that have a character of prisoner's dilemma, which are similar to those that exist between the clubs (Haugen & Solberg, 2010). Domestic leagues can therefore benefit from implementing regulations that are softer than rival leagues. This also includes monitoring systems.

These forces also exist between the different sports, for example between football and other team sports. It is important to bear in mind that football competes with other sports for the attention of spectators, TV viewers, sponsors, and the media. Hence, the rivalry that exists between football governing bodies and other sports federations has similarities to the rivalry between the respective domestic football leagues. This can prevent international sport governing bodies, such as UEFA, from implementing regulations that affect their popularity relative to other sports.

SBC Behaviour Underpinned by a Self-destructive Financial Logic

We have argued that the two soft budgeting practices discussed constitute a self-destructive financial logic, as illustrated in Figure 2.2. The logic is described by a sequence of reciprocal cause and effect in which the two practices intensify and aggravate each other. This inexorably leads to the preservation of the problematic financial situation in European football clubs over time. Many clubs do not possess the financial resources necessary to fund their ambitious sporting aspirations. Therefore, they are rescued after incurring excessive financial risks.

Although overspending is not sustainable in itself, clubs will benefit if they are financed by external stakeholders (i.e., bailout practice). Similar effects can occur if domestic leagues fail to implement regulations that are sufficiently strict. When studied through financial lenses, each practice seems neither legitimate nor sustainable. However, when studied as budgeting practices that scaffold a dominant sporting logic, they both seem de facto legitimate and sustainable at the club level. Clubs and leagues unwilling to adopt SBC practices will be exposed to a competitive disadvantage. Many clubs have been living under constant financial distress because of the soft budgeting practices employed. Consequently, regulations are necessary to break the vicious financial circle illustrated in Figure 2.2 (Storm & Nielsen, 2012).

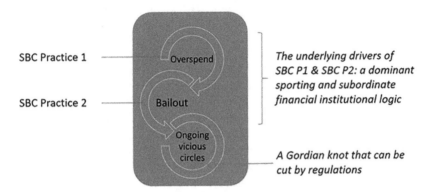

Figure 2.2   *European football is subject to a self-destructive financial logic underpinned by soft budget constraints*

CONCLUDING REMARKS

This chapter has shown that two seemingly unsustainable soft budgeting practices have been institutionalised in European club football. The clubs operate as hybrid organisations where sport performance (SBC) is prioritised above financial performance (HBC). Although the formal owners emphasise financial performance, their choices are also influenced by the supporters who operate as the social owners of the clubs. By standing together, often in company with the local media, they can push clubs to spend more on talent than is financially healthy. In that way, clubs operating under an SBC regime have the character of a dual ownership.

One reason for this is that many clubs operate as social institutions within their local communities. Therefore, they have been saved from bankruptcy by 'sugar daddies', who among others can be wealthy supporters, sponsors, but also the local public sector. The institutionalisation of such a bailout practice has encouraged clubs to behave in a riskier way than they otherwise would do. Additionally, the system of promotion and relegation, combined with the possibilities of qualifying for international tournaments, has triggered European clubs to take more risks than those operating in hermetic leagues, as for example in North American and Australian team sports (Haugen & Solberg, 2010).

Nevertheless, the financial problems have been reduced in recent years. One reason for this is the implementation of FFP regulations both by UEFA and domestic football governing bodies. Another reason has been the strong growth in media revenues, which has particularly benefited the biggest leagues. Despite this, the figures in Table 2.2 show that a large number of clubs are still in the red. This illustrates that the regulations are necessary.

However, it does not automatically follow that national and international football governing bodies are able to regulate themselves. European club football consists of more than 50 elite leagues. These leagues compete with each other for talent. Therefore, the leagues will find themselves in the situation where individual preferences do not correspond with collective efficiency. This applies to both the implementation and the monitoring of the regulations. International football governing bodies such as UEFA will find themselves in a similar situation as other international sports federations. Football competes with other sports to attract the attention of spectators, TV viewers, sponsors, and the media. Hence, the rivalry that exists between clubs and domestic leagues also exists between UEFA and other sports federations. The literature has used the term 'financial doping' to describe performance-enhancing social practices and compare these practices to medical doping in sports (Schubert & Könecke, 2015: 73). 'While classical doping aims at increasing sporting success by the use of prohibited substances and methods, financial doping implies the use of financial means for the same ends' (ibid.: 76).

The many losses in Table 2.2 give reason to ask if national and international football governing bodies should be the regulators. In other words: Is the football industry capable of investigating itself? When governing bodies are set to look after themselves, it is tempting to pursue a policy that benefits themselves. However, such behaviour may be collectively irrational and inefficient, and the incentives to feather one's own nest are reduced if the job of being regulator is given to independent governing bodies. Our main proposal for that reason is to establish a regulating body that is modelled after the World Anti-Doping Agency (WADA) and funded accordingly, i.e., sourced equally from the clubs and governments of the clubs participating in the competitions.

NOTES

1.   Acknowledgement: Associate professor Elin Anita Nilsen at UiT The Arctic University of Norway has provided constructive input to and valuable comments on an early version of this chapter.
2.   https://offthepitch.com/a/premier-league-overseas-broadcasting-deal-exceed -ps4-billion.

3. https://www.uefa.com/MultimediaFiles/Download/OfficialDocument/uefaorg/
    Clublicensing/02/53/00/22/2530022_DOWNLOAD.pdf.
4. https://www.uefa.com/MultimediaFiles/Download/OfficialDocument/uefaorg/
    Clublicensing/02/64/06/95/2640695_DOWNLOAD.pdf.
5. https://www.theguardian.com/football/2012/aug/05/spl-counts-cost-of-rangers
    -banishment.
6. https://www.theguardian.com/football/2015/sep/30/celtic-rangers-english
    -premier-league-dermot-desmond.

REFERENCES

Alderfer, C. P. (1972). *Existence, Relatedness, and Growth: Human Needs in Organizational Settings*. New York: The Free Press.

Alford, R. R., & Friedland, R. (1985). *Powers of Theory: Capitalism, the State and Democracy*. Cambridge: Cambridge University Press.

Andreff, W. (2007). French football: A financial crisis rooted in weak governance. *Journal of Sports Economics*, *8*(6), 652–661.

Andreff, W. (2015). Governance of Professional Team Sports Clubs: Agency Problems and Soft Budget Constraints. In W. Andreff (Ed.), *Disequilibrium Sports Economics* (pp. 175–228). Cheltenham: Edward Elgar Publishing.

Barajas, Á., & Rodríguez, P. (2010). Spanish football clubs' finances: Crisis and player salaries. *International Journal of Sport Finance*, *5*(1), 52–66.

Beech, J., Horsman, S., & Magraw, J. (2010). Insolvency events among English football clubs. *International Journal of Sports Marketing and Sponsorship*, *11*(3), 53–66.

Boeri, T., & Severgnini, B. (2014). The Decline of Professional Football in Italy. In J. Goddard & P. Sloane (Eds.), *Handbook on the Economics of Professional Football* (pp. 322–335). Cheltenham: Edward Elgar Publishing.

Brown, A., Crabbe, T., & Mellor, G. (2008). Introduction: Football and community–Practical and theoretical considerations. *Soccer and Society*, *9*(3), 303–312.

Carlsson-Wall, M., Kraus, K., & Messner, M. (2016). Performance measurement systems and the enactment of different institutional logics: Insights from a football organization. *Management Accounting Research*, *32*, 45–61.

Cocieru, O. C., Delia, E. B., & Katz, M. (2019). It's our club! From supporter psychological ownership to supporter formal ownership. *Sport Management Review*, *22*(3), 322–334.

Deloitte (2016). *Annual Review of Football Finance*. London: Deloitte LLP.

Deloitte (2018). *Annual Review of Football Finance*. London: Deloitte LLP.

Dietl, H. M., & Franck, E. (2007). Governance failure and financial crisis in German football. *Journal of Sports Economics*, *8*(6), 662–669.

DiMaggio, P., & Powell, W. (1983). The iron cage revisited: Collective rationality and institutional isomorphism in organizational fields. *American Sociological Review*, *48*(2), 147–160.

Dobson, S., & Goddard, J. A. (2001). *The Economics of Football* (pp. 106–130). Cambridge: Cambridge University Press.

Fort, R. (2000). European and North American sports differences(?). *Scottish Journal of Political Economy*, *47*(4), 431–455.

Fort, R. (2003). Thinking (some more) about competitive balance. *Journal of Sports Economics*, *4*(4), 280–283.

Frank, E. & Lang, M. (2014). A theoretical analysis of the influence of money injections on risk taking in football clubs. *Scottish Journal of Political Economy, 61*(4).

Gammelsæter, H. (2010). Institutional pluralism and governance in 'commercialized' sport clubs. *European Sport Management Quarterly, 10*(5), 569–594.

Gerrard, B. (2000). Media ownership of pro sports teams: Who are the winners and losers? *International Journal of Sports Marketing and Sponsorship, 2*(3), 20–39.

Giulianotti, R., & Robertson, R. (2004). The globalization of football: A study in the globalization of the 'serious life'. *The British Journal of Sociology, 55*(4), 545–568.

Gratton, C., & Solberg, H. A. (2007). *The Economics of Sports Broadcasting.* Abingdon: Routledge.

Guttmann, A. (1986). *Sports Spectators.* New York: Columbia University Press.

Hanson, M. (2001). Institutional theory and educational change. *Educational Administration Quarterly, 37*(5), 637–661.

Haugen, K. K., & Solberg, H. A. (2010). The financial crisis in European football—a game theoretic approach. *European Sport Management Quarterly, 10*(5), 553–567.

Johansen, S. T., Olsen, T. H., Solstad, E., & Torsteinsen, H. (2015). An insider view of the hybrid organisation: How managers respond to challenges of efficiency, legitimacy and meaning. *Journal of Management & Organization, 21*(6), 725–740.

Kaplan, V. (2015). UEFA Financial Fairplay regulations and European Union antitrust law complications. *Emory International Law Review, 29*, 799–857.

Késenne, S. (1996). League management in professional team sports with win maximizing clubs. *European Journal for Sports Management, 2*(2), 14–22.

Késenne, S. (2007). *The Economic Theory of Professional Team Sports: An Analytical Treatment.* Cheltenham: Edward Elgar Publishing.

Kornai, J. (1986). The soft budget constraint. *Kyklos, 39*(1), 3–30.

Kuper, S., & Szymanski, S. (2009). *Why England Lose & Other Curious Football Phenomena Explained.* London: Harper Sport.

Lago, U., Simmons, R., & Szymanski, S. (2006). The financial crisis in European football: An introduction. *Journal of Sports Economics, 7*, 3–12.

Maslow, A. H., Frager, R., & Fadiman, J. (1970). *Motivation and Personality.* New York: Harper & Row.

Morrow, S. (2003). *The People's Game? Football, Finance and Society.* Basingstoke: Palgrave Macmillan.

Morrow, S. (2014). Football Finances. In J. Goddard & P. Sloane (Eds.), *Handbook on the Economics of Professional Football* (pp. 80–99). Cheltenham: Edward Elgar Publishing.

Morrow, S. (2015). Power and logics in Scottish football: The financial collapse of Rangers FC. *Sport, Business and Management, 5*(4), 325–343.

Neale, W. C. (1964). The peculiar economics of professional sports: A contribution to the theory of the firm in sporting competition and in market competition. *The Quarterly Journal of Economics, 78*(1), 1–14.

Nier, E., & Baumann, U. (2006). Market discipline, disclosure and moral hazard in banking. *Journal of Financial Intermediation, 15*(3), 332–361.

Reay, T., & Hinings, C. R. (2009). Managing the rivalry of competing institutional logics. *Organization Studies, 30*(6), 629–652.

Rosen, S. (1981). The economics of superstar. *American Economic Review, 71*(5), 845–858.

Rottenberg, S. (1956). The baseball players' labor market. *Journal of Political Economy, 64*(3), 242–258.

Scelles, N., Szymanski, S., & Dermit-Richard, N. (2016). Insolvency in French soccer: The case of payment failure. *Journal of Sports Economics*, *19*(5), 603–624.

Schubert, M., & Könecke, T. (2015). Classical doping, financial doping and beyond: UEFA's financial fair play as a policy of anti-doping. *International Journal of Sport Policy and Politics*, *7*(1), 63–86.

Scott, W. R. (2008). Approaching adulthood: The maturing of institutional theory. *Theory and Society*, *37*(5), 427–442.

Selznick, P. (1957). *Leadership in Administration*. Berkeley, CA: University of California Press.

Shull, B. (2012). Too Big to Fail: Motives, Countermeasures, and the Dodd-Frank Response, *Levy Economics Institute*, Working Paper, No. 709.

Sloane, P. J. (1971). The economics of professional football: The football club as a utility maximiser. *Scottish Journal of Political Economy*, *18*(2), 121–146.

Sloane, P. J. (2015). The economics of professional football revisited. *Scottish Journal of Political Economy*, *62*(1), 1–7.

Solberg, H. A. (2017). The Battle for Media Rights in European Club Football. In U. Wagner, R. K. Storm, & K. Nielsen (Eds.), *When Sport Meets Business: Capabilities, Challenges, Critiques* (pp. 92–107). London: Sage.

Solberg, H. A., & Haugen, K. K. (2010). European club football: Why enormous revenues are not enough? *Sport in Society*, *13*(2), 329–343.

Storm, R. K. (2012). The need for regulating professional soccer in Europe: A soft budget constraint approach argument. *Sport, Business and Management: An International Journal*, *2*(1), 21–38.

Storm, R. K., & Nielsen, K. (2012). Soft budget constraints in professional football. *European Sport Management Quarterly*, *12*(2), 183–201.

Szymanski, S. (2003). The economic design of sporting contests. *Journal of Economic Literature*, *41*(4), 1137–1187.

Szymanski, S. (2012). Insolvency in English Professional Football: Irrational Exuberance or Negative Shocks? Working Paper, No. 12-02. International Association of Sports Economists.

Szymanski, S. (2017). Entry into exit: Insolvency in English professional football. *Scottish Journal of Political Economy*, *64*(4), 419–444.

Terrien, M., & Andreff, W. (2019). Organisational efficiency of national football leagues in Europe. *European Sport Management Quarterly*, 1–20.

Terrien, M., Scelles, N., Morrow, S., Maltese, L., & Durand, C. (2017). The win/profit maximization debate: Strategic adaptation as the answer? *Sport, Business and Management: An International Journal*, *7*(2), 121–140.

Thornton, P. H., & Ocasio, W. (1999). Institutional logics and the historical contingency of power in organizations: Executive succession in the higher education publishing industry, 1958–1990. *American Journal of Sociology*, *105*(3), 801–843.

Thornton, P. H., Ocasio, W., & Lounsbury, M. (2012). *The Institutional Logics Perspective: A New Approach to Culture, Structure, and Process*. Oxford: Oxford University Press.

UEFA (2012). *UEFA Club Licensing and Financial Fair Play Regulations, Edition 2012*. Nyon: UEFA.

UEFA (2017). *Club Licensing Benchmarking Report: Financial Year 2016*. Nyon: UEFA.

UEFA (2019). *Club Licensing Benchmarking Report: Financial Year 2018*. Nyon: UEFA.

Vroman, J. (1997). A unified theory of capital and labor markets in major league baseball. *Southern Economic Journal, 63*, 594–619.

Wann, D., Royalty, J., & Roberts, A. (2000). The self-presentation of sport fans: Investigating the importance of team identification and self-esteem. *Journal of Sport Behaviour, 23*(2), 198–206.

3. Hardening the soft budget constraint in professional team sports: why is it so hard?

Wladimir Andreff

Since its emergence in 1874, in Léon Walras' *Eléménts d'économie politique pure*, the concept of a budget constraint has become standard in neoclassical microeconomics to express that a consumer cannot spend more than his/her current income. In a general equilibrium theory, at the end of the day, consumer's expenditures and revenues converge to equality at the equilibrium point. János Kornai slightly twisted this microeconomic concept in such a way as to make it suitable both for producer (enterprise) microeconomics and for a whole (macro) economy in disequilibrium, the shortage economy that he has empirically observed in socialist countries. As long as an actual economy has not converged to equilibrium, most markets witness either an excess demand that soften the suppliers' (enterprises) budget constraints or an excess supply which makes their budget constraints hard.

Over two decades or so, the soft budget constraint (SBC) remained associated with centrally planned economies and their shortages, then to their transition to market economy. However, since the mid-1990s, the concept was extended to some specific markets or industries, such as banking, up to the idea that, under given preconditions, any market in any economy could happen to operate with soft budget constrained entities. In the wake of this extension, the concept was first introduced in sports economics in 2005; a brief literature review of SBC in sports economics is the launch pad of this chapter.

Then, digging deeper into the theoretical literature about the SBC, one detects that its determinants were analysed as being macroeconomic (nationwide in socialist and transition economies), then microeconomic (softness of a firm's budget), and finally mesoeconomic (at industry level or in the banking business). From there the conclusion is derived that hardening the SBC calls for measures taken at macro-national, meso-industrial, and micro-entrepreneurial levels.

Consequently, when it comes to knowing how the SBC could be hardened in professional team sports, a first step is to analyse its determinants at club level and infer which measures are likely to harden it. Then at mesoeconomic level, i.e., that of the professional sport league, the SBC determinants pertain to the league rules, regulations, supervision and monitoring of clubs; hardening SBC measures must be thought of as changing some league rules or better enforcing the existing ones. At macro level, institutions, laws, macroeconomic regulation and policies are at stake which, in order to harden the SBC, implies some change in policies or behaviour on the side of regional and national governments, financial institutions and law enforcement.

JÁNOS KORNAI'S LEGACY IN SPORTS ECONOMICS

In his autobiography, János Kornai (2005) spent only 12 (pp. 309–20)[1] out of 566 pages discussing the concept of SBC. Why it is so few, given that it may be the most typical 'Kornaian' concept? In these pages, Kornai of course comes back to his own understanding of SBC as of 2005 (2 below) – he reminds us that his intuition about the SBC dates back to an old paper (Kornai, 1958), calls for the practical significance and empirical evidence of SBC – and notes how SBC modelling materialised when he was working with Erik Maskin and Mathias Dewatripont. However, he also stresses his frustration due to the fact that his most elaborate paper on SBC (Kornai, 1986) was rejected from publication in the *American Economic Review* (*AER*), and eventually published in *Kyklos*, while an article with a bulk of mathematical technicalities about the SBC by Qian (1994), his former student at Harvard, was accepted in the *AER*. Kornai understandably goes on (pp. 320–6) with a critical assessment of the process through which articles are selected for publication in the most famous mainstream economics journals.

Assessing Kornai's autobiographical book, Andreff (2014a) ends up considering the SBC concept as his major breakthrough in the economics literature while mentioning how wide the empirical area could stretch for extending the concept because the SBC is relevant each time an economic decision maker is able to survive his/her permanent over-expenditures compared to his/her revenues. In the same paper, it is also contended that the sports industry is often plagued with expenditure overruns beyond the break-even point, and professional team sports are highlighted as one of the most promising avenues for further SBC studies in the near future.

Indeed, a brief literature review confirms that the SBC is a newly spreading concept in the economics of professional team sports leagues. The SBC was first referred to in sports economics by scholars previously acquainted with work on former centrally planned economies in a theoretical framework in which they were coined shortage economies since Kornai (1980). In particular, Andreff (2005, 2007a) started referring to the SBC when explaining both the financial mismanagement of some French professional football clubs and recurrent deficits and net debts[2] of the French professional league – meaning that the cumulative deficits of all clubs in the red are higher annually than the cumulative profits of all clubs in the black. From that came criticism of football clubs' lack of accounting and financial transparency, and of their reluctance to comply with the disclosure[3] requirement of their accounts by the French football auditing body. Moreover, French football clubs could rely on the league's bargaining power with TV channels for recurrently rising TV rights revenues in such a way as to recoup ex post a part of their deficits and debts, thus softening their budget constraints (Andreff, 2007b).

Persistent deficits and growing debts in the majority of European top league football clubs were underlined together with clubs' abnormally high survival rate (Storm, 2010). The SBC concept helped in explaining why only very few among such European professional football clubs go out of business while being on the brink of bankruptcy, as was happening to state-owned enterprises in former socialist or post-socialist economies.

Then it was shown that taking on board the SBC in the standard economic model of an open team sports league necessarily transforms it into a disequilibrium model (Andreff, 2009, 2011). Késenne (1996) published a Walrasian model which, since then, became the standard for open leagues such as:

$$Max\ ti \tag{3.1}$$

$$R_i(m_i, t_i) - s.t_i - c_i^0 = 0 \tag{3.2}$$

where *ti* stands for the quantity of talent recruited by team *i*, R_i for team *i*'s revenue function, m_i for its market size, *s* for the salary per unit of talent taken by team *i* from the (assumed perfect competition) market, and c_i^0 for fixed costs (stadium, management). One crucial assumption is enshrined in the above constraint (3.2), which says that team *i* exactly covers its expenditures with its revenues, that is the minimal theoretical definition of a hard budget constraint – the constraint would be hard too, even harder if instead of having = we had > in (3.2). From a team *i* accounting standpoint, the above constraint (3.2) means that it breaks even.

Now imagine that one intended to insert an SBC in the previous model, the constraint should be rewritten as:

$$R_i(m_i, t_i) - s.t_i - c_i^0 < 0 \tag{3.2'}$$

If (3.2') were to pertain to all teams in an open league, then neither a single team nor the league (as an accounting aggregate of all teams) would break even, and all would be run under an SBC economic regime with persistent deficits. Andreff (2011)[4] stresses two consequences of the SBC. First, the league does not reach the Walrasian equilibrium point any longer and is stuck in non-Walrasian equilibrium[5] (unable to clear excess demand) or, better, economic disequilibrium. Moreover, persistent excess expenditures should spill over on to the labour market for talent in the form of sustained excess demand (Andreff, 2018).

In tune with Storm (2010), a further article starting again from the paradox of co-existing persistent losses with high club survival rates in European football refers more extensively to the SBC literature (Storm & Nielsen, 2012). It is considered that the SBC syndrome is not confined to socialist economies and can be found in the different activities of capitalist economies (Kornai et al., 2003), namely in those non-profit organisations which are bailed out by public authorities as well as in the banking and financial intermediaries sector where a 'too big to fail' concern nearly always results in rescuing large banks in financial trouble (Berglöf & Roland, 1998). Storm & Nielsen contend that many European football clubs are similarly seen as too big to fail by their stakeholders, be they fans, TV viewers, sponsors, sugar daddy investors, local governments, tax authorities, local banks, or any other benefactors, most of whom are ready to pay the price (and inject the required streams of money) for rescuing a club in financial jeopardy. This is exactly what the SBC syndrome is all about from a club standpoint: being certain that someone will step in financially and bail it out. The authors list a number of football clubs' bailouts in Europe and correctly stress the institutional framework of European football market as providing strong incentives to overspend in addition to spending pressures deriving from fans' emotions and the social attachment of local communities.

A two-market disequilibrium model of team sports leagues takes on board the SBC in which clubs' financial disequilibrium $(R_i \ (m_i \ , \ t_i) - s.t_i - c_i^0 < 0)$ spills over on to the labour market for talent where the SBC triggers an overall excess demand, and to the output market for sport events in excess demand too – i.e., short supply (Andreff, 2014b). Such a double excess demand model corresponds to Kornai's shortage economy or Benassy's suppressed inflation regime. In more detail, a dual labour market (Piore & Doeringer, 1971)[6] is modelled, disentangling a primary segment for superstar players from a secondary segment for journeymen players. In the primary segment, each superstar is in a monopoly position on the supply side since his specific talent is unique (non-substitutable), while on the demand side, clubs are compelled to outbid each other with a view to signing a given superstar – the famous arms' race for talent. Consequently, including a monopoly rent, superstar salaries are excessively high (higher than at the Walrasian equilibrium point), as are transfer fees. In the secondary segment, journeymen players are facing the monopsony or oligopsony power of top leagues' recruiting teams and are in excess supply with two consequences: they are exposed to queuing for a job (unemployment) or, more often, to spilling over to a lower division or a foreign league's lesser-quality demanding market.

The output market is also segmented into a fan market where fans demand stadium seats (tickets), a market for televised games supplied by free-to-air TV channels and a market for televised games supplied by pay-per-view channels. With the first two markets, consumers are rationed (excess demand). For the fan market, rationing is due to a limited number of high-quality games supplied by a monopolistic league with a small number of clubs (about 20);[7] for high-quality matches, fan demand may even be more tightly rationed given the fixed stadium capacity. Moreover, since all the fixtures must be played in a season, a number of games will be unattractive or even boring with the result that fan demand concentrates on a fewer number (than 380 home-away games in a 20-team league) of attractive high-quality matches which end up being in excess demand. The same applies to free-to-air televised games; a proportion of them are unattractive or boring even though they are usually supplied at a relatively low and fixed price or for free. It is only in the market for pay-per-view televised games, where ticket price (or subscription fee) may vary, that demand–supply equilibrium may be reached, in particular if TV channels adopt a strategy of dynamic pricing over time.

In a paper explaining how and why the UEFA Financial Fair Play (FFP) regulation tackles the issue of many European football clubs that actually do not break even, Franck (2014) explicitly contends that such a situation comes from clubs facing a soft – instead of hard – budget constraint. The SBC results in detrimental managerial incentives for football clubs' decision makers and triggers a runaway demand for talent and the emergence of a salary bubble (Franck, 2015). Managerial moral hazards and rent-seeking crowd out incentives for good management and fuel a kind of financial doping of football clubs. FFP regulation is an attempt at hardening budget constraints for football club managers and, by the same token, at indirectly capping payroll injections made by football club benefactors.

In North American closed team sports leagues, it is usually assumed that all teams, and consequently the league, are profit-maximisers. It seems that such an assumption excludes the SBC from the very beginning since a profit means that $R_i(m_i, t_i) - s.t_i - c_i^0 > 0$, i.e., opposite to SBC, a very hard budget constraint which fuels profit making. However, though they do not claim that the SBC syndrome exists in North American team sports leagues, Storm & Nielsen (2015) contend that budget softening in the American league context takes the alternative shape of 'income generating activities that merely increase the budget rather than soften budget constraints' (p. 157), which distorts the market mechanism. They refer to institutional arrangements privileging the monopoly power of team franchises and league organisations.

Ex ante soft environmental conditions consist first of soft pricing: a closed league is a cartel-like monopoly whose franchises behave as price-makers in their local urban areas while labour cost is kept low through the league's monopsony power on the market for talent where it is a wage-maker. A second condition is soft taxation: franchises are used to negotiate taxes with local authorities, and taxes are eventually discounted or franchises exempted. Third, soft subsidies and soft investment finance result from the willingness of local politicians to subsidise franchises and even build stadiums for their teams under the franchise monopolist threat of relocating elsewhere. A last SBC feature in North American closed leagues lies in soft credit (issuing tax-free bonds, low interest rates) in the public financing of major league sport facilities. Therefore, even in a profit-maximising context, a number of SBC determinants may prevail and help franchises to be profitable or even to make extra profit.

That SBC is a relevant concept for North American closed leagues is exemplified in a different, much simpler though less general, way in Andreff (2015). Checking all operational profits or losses in the Big Four North American leagues (MLB, NBA, NFL, NHL), from 2003 to 2014, 370 occurrences of team losses (26% of all observed net operating incomes) overall were found. Soft pricing, soft taxation, soft subsidies and soft credit were not enough for a number of teams to avoid being in the red. The least SBC-affected teams are the NFL's, with only 15 occurrences of team deficit over 12 years (4% of net operating incomes), basically concentrated on one team, the Detroit Lions (six years in the red). Seventy-seven deficit occurrences (21%) were witnessed in the MLB, 124 deficit occurrences (34%) in the NBA and 154 (47%) in the NHL, the latter coming closer to what was observed in European soccer leagues in 2010. Although having typical features of the SBC syndrome, North American professional team sports leagues may even exhibit classical or pure evidence of teams unable to break even or make profit.

Nielsen (2017) presents SBC case studies in European football and stresses the following implication: clubs that do not bother much about balancing the books or making profit will pay less attention to efficiency, and will hoard scarce resources rather than properly manage their resources. Assuming that clubs and leagues have multiple objectives – and not only win or profit maximising – a scattered inefficiency across European football leagues is exhibited on a sample of 36 observable leagues out of 55 UEFA member leagues from 2010–2015 (Terrien & Andreff, 2020). Such widespread inefficiency provides another index of prevailing football club bad management under the SBC.

With the research note of Havran & Andras (2016), the SBC concept which first emerged in Hungary returns back to its homeland, though adapted for the first time to football economics in nine Central Eastern European countries (CEECs) where clubs are still often non-profit organisations mostly supported by public authorities. However, in some CEECs, due to transition, economic austerity and cuts in government budget, their budget constraints became so hard that clubs could only survive by means of selling their best players on the global market for football talent, as do some Croatian clubs for instance (Gudasic, 2018).

Approaching team sports leagues' financial troubles through the SBC lenses sheds a new light on recurrent economic issues which require resolution through a process of hardening clubs' and leagues' budget constraints. Before addressing this point, a detour is needed to check which factors are determinants of the SBC.

UNDERSTANDING THE DETERMINANTS OF A SOFT BUDGET CONSTRAINT

Kornai first empirically observed the SBC syndrome in the Hungarian economy at a time when market reforms were introduced in 1968: Consumers were queuing for goods and enterprises were missing planned though undelivered inputs, and rationing and shortages (excess demands) were plaguing the whole centrally planned economy. Thus, he first dubbed pervasive shortages as "suction" economy (Kornai, 1971), though in this book neither shortage nor the SBC explicitly show up as concepts. The major cause of suction was the socialist state macroeconomic policy and not the state-owned enterprises' microeconomic behaviour. In the same vein, Kornai (1972) contended that the 'rush' macroeconomic policy was the major source of shortage. Therefore, the SBC was introduced as a macroeconomic (or 'systemic') concept required for understanding dysfunctions of centrally planned economies. The SBC concept, properly speaking, first emerged in Kornai (1979) when he looked for microeconomic foundations of shortages – excess demands – of different products as the normal state of a socialist centrally planned system. From this first step one could infer that it is for explaining macroeconomic issues that the SBC was used, even though the notion of budget constraints was 'borrowed' by Kornai from mainstream neoclassical microeconomics. Therefore, a debate followed about the SBC as a consequence of macroeconomic policy (central planning, job and wage security) or the cause of shortage rooted in microeconomic behaviour of firms operating in such a macroeconomic context (Vahabi, 2014).

As early as Chapter 2 of Kornai's masterpiece (1980) is devoted to the producer's adjustment to the mandatory central plan, the socialist enterprise meets the SBC since, whatever its residual operating income (even a permanent loss), it will go on producing, investing and recruiting; its probability of going bankrupt is zero because the state (central authorities) will step in to bail it out at any cost. In Chapter 5, dealing with the seller in a shortage economy, the enterprise can always take it easy and sell whatever it wants since it is facing a long queue of unsatisfied and rationed potential buyers; being on the short (supply) side of the market, the seller does not even have to adjust to planners' commands.[8] Again, when analysing the enterprise as an investor, the latter meets the SBC because it never feels any financial risk due to soft credit delivered by banks in centrally planned economies and bailing-out subsidies. From there comes an investment 'thirst' – always invest more and more, which looks like the recruitment strategy of European football clubs. Then the enterprise's (hard and soft) budget constraints are analysed in detail (chapter 13); a hard budget constraint (HBC) prevails as soon as the enterprise currently breaks even and, of course, when it is able to make profit; whereas an SBC characterises socialist enterprises that do not break even (expenditures > revenues) and do not suffer from it due to centrally decided subsidies and bailouts. The softness of a firm's budget constraint is to be measured by the frequency of bankruptcies and bailouts in a given economy, which indicates an SBC macroeconomic dimension. Further, Kornai contends that the HBC pertains to enterprises operating in a capitalist economy context while the SBC is a normal state for enterprises[9] operating in a socialist planned command economy and is assessed as a cause of its inefficiency.

Therefore, the SBC has *both macro- and microeconomic*[10] dimensions, and its determinants are to be found at both levels. However, a third dimension of the SBC underlies Kornai's criticism against the so-called Clower (1965) and Barro–Grossman (1971) post-Keynesian school of disequilibrium economics. Kornai (1980) contests the relevance of conceiving an aggregated excess demand, aggregating together all the product shortages into an overall excess demand variable. Based on his experience of typical shortages on the intermediary (inputs) and consumption goods markets in centrally planned economies, Kornai criticised the market short-side rule that aggregates all specific goods' or industry's shortages into a single macroeconomic excess demand variable.

For Kornai, for each good or industry, a specific good demand must be compared to its supply so that the shortest side determines whether the market for each specific good is in short demand (excess supply) or in short supply (excess demand). When consumers and enterprises are suffering an excess demand (shortage) of a specific good, they adjust to market disequilibrium basically through waiting (queuing), postponing their purchase or accepting a forced substitution through spilling over to the market for another good. When they are plagued with excess supply of a specific good in the face of too few demanders, they adjust by means of a sale activism (publicity, selling effort and marketing) and stockpiling unsold goods with a view to selling them later. With aggregating excess demands or supplies as in the Barro–Grossman model such micro-adjustments would be unheeded and remain unanalysed. Thus, Kornai rejects the short-side rule assumption.

In addition, Kornai (1980) correctly considers that the core and origin of shortages are not rooted in the consumption goods market but are generated upwards on the input 'market' of centrally planned inter-enterprises, inter-industry input supplies and deliveries – a non-existing market in aforementioned post-Keynesian disequilibrium models. Although shortage is the normal state of a centrally planned economy, shortages are not evenly widespread nor of the same intensity for different products in different industries.[11] The state industrial policy was deciding about which strategic industries would have a preferential access to inputs and capital goods and which non-strategic industries would not (Andreff, 1993; Vahabi, 2014). Therefore, specific product shortages pertain to an industry's excess demand associated with the SBC at industry level that we can coin a *meso-economic* dimension[12] of SBC. Kornai (1980) even self-criticises one of his earlier texts (1971) for having neglected the fact that shortage (excess demand) and excess supply may show up together in the same economy, in different industries or even in the same industrial market due to adjustment time lags.

Kornai (1986) lists the different ways and means to soften the budget constraint as being soft subsidies, soft taxation, soft credit and soft administrative prices, meaning that all of these can be bargained for by a firm with its supervising authorities. This implies some impact of the SBC on the firm: its price responsiveness declines; its efficiency reduces; it forms an excessive demand of inputs – and if all firms behave this way, a runaway demand will appear, generating the shortage economy. He also extends the SBC syndrome to some specific activities or industries in mixed, i.e., regulated market economies.

Later Kornai (1992), though more geared towards institutional dimensions of the socialist system, still keeps the SBC concept in its core analysis. Regular external assistance to a firm can take four forms: (a) soft (ex post bargained) subsidy; (b) soft (ex post bargained) taxation; (c) soft (ex post bargained) credit and (d) soft administrative pricing bargained with central authorities. All four are firms' budget softening methods. Here emerges an institutional view about SBC determinants, since in the background of (a), (b), (c) and (d), SBC is respectively determined by the government with its fiscal and taxation policy, the socialist banking system and the central planning pricing office. Obviously, this is only an institutional specification of the SBC macroeconomic or systemic dimension that Kornai associates with state paternalism: 'Paternalism, and soft budget constraint as one manifestation of it, is a typical social relation between superior and subordinate, higher authorities and management of the firm' (Kornai, 1992, p. 144). Paternalism may motivate the state or a supporting organisation to bail out an ailing enterprise in a centrally planned economy; a variant of this is cross-subsidisation serving as insurance against failure, as in Japanese *keiretsu* and *zaibatsu* or Korean *chaebol*... as well as hedging against a team's financial dire straits in North American team sport leagues (Fort & Quirk, 1995).

In the same text, Kornai (1992) also introduces the idea of degrees of softness and hardness, from extremely soft to extremely hard budget constraints; as well as the lack of credible commitment that is a pivotal component in the SBC game-theoretical modelling developed by some of Kornai's followers (Qian, 1994; Dewatripont & Maskin, 1995). Finally, Kornai (2005) supports the view that the SBC concept became famous enough because it fits well in a mainstream (micro-)economics framework, and concludes that, beyond different evolving presentations of the SBC, his final standpoint is the one published in the last synthesis article on it (Kornai et al., 2003).

Turning now to the SBC in the works of Kornai's followers, Gomulka (1985) contends that if prices are sufficiently (infinitely) flexible, the SBC need not result in shortages. When considering the professional team sports industry, most prices do not appear to be very flexible: the price is fixed over a whole season in the case of season tickets; the price is very sticky for other tickets since their price does not vary until the very last minute before kick-off (even with dynamic pricing); and player salaries are fixed over the whole season and in some leagues a salary cap curbs them down. Gomulka's contention does not prevent using the SBC in the context of professional team sports, rather it is quite the contrary.

Next, a crucial task is to empirically test a major consequence of the SBC, which is the spillover of disequilibria (shortages) from one market or industry to others. This job was done by Goldfeld & Quandt (1988, 1993) who successfully tested that firms run with an SBC form an excess demand for inputs that is coined a 'Kornai effect'. When applied to a football league, the same theoretical story says: clubs that are run with an SBC recurrently develop an excess demand for their major input, i.e., players' talent. In practical terms, they overbid for talent on the players' labour market and engage in an arms race for inputs that are in short supply, particularly superstar players. Consequently, the players' market is in a permanent state of excess demand, at least for superstar players (Andreff, 2018). Firms' or football teams' ability to buy inputs without footing the bill – costs being borne by some supporting organisation – can dramatically augment their demand for inputs; this in turn can lead to serious shortages. Therefore, SBC boosts the propensity to permanently invest in more and more inputs (over-investment). Consequently, as Woo (2017) argues, the existence of the SBC guarantees the creation of excess capacity and zombie firms in China, and he infers that macroeconomic stimulus and supply-side structural reforms are not enough to mop up excess demands as long as the termination of the SBC will not occur.

The macro-interpretation of the SBC is stressed by Schaffer (1998, p. 81): 'The definition of the SBC that is used most often by Kornai is a subsidy paid, typically by the state, to loss-making firms to guarantee their survival'; the cause of SBC is associated with paternalism by the state and its empirical effect is an ex post bailout of loss-makers since a paternalistic state is unable to commit credibly to not rescue firms in financial distress. Then Schaffer's focus switches to inter-enterprise payment arrears, overdue debts, tax arrears and bank bad (irrecoverable) debts as a means of ex post financing and rescuing unprofitable firms.

Although basically developing a microeconomic game-theoretical analysis of banks and their business relations with firms, Dewatripont & Maskin (1995), in focusing on one specific (the banking) industry, adopt a background mesoeconomic view of SBC. Microeconomic theory is used in a mesoeconomic context where a bank accepts its client's payment arrears because of previous investments or loans that it would lose were the indebted firm's operations to discontinue. The tax authority may deliberately overlook mounting tax arrears, or the bank may willingly tolerate non-performing debt. From the standpoint of the Dewatripont–Maskin model, hardening the budget constraint means creating conditions in which the government can credibly commit to refinance an enterprise. Note that the hardness of the budget constraint is not a matter of direct policy choice, but rather the indirect result of putting institutions in place that discourage or interfere with refinancing. The model stands in sharp contrast with ex post bailouts due to paternalism and shows that the latter is neither a necessary nor a sufficient condition for SBCs to emerge. The crux of the story is lack of dynamic commitment.

In the wake of Dewatripont–Maskin analysis and chasing the SBC in the banking industry in transition economies, Berglöf & Roland (1998) deliberately adopt a meso approach, concentrating on trade arrears in that industry, bank passivity – bailouts of banks affect their incentives to harden budget constraints of their client enterprises – and banks' gambling for resurrection by means of bailout. Then the focus moves to the SBC as a commitment problem due to ex post renegotiation of firms' financial plans and a close relationship between firms and central authorities (Maskin & Xu, 2001), while such a problem is extended from centralised and transition economies to market economies.

According to Kornai, the article by Kornai et al. (2003) represents his last word about the SBC. The concept is increasingly acknowledged to be pertinent well beyond the realm of socialist and transition economies. SBCs are confined neither to socialist economies nor to government–firm relationships. The SBC syndrome is truly at work only if firms or organisations can *expect or be guaranteed* to be rescued from financial trouble, which creates an SBC mentality. The SBC phenomenon occurs if ex ante a budget-constrained entity knows, guesses or is aware of the fact that one or more supporting organisations will be persistently (even sometimes unwillingly) ready ex post to cover all or part of its deficit (or debt). Surrounding institutions make supporting organisations ready and allowed to bail out.

Kornai et al. (2003) list all entities that may happen to be rescued from financial dire straits: state-owned enterprises, firms in private ownership in agriculture and 'rustbelt' industries, a number of non-profit organisations (hospitals, schools and universities), local government authorities and even insolvent national economies. Politicians may obtain subsidies for firms in financial difficulty – which was indeed observed in European football before the 1990s but seems to be less relevant in the 21st century due to both EU competition policy and bailouts now preferably made by private benefactors or sugar daddies. Bailouts may be motivated by an effort to avoid negative economic spillover effects, a motivation captured by the phrase 'too big to fail'. Finally, there may be corrupt influences whereby 'crony' relationships do exist between the bailed-out entity and supporting organisations, an occurrence which is not that rare in professional team sports (Andreff, 2019b).

Whatever the economic system (socialist, transition, capitalist), the means of softening the budget constraint are always the same as in Kornai et al. (2003). They first consist of fiscal means in the form of subsidies from the state budget or tax concessions (remission, reduction or postponing of tax obligations, tolerance of tax arrears). The second group of softening instruments encompasses some form of lax credit (too much credit extended, bad loans and loan repayment arrears). A third group consists of various indirect methods of state support (imposing restrictions on imports or erecting a deterrent tariff barrier, relaxed discipline in tax collection and, this way, providing financial support to loss-making firms), a low frequency of bankruptcies and liquidations and a high frequency of bailouts.

To cure the SBC syndrome, there is one crucial recipe in a Kornaian framework of analysis which consists of HBC. The hard budget constraint is a form of economic coercion where 'proceeds from sales and costs of input are a question of life and death for the firm' (Kornai, 1979, p. 806; Kornai, 1980, p. 303). In addition, the budget constraint is hard if the growth of the firm is dependent on what it can derive from its own profits, or what it can take out from creditors for investment purposes under conservative conditions. Hardening the budget constraint is supposed to promote restructuring, raise total factor productivity and encourage the shedding of surplus labour (Kornai et al., 2003) through improving how an entity (a firm, an organisation, a state) is run.[13]

Finally, a political economy model shows how the SBC may arise as an efficient political – though not economic – strategy (Robinson & Torvik, 2009), and this would be a major reason why SBCs are so hard to eradicate. Where politicians cannot commit to arbitrary forms of redistribution, the commitment problem isolated by Dewatripont–Maskin may be politically advantageous because it allows politicians to deliver benefits in the form of transfers to potential supporters and fans. Then politicians will finance poor projects that they anticipate they will have to bail out in the future because that is the only way to deliver redistribution that can influence electoral outcomes.

To sum up: Macro-determinants of the SBC relate to institutions (for example, ownership), the law (for example, bankruptcy law) and the rule of law and current macroeconomic policy. Hardening the SBC at this level must target institutional or legal change, better law enforcement and adjusting and tightening macroeconomic (primarily tax and fiscal) policies.

Meso-determinants of the SBC pertain to specific macroeconomic policies geared towards a given industry (for example, anti-trust exemption), management rules and economic regulation that apply to all participants in the industry and, when there is a governing or supervising body over the industry, supervision and auditing of industry members by the aforementioned body (a league or a federation in team sports). Hardening the SBC in an industry implies a change in either the macroeconomic policy that targets this industry or in internal rules, regulation and supervision by the industrial governing body.[14]

Micro-determinants of the SBC are found at the firm (club/team) level as regards weak governance structure and subsequent mismanagement, possible agency issues, credible commitment, lack of transparency, lax enforcement of the industry's rules and regulation at firm level and, in the worst case, illicit or illegal firm behaviour. Hardening the SBC at this level must improve the governance structure, resolve agency issues, create conditions for credible commitment, increase transparency and tighten supervision by governing bodies.

Politicians' redistribution or transfer behaviour that facilitates the SBC may emerge at the three levels. At a macro level, they may influence institutions: passing new laws, proceeding with a lax law enforcement and redistribution policies. At a meso level, 'politicians', including those people elected at the top of sports governing bodies, may attempt to change the industry's regulation and rules in a way that favours the SBC. At a micro level, politicians may promise to a firm (a club) an additional injection of resources through transfers or may simply get elected as a club's CEO or staff member who will take advantage of his/her crony or political networks to attract rescue money when necessary.

In the following sections, the chapter highlights how to harden the professional team sports' SBC in the macro context of European football (soccer), where major EU institutions are relevant for most domestic football leagues and clubs – those located in all EU member nations and in Eastern European countries having signed an association or a partnership agreement with the EU. The meso context is the professional football industry ruled by UEFA and domestic football leagues, while the micro level is made up of professional football clubs and their strategies.

HARDENING THE SOFT BUDGET CONSTRAINT AND CLUBS' MANAGERIAL STRATEGIES

Lax management is quite common in non-profit organisations,[15] reflecting an SBC which is determined by various inner and external factors. In a professional football club, the SBC shows up when expenditures permanently exceed current business revenues drawn from match day and season ticket receipts, current sponsorship fees, merchandising revenues, TV rights revenues and transfer fees gained from selling players. Therefore, a managerial strategy to hardening a club's SBC is one that targets reducing, and eventually phasing out, the accounting imbalance between incomes and expenditures with the consequence of stopping the club's net debt rise. On one side of the coin, combating or curing extra expenditures is a major lever for hardening clubs' SBCs. From the standpoint of the balance sheet expenditure side, the budget constraint basically is hardened by cutting excess expenditures such as over-investment in player talents, putting a halt on lax management and managerial expensive malpractices and improving club governance and economic efficiency. On the revenue side, softening the club budget constraint consists of successfully bargaining and collecting additional revenues that do not derive from current business, basically public subsidies, fake or ex post inflated sponsorship fees (which are often hidden bailouts) and bargained bailouts ending in some ex post benefactor's injection of cash; therefore, hardening the SBC implies putting a halt on such ex post[16] bargaining. A change in club's ownership does not necessarily harden an SBC; all depends on the new owner's managerial strategy.

Hard to Handle Stakeholders' Pressure that Fuels Over-investment in Player Talents

Stakeholders of a football club identify to a greater extent with their 'company' (team) than they would with ordinary firms in other industries and, consequently, clubs are to a great extent influenced or dominated by their members and even more so by their fans and supporter trusts. Storm & Nielsen (2012) contend that stakeholders – members, fans, club owners, sponsors and investors – consider 'their' club as too big to fail, with the meaning that it is socially 'big' as an identity marker of common interests and loyalty – though even the richest European clubs are not big companies in financial terms. A club generates such deep social attachment and emotions that stakeholders are always ready to support it, including with financial help. Soft money injections by sugar daddy benefactors and investors, soft taxation, public subsidies (including using the municipal stadium for free or below the market price) by local governments and soft credit by local banks without expectation or enforcement of repayment (bad loans) are determinants of the SBC puzzle for which empirical evidence is well covered in the literature.

Hardening the SBC fuelled by such stakeholder behaviours cannot succeed only at the microeconomic level of a club and must be attempted either at the meso and macro level (see the subsequent sections: 'Hardening the soft budget constraint and the enforcement of leagues' rules' and 'Hardening the soft budget constraint and team sports leagues' macro-environment'), except for one group of stakeholders that is the crowd of ordinary fans attending matches or purchasing season tickets. While owners, sponsors, local governments and banks are stakeholders who act to soften the budget constraint on the revenue side of the balance sheet, fans and season ticket holders act on its expenditure side as well. Why is this so? Usually, fans exert a strong pressure on club management in favour of recruiting as many player talents as possible (or even more than budgetarily possible) because they want 'their' team to win more than lose,[17] or to win highly contentious matches (Andreff & Scelles, 2015; Scelles et al., 2013). They always gamble on the success of their team on the pitch, whatever price must be paid for it. This trend towards gambling on success critically leads to a club's insolvency if no new investor or additional cash can be found.

More than the socially significant character of the club, this kind of fan pressure fuels an over-investment 'thirst' (in Kornai's wording) in player talent that is so strong that club managers cannot escape it. The more a club is successful on the pitch, the stronger the fan pressure and the harder it is to handle it. It is very hard to curb such fan pressure in view of hardening the SBC. Consequently, European football clubs are known for a management culture which prioritises on-field success over financial performance, and this creates a context within which most clubs endlessly operate, producing deficits and debts. In such a context, making fans and supporters feel part of the financial dire straits of their team through providing them with the club's financial information, as suggested by Morrow (2013), might well be no more than wishful thinking.[18]

In the wealthiest clubs, owners and shareholders often behave as fans, which boils down to non-profit-seeking investment by patrons and tycoons always ready, or even eager, to pour more money streams into 'their' club. Among them, sugar daddy benefactors are those who most soften the club budget constraint and relax financial discipline over managers. It is nearly impossible to harden the SBC at club level when the club regularly benefits from financial rescue by sugar daddies; then the pressure to harden the SBC must come from a higher level, i.e. league regulation, in particular in the face of foreign sugar daddies.

Due to the aforementioned fan and stakeholder pressures, clubs are compelled to invest heavily in players to increase their chance of winning on the pitch and, consequently, of earning higher revenues. But since a club's success depends on its relative investment compared to all other clubs, investment decisions are always risky and entail an element of gambling on success while rising expenditures for sure lead to greater financial deficits.

Giving a voice to fans, as in German clubs which are registered as associations (*eingetragener Verein*) or incorporated with 50% plus one vote kept by the *Verein*, is not a highway to hardening an SBC, quite the opposite (Dietl & Franck, 2007). When fans were given more power through club ownership, which is a popular idea, it was shown that this might increase the financial instability of professional clubs (Scelles et al., 2018). Simply because fans are those stakeholders exerting the strongest spending pressure on clubs' managers and the least controllable, or the least easy to bargain with, by clubs' managers. Even without ownership, giving a say to fans on what the club's strategy should be, as with *socios* in some Spanish football clubs, though a democratic solution, will fuel the club's demand for the best players and consequently press on softening the SBC further – FC Barcelona's and Real Madrid's resulting deficits and debts are cases in point.

'The leading clubs have mainly sporting aims and economic and financial constraints; … [they] aim at obtaining sporting results with almost unlimited economic resources' (Baroncelli & Lago, 2006, p. 24); this may well summarise the standpoint of most stakeholders, managers and club owners and clearly means that, without such constraints, they all are eager to spend to the infinite to enable 'their' club to win on the pitch. Such very deep roots of the SBC are definitely hard to eradicate, even in a dream. One can conclude that as long as stakeholders, in particular fans, whoever they are, fiercely support a club to the point of being ready to pay the price for gambling on success (even losing their money placed in club shares), it would remain very hard to harden the SBC.

Hard to Combat Management Malpractices

Embezzlement, hidden money transfers, slush funds, funds diversion, fictitious player transfers and bungs were growing economic dysfunctions in European football during the 1990s (Andreff, 2000). For instance, bungs can be used for grabbing a club's assets, funds can be diverted in a manoeuvre of abusing social benefits and social contributions can be redirected to fuel clubs' secret slush funds (Poli, 2007). Mismanagement practices were usually hidden by means of fake accounting. In the worst cases, managerial malpractices went as far as systematic tax evasion (Turner, 2016) and money laundering (Verschuuren & Kalb, 2013).[19] Some clubs were convicted of fake accounting (or creative bookkeeping), fake invoicing and holding secret funds, and their chairmen were sentenced for abusing social benefits; Andreff (2000) points at the chairmen of AS Saint-Etienne, Girondins de Bordeaux, RC Toulon, Olympique de Marseille and Paris-Saint-Germain in French football. In 2004, 51 Italian football clubs were suspected of fake accounting; in 2005, a dozen

were relegated to a lower division for not paying taxes and two were seques-
tered due to their tight relationships with the *Camorra* (Andreff, 2006). In
January 2016, 64 club managers in Italian football *Serie* A and *Serie* B were
sued for wrong managerial practices in the Naples court. Since the Lux Leaks
and Panama Papers disclosures, a number of superstar players have been suspected of tax evasion. Such practices must be combated everywhere in society,
including in professional football where one of their outcomes is to soften
clubs' budget constraints.

Since the late 1990s, in some domestic leagues, stricter regulations were
introduced to hinder such mismanagement practices which still survived in
a number of Eastern and Southern European football clubs. Such malpractices were disregarding and circumventing any kind of budget constraint;
eradicating them would align those football clubs concerned on common law
and regular managerial rules and, by the same token, harden their budget constraint. However, it is difficult to harden the latter in circumstances of criminal
behaviour except through ex post heavy sanctions and suing the guilty parties
in court. Although, when the SBC is based on fraudulent managerial practices, hardening it can only end up coming under a lawsuit (Andreff, 2019b).
A better solution is to ex ante prevent criminal behaviour through improving
clubs' corporate governance.

Bad governance may go as far as match fixing and corruption as with, for
instance, Offenbach and Bielefeld (*Bundesliga*) bribing some of their oppo-
nents' players in 1970–1 to avoid their teams' relegation. Many other occurrences are known of, some of which are surveyed in Andreff (2019b). Match
fixing and corruption are not determined by, or even tightly linked to, the SBC
in all cases, but they fuel over-expenditures and exhibit bad management practices; the latter are extremely favourable to sustaining a club's SBC.

Hard to Improve the Quality of Clubs' Corporate Governance

Some peculiarities relative to the other companies make the issue of good
governance more important for professional sports clubs (Michie & Oughton,
2005). Governance practices are based on codes and rules about the role
and composition of a company's board of directors, relationships within it,
internal auditing and information disclosure and the recruitment and dismissal
of directors and senior managers. Two barriers are likely to hinder club bad
governance and put a halt on lax management or mismanagement related with
the SBC. The first one is based on linking managers' (also coaches') pay to
performance, which may be achieved by means of pay–performance contracts.
The other one, in line with the principal–agent model, is considered to consist
in floating a club's shares in order to submit its management to stock market
discipline: profitability and good governance should phase out the SBC. The

discipline imposed by financial markets is supposed to be a powerful tool for reaching strong club governance in European football (Barros, 2006) and maximising shareholder value. Those listed clubs should be in the black nearly every year and should be able to distribute dividends to shareholders.

As regards the first hypothesis, it was found that, in Portugal, the football earnings of the club's managerial director are a function of accountancy performance variables, board's composition and directors' individual characteristics (De Barros et al., 2007). The board composition revealed agency problems since directors' earnings increased with board size, the number of insiders, older and politically related managers on the board, the number of friends on the board, the duration of a manager on the board and the managerial director also being the chairman. Not only are conflicts of interests at stake with such board configuration – which can be witnessed in European football far beyond only the Portuguese clubs – but all the premises for softening the budget constraint are there.

In turn, the quality of clubs' corporate governance can impact the quality of published accounting information. Firms with efficient corporate governance practices are resorting less to accounting fraud and are reporting accounting disclosures with better reliability. Dimitropoulos (2011) found that expropriation of wealth by football clubs' managers is mitigated in clubs with increased board independence, managerial ownership, institutional ownership and small board size, which are associated with high-quality financial reporting and lower management earnings. In a sample of football clubs from 10 European countries, increased board size and independence and the separation of the CEO and chairman roles, and increased ownership by managers and institutions, lead to greater levels of profitability and viability (Dimitropoulos & Tsagkanos, 2012).

Examining the second hypothesis, one can observe those European football clubs (44 as of 2015) which have experienced an initial public offering (IPO). Basically, the hypothesis that floating clubs' shares will financially discipline their management is not confirmed (Andreff, 2015) since most listed European football clubs were continuously or very often in the red, with the exception of Benfica, Galatasaray, Fenerbahce and Trabzonspor.[20] Public trading of their shares was mainly undertaken by European football clubs in order to repay their debts in the early 2000s, that is to clean a residual outcome of the SBC; but IPO is a one-shot, short-term solution if it does not trigger improved inner club governance.

Governance did not change since most IPOs' revenues were invested by clubs in an SBC-relaxing way; that is, in recruiting superstar players instead of educating new players and acquiring stadiums, sporting infrastructures and other tangible assets. Public trade of shares alone should not be understood as a tool for hardening the SBC. Eventually, 21 English football clubs were delisted after continuous operating losses. IPOs did not either trigger the disciplining shock on to former bad governance practices or harden clubs' SBCs. The continuous decline of the DJ STOXX Football Index seems to be structural due to market illiquidity, low club profitability and the uncertainty attached to the fundamental value of football clubs; this value is heavily dependent on clubs' intangible assets – the non-amortised value of players' contracts (Aglietta et al., 2008).

Finally, European football's experience of raising capital through flotation on the stock market was not convincing as a tool for promoting financial discipline and did not put a halt on clubs' SBCs. The influence of stock exchange listing was found to be nil in terms of clubs' financial performance (Leach & Szymanski, 2015). Empirical evidence confirmed that being listed or not in the stock market has no effect on clubs' financial performance (Sanchez et al., 2017): the agency theory does not fit well with football clubs. The SBC theory is an interesting substitute.

Slowing Down Football Clubs Begging for Public Subsidies

Sports clubs managers usually push forward a demand for attracting subsidies from the local, regional or national government, which will meet the state paternalistic attitudes, the preferences of a benefactor local government and the influence of special interest groups with, often, some politicians as their go-between and speakers motivated with their own re-election motives. Then club managers adapt to the government's objectives: the probability of receiving a public subsidy is statistically significant and positively associated with the number of club members and managers' income and, though less significantly, with voting for the incumbent political party (Barros & Lucas, 2001). The bigger a club and the wealthier its managers, the higher is the probability of attracting public subsidies. However, public subsidies have been decreasing in importance in European football since 1999 as a result of EU competition policy enforcement. This determinant of the SBC is dying out for professional sports clubs in the long run, which is one step, though not the most important, on the path towards hardening the SBC.

Does a New Club Owner Harden the Budget Constraint?

Although it was not tested in European football to the best of our knowledge, a new club owner is not a guarantee for switching from SBC to HBC. For instance, in North American leagues, a recurrently non-profitable team (i.e., with an SBC) eventually ends up being sold by its incumbent owner to a new owner. It has been tested that change in ownership increases the odds of general manager and manager dismissals in the MLB (Hersch & Pelkowski,

2019). However, since a temporary 8% bump in players' payroll is observed in the first few years with a new owner, it is not a sign that the budget constraint is actually hardening. Among teams which were sold to a new owner from 2000 to 2014 (12 in NFL, 15 in MLB, 16 in NBA, 13 in NHL), some did not recover after-sale profitability (Andreff, 2015). In some cases, the deficit worsened with a new owner as with the Boston Red Sox after 2002, Tampa Bay Lightning and Nashville Predators after 2008, Arizona Coyotes and Brooklyn Nets after 2009 or New Jersey Devils after 2013. All depends on the new owner's strategy: whether he/she behaves as a sugar daddy benefactor or a harsh tycoon eager to make money, and his/her effective control over appointed staff. This is exactly the point where European football stands, with an increased number of new – including foreign – owners taking over a variety of clubs.

In fact, the outcome of a new owner's takeover or new ownership concentration, in terms of hardening or softening a club's budget constraint, depends on the strategy of those financial interests that invest in bailing it out. Some new owners (of a fan kind) acquire a club with a view to improving its sporting performance disregarding budget constraints; some invest to rescue a club that will be used as a tool for the new owner's prestige, pride, reputation and publicity (the kind of sugar daddy benefactor); in both cases, the SBC will not be phased out. Finally, some new owners act as businessmen willing to earn money – or at least not lose money – from their investment in the club, in which case the SBC may be hardened.

For instance, among those foreign investors in the English Premier League (EPL), Stan Kroenke was likely to have bought Arsenal with a view to making money and, indeed, Arsenal have not exhibited deficit, net debt and soft loans in the past few years; to some extent Harris and Blitzer's investment in Crystal Palace, Radrizzani's in Leeds, Dai Yongge's in Reading or Kaplan and Levien's in Swansea can compare as well as Rybolovlev's in Monaco, Kita's in Nantes, Chinese-American investors' in Nice and Gary Allen's in Troyes. On the other hand, Abramovich's takeover did not cure the deficit, net debt and soft loans in Chelsea, which compares to Glazer's in Manchester United, Vincent Tan's in Cardiff, Shahid Khan's in Fulham and Ellis Short's in Sunderland; while the acquisitions of Auxerre by James Zhou, Bordeaux by the GACP investment fund, Lens by Joseph Oughourlian, Lille by Mangrove Capital, Marseille by Frank McCourt, PSG by Qatar Investment Authority and Sochaux by Baskonia Alavès did not stop current deficit. Most English football clubs have been rescued at least once by wealthy patrons and patriarchal figures saving clubs from financial collapse, partly as a result of civic pride and partly because of the favourable publicity (Buraimo et al., 2006). Nowadays local businessmen with small fortunes have been replaced in this role by sugar daddies from the Middle East, tycoons in the oil industry and oligarchs from Russia and other transition economies.

Concentration of clubs' ownership (in the hands of a family group as with Agnelli, or a tycoon or a sugar daddy benefactor or an investment fund) empirically resulted in different results: Dimitropoulos & Tsagkanos (2012) found a positive relationship between concentrated ownership and a club's financial profitability, i.e., a vanishing SBC, while Sanchez et al. (2016) found the opposite relationship: a greater ownership concentration has a negative effect on financial profitability. All clubs with foreign ownership are capital companies with concentrated ownership. With increasing ownership concentration of economic investors, tested by Buchholz & Lopatta (2017) differentiating between economic and sporting investor types in European football, even the former investors favour sporting over economic performance, so that the sporting performance of a club increases; thus the SBC is therein since investments in player talent are made under a high risk of outcome uncertainty, and investors do not monitor (or not enough) club managers' actions.

HARDENING THE SOFT BUDGET CONSTRAINT AND THE ENFORCEMENT OF LEAGUES' RULES

At league (meso or industry) level, several countervailing factors could be mobilised against the SBC with more or less successful results: revenue redistribution across the clubs, league supervision and auditing, improving club efficiency based on benchmarking, attempting to curb wage and transfer fee inflation fuelled by an arms race for player talents, whereas the league bargaining TV rights for all clubs had been used to soften the SBC. Changing the league system, from open to closed leagues, is an often-debated topic which does not necessarily resolve the issues triggered by the SBC.

Hard to Use Revenue Redistribution With a View to Hardening All Clubs Budget Constraints

In former communist planned economies, revenue redistribution from profitable to loss-making state-owned companies was the rule of the game. It was the lever used to subsidise and keep weak and uncompetitive firms alive through 'taxing' the strongest and most competitive ones. In a cartel, which is what a team sports league is at the end of the day, revenue redistribution is also the rule and a tool for sustaining enough solidarity among the firms coordinated in the cartel. North American leagues are directly inspired from such principles with TV rights revenues and gate receipts' redistribution from big-market wealthier teams to small-market poorer teams (Fort & Quirk, 1995). In European football, until the 1990s, for the sake of solidarity between big and small clubs, an egalitarian share of TV rights revenues was redistributed among all clubs by the league. However, an equal share of revenues was redistributive since it was a small percentage of big club budgets while being a significant percentage of small club budgets. This helped many small clubs to stick to their budget constraint, whereas big clubs were complaining of an unfair redistribution to them and were always tempted to spend more; egalitarian redistribution indirectly fuelled the SBC syndrome in big clubs.

Since the late 1990s, two evolutions were noticed (Andreff & Bourg, 2006). Few European leagues adopted a model of individual club ownership over TV rights revenues. In most leagues, though keeping TV rights pooling by the league, the criteria used for the redistribution of TV rights revenues evolved, under the pressure of big clubs, towards a less egalitarian model: an increasing significance was given to past and current ranking (sporting performance) and to TV appearances in the calculation of each club's share. As a result, budget constraints softened for big clubs and should have hardened for small clubs. However, the latter effect was largely swamped by a rapid increase of overall TV rights revenues during the past two decades so that the SBC was still the context in which small clubs were run.

The distribution of those TV rights revenues related to club participation in continental competitions (such as UEFA Champions League and Europa League) deepened the revenue gap between wealthier and poorer clubs on the one hand and, on the other hand, softened the budget constraint of big clubs that often qualified for such competitions.

In order to combat the SBC syndrome, a new redistribution criterion should be accounted for: a club's share in overall TV rights revenues should be reduced when it is in the red, it should be maximal when it breaks even and it should be average when the club is profitable; with such league regulation, more clubs would have an incentive to harden their SBC and break even. Of course, such criterion would infringe the solidarity principle between clubs and distort competition,[21] which is the price to pay for hardening the SBC. This is the reason why this suggested new league regulation would be very hard to be accepted and implemented.

Every season the SBC should harden for those clubs relegated to a lower league; depending on the country, a relegation from the top division translates into a five-to-ten times reduction of the relegated clubs' budget. However, if the year after relegation, despite selling its star players, the club appears to be in the red, which often happens, the SBC syndrome is lasting in the lower tier. Moreover, in over half of European football top leagues, the financial hardship of relegation is alleviated by parachute payments – over three years in the English Premier League – whose aim 'is primarily to soften the financial blow of relegated clubs no longer having access to the broadcasting money available to clubs in the top league' (Wilson et al., 2018). This regulation obviously fuels the SBC syndrome for those weakest clubs in the top league and spreads it over a three-year period in the EPL. Yet these clubs are overspending on wages (greater than their total revenue) in an attempt to reach the EPL again.

Hard to Strengthen Domestic and International League Supervision and Auditing

Many domestic football leagues in Europe and most typically in the German *Bundesliga* have implemented a licensing system to prevent the financial collapse of a club before the end of a season. In 1965, Hertha Berlin was relegated because the management had paid higher wages and signing bonuses than was allowed under the statutes of the German Football Federation (Frick & Prinz, 2006). In the *Bundesliga*, the clubs' financial stability is usually attributed to the licensing system practised by the league's organisation since the 1960s. Clubs are required to submit budgets, financial data and business plans for the forthcoming season, including forecasts of their expected revenues, and provide external auditing reports according to predefined standards. This system ensures that there is continued control over costs, in particular wage costs. However, league supervision and auditing are not enough to harden the SBC in current circumstances. The German licensing system reduces the risk of clubs running into mid-season insolvency, though not down to zero, but it does not encompass guarantees that a club will not run into deficit. The *Bundesliga* licensing procedure is less effective than expected because it is based on inner and not any form of external financial control; the league is not allowed to interpret or question the quality of data provided by the clubs and has no power to sanction a club. Clubs are not even required to publish their accounts (Dietl & Franck, 2007).

A club too heavily or recurrently in the red may be more severely sanctioned, as happens in the French DNCG. Sanctions may range from warnings, advice and recommendations with regard to urgent policy measures to be taken by the club's management. If the financial deficit is persistent, the DNCG is allowed to audit the payroll in detail, to prohibit the recruitment of new players for a certain period, to impose fines and, as a last resort, to relegate the club to a lower division. However, this was not enough to avoid the French league being in the red nearly every year. Seventeen years out of twenty, 1997–2017 (Table 3.1), the entire league was in the red (Andreff, 2018).

Table 3.1   *French league operating profit/loss and transfer fee balance,*
               1997–2017

Season	Operating profit/loss (million €)	Transfer fee balance (million €)
1996–7	-7.0	25.1
1997–8	-46.0	51.1
1998–9	-70.0	65.9
1999–2000	36.0	8.1
2000–1	-41.0	-19.3
2001–2	-98.0	-68.1
2002–3	-61.0	-100.2
2003–4	-102.0	17.9
2004–5	-15.0	3.0
2005–6	37.0	14.7
2006–7	23.0	31.7
2007–8	-84.0	58.8
2008–9	-64.0	41.9
2009–10	-102.0	-91.7
2010–11	-97.0	73.4
2011–12	-67.0	38.9
2012–13	-3.0	-26.8
2013–14	-208.1	-184.5
2014–15	-57.3	114.7
2015–16	42.6	147.2
2016–17	-31.8	-12.1

Source: DNCG.

The trick is that the 18 experts sitting in the DNCG all derive their revenues from professional soccer since they are appointed by the football federation, leagues, coaching unions, player unions and football club owners' representatives (Andreff, 2007a), which may result in decisions undermined by a conflict of interests. For instance, PSG was never relegated to a lower division in spite of its repeated deficits while some other clubs were. The independence of the DNCG should be reinforced, which requires cutting the umbilical cord between the auditing body and major stakeholders of the soccer industry. The auditing body should no longer have members exclusively nominated by football governing bodies and representatives, some of whom should be replaced with independent chartered accountants, financial experts, lawyers and professional (sports) economists, as is usual in the external auditing of any other industry or business. Otherwise, it will remain difficult to harden the SBC.

Quite the opposite is observed in the Spanish *Liga*. Insolvent clubs have gone into administration but the *Concursal* law 22/2003, designed for other industries, relies on the principle of trying to guarantee the continuity of the business when it emerges from the administration process. For that reason, the Spanish High Court of Justice set the principle that clubs could not be punished with relegation or other sporting punishment because that would alter their business conditions and would make it almost impossible for the club to survive. This pushes forward the clubs' dynamic of losing money due to excess expenditures on players (Barajas & Rodriguez, 2014). Such legislation obviously fuels the SBC syndrome. Moreover, the Spanish *ley del deporte* (law on sports) did not accomplish its goals partly because the national football league actually had no coercive power over the clubs, although it had to supervise and control the balance sheets of the SADs (*sociedad anonima sportiva*).

At a continental football league (here UEFA) level, since 2004 the league football clubs began to have concerns about spending money, that was not earned through their own business, i.e., the SBC. Such practices were suspected of providing a few clubs with what is felt to be an unfair advantage and, possibly, a distortion of competition (Schubert & Hamil, 2018). Labelled financial doping (Müller et al., 2012), indeed they significantly softened the budget constraints of those clubs benefiting from benefactors' money. Later, UEFA adopted the Financial Fair Play (FFP) rules in 2010, and actually implemented them starting from 2012; its objectives were designed to ensure financial stability, not explicitly to harden the clubs and leagues SBCs. However, when encouraging clubs to improve their financial management and performance and to achieve a sustainable balance between income, spending and investments, FFP rules should come out with harder budget constraints. The break-even requirement, in tune with the above model constraint (3.2), would absolutely put an end to SBC (in 3.2') if the requirement is fulfilled.

Hardening the SBC is sometimes wrongly confused with a salary cap or a budget cap, which is then criticised for its distortive effects on sporting competition – competitive balance – and economic competition, namely in critical debates about the UEFA FFP (Budzinski, 2018). When the above constraint (3.2) is fulfilled for all clubs, absolutely nothing is capped, budget expenditures are simply equalised to budget revenues ex ante and ex post and competition is no more distorted than it used to be in an open league system represented by the Késenne model. Moreover, breaking even is the rule rather than the exception in all industries and for all enterprises in a competitive market, it is recommended in all accounting codes and it is the rule of law in all business laws. Equalisation of expenditures to revenues should be the objective of any domestic or international league attempting to harden clubs' budget constraints.

If something is wrong with UEFA FFP, this is not due to its attempt at hardening the SBC but in tolerating a €5 million deficit per year, a threshold that wealthy European clubs take advantage of and which indeed distorts sporting and economic competition to the detriment of clubs that break even; the UEFA FFP has not gone far enough on the path to fulfilling exactly an HBC that is not distortive when $R_i\ (m_i, t_i) - s.t_i - c_i^0 = 0$ exactly.

Now if all clubs in a professional team sport league break even, then the SBC will vanish in the league and, by the same token, the league will gain a warranted financial stability and, last but not least, it will reach its economic equilibrium point – fulfilling the model constraint (3.2) which is the objective of those mainstream economists who usually criticise the UEFA FFP as distortive. Since the FFP really hardens clubs' SBCs (Table 3.2), either their criticism against such regulation is misleading or they have to give up the equilibrium model of open team sports leagues for a disequilibrium model (Andreff, 2014b). As a result of FFP enforcement, the number of leagues with a loss decreased, as also did the percentage of clubs exhibiting a net debt in Table 3.2. Many European football clubs became financially much healthier, and a first step was reached in hardening the SBC, but it is very hard to go further.

Table 3.2   Financial performance in UEFA member leagues, 2010–17

(in € million)								
Performance	2010	2011	2012	2013	2014	2015	2016	2017
Club operating profit/loss	-336	-382	-112	339	799	727	832	1,386
Net bottom-line losses*	1,634	-1,670	-1076	-792	-676	-456	-350	615
Number of leagues with a loss	47	43	41	35	35	30	30	30
Clubs with net debts/total (%)	60	51	52	46	42	40	35	34

Note: * Financial audited statement after tax, adjusted for unrealised foreign exchange gains and losses.
Source: UEFA (2019).

At the end of the day, the credibility of FFP is essentially dependent on UEFA's ability and willingness to sanction some of the most famous clubs in Europe if they breach the rules (Drut & Raballand, 2012). The fact that UEFA's Club Financial Control Body (CFCB) has the ability to impose disciplinary sanctions in case of non-fulfilled requirements makes the FFP enforcement credible. Some clubs have been sanctioned for significant overdue payables. Although behind an apparent statistical success story, one may ask whether the

FFP has entirely succeeded in reaching an HBC at the level of any and every soccer club. The response is probably no.

First, a number of clubs have been sanctioned every year for violating UEFA FFP rules which should not have occurred. Although UEFA FFP has sent a signal in the right direction of hardening clubs' budget constraints, it might not be sufficiently onerous for clubs to put a definite halt on bad managerial practices and their resulting deficits and debts.

Creative bookkeeping,[22] which is a variant of fake accounting, has been one of the clubs' reactions in order to meet UEFA's financial criteria (Schubert, 2014). This calls for stricter club supervision and auditing by the CFCB rather than the opposite if hardening the SBC is targeted. Despite UEFA monitoring processes, Dimitropoulos et al. (2016) demonstrated with a sample of 109 European soccer clubs that, at the expense of accounting quality, club management seeks to promote the image of a financially robust organisation in order to secure licensing and, consequently, much needed funding from UEFA. This way the management culture which impairs financial performance is further cemented, and the SBC is consolidated. According to the authors, UEFA's supervision should be accompanied by the imposition of a corporate governance framework which would aim to rearrange club management priorities. When institutional monitoring is tied to accounting data, managers may be susceptible to disregarding their duty to produce credible financial statements in favour of demonstrating the desired levels of financial capacity required by regulatory agencies.

Finally, it was discovered through Football Leaks that a few clubs, namely Manchester City and PSG, have circumvented the FFP rules (Andreff, 2019b). Both clubs were allowed to artificially write off part of their financial deficits and were not sanctioned[23] as they should have been. This sent a clear incentive not to harden their SBC. Uneven and negotiated enforcement of the rules from club to club is the most pervasive SBC sustaining mechanism. In particular, if those unsanctioned clubs had transfer fee payment overdue payables, the SBC would propagate from club to club which, as in a banking system, would degenerate into a so-called systemic crisis of the league that would jeopardise the long-run viability and sustainability of European club football.

Hard to Impose a Better Efficiency Benchmark at League Level

All football clubs are not evenly efficient partly due to their governance and management, and partly because of other factors. If club efficiency increases, the growth of total output, and thus revenues, is more important than the growth of total input, and thus expenditures. Therefore, improving efficiency helps in coming closer to the break-even point or making profit and counteracts the negative managerial effect of SBC. Consequently, if a league were to recommend that all clubs align on its most efficient members, and provide incentives to do so, this must help all clubs sticking to a harder budget constraint than otherwise; in the same vein, a continental league (for example, UEFA) might counteract a too-harsh SBC effect on some of its national member leagues by advising them to align with the performance of its most efficient leagues. However, it is hard for a league to impose better efficiency and resulting HBC simply through benchmarking accompanied with a watchword such as 'follow the leaders' (in terms of efficiency).

Assessing club and league efficiency in team sports leagues is an area of robust studies in sports economics, namely by Barros et al. (2009), Barros & Leach (2006), Collier et al. (2011), Einolf (2004), Guzman (2006), Guzman & Morrow (2007), Haas et al. (2004) and Zambom-Ferraresi et al. (2017). Such studies offer an opportunity for improving clubs' and leagues' organisational performance and help in sticking to a harder budget constraint. To the best of our knowledge, the results of such studies are not used in any league with a view to improving club efficiency, and therefore countervailing the SBC. Focusing here on the French football league, Miningou & Vierstraete (2012) – considering club payrolls and all other expenditures (transportation costs, commodity purchases) as inputs, and the number of points at the end of season and game attendance as outputs – have exhibited, using a Data Envelopment Analysis (DEA), that the average efficiency score for French football clubs was only 0.625, suggesting that they could have obtained the same output level with 37.5% less input. Among the least efficient, PSG could have saved 80% of its inputs and achieved a similar outcome by operating at maximum efficiency. This probably would have helped PSG avoid being in deficit every year and being managed under an SBC.

Now, at league level, peer groups of national football leagues can be delineated and used as an international benchmark for assessing league organisational and managerial efficiency (for instance by the UEFA over its member leagues) which has been done for European football leagues (Terrien & Andreff, 2020). Retaining three inputs – GDP, population and the number of soccer players in each sampled nation – and five outputs – the UEFA ranking index, a payroll to turnover ratio, a Herfindahl index for the concentration of sporting performances, the market value of talents gathered in a league and average game attendance – it can be seen that no national league shows a pure managerial efficiency equal to one over the 2010–15 period. Therefore, some significant efficiency improvements are possible because each league can optimise its performance after identifying the best practices. This kind of benchmarking could reduce the SBC effect on club management if adopted as a policy tool by football leagues, but it remains to be imposed or, at least, clubs should be provided incentives by leagues to improve efficiency – and national leagues should receive incentives from their umbrella continental league (UEFA). It would probably be hard to implement.

Hard to Halt the Arms Race and Subsequently Curb Salary and Transfer Fee Inflation

Since the Bosman case, the international mobility of soccer players has increased tremendously and, at the superstar segment of the global player talent market (Andreff, 2014b), wages have skyrocketed while ever higher transfer fees have concentrated on a handful of big wealthy European clubs (Andreff, 2018). Clubs are inclined to embark on risky strategies to keep up with these big teams while the latter pay increasingly higher sums for player services due to the rat race for sporting success and the arms race for superstar players (Hamil & Walters, 2010). The arms race between clubs overbidding for superstar talents, which anticipate all their future income in an attempt to put together and develop winning teams, triggers a situation in which only the leading and most solid (wealthiest) clubs are capable of holding out, whereas those that are financially less solid sink into a level from which it is difficult to recover (Baroncelli & Lago, 2006).

In European football, wage increases tend to speed over club revenue increases, in particular in some unprofitable and heavily indebted clubs among the richest and sportingly most successful ones; in 'normal' industries, such clubs would fall under bankruptcy (Müller et al., 2012). For instance, the consequence of overspending on salaries has been sustained losses in Scottish football and half of clubs being technically insolvent – with liabilities greater than their assets (Morrow, 2006); this applies to most national European football leagues. Such a growing overspending trend is even more visible and sensitive as regards the skyrocketing transfer fees of superstar players. In 2010, two-thirds of European top-tier professional football clubs were in the red while one-third disclosed negative equity – debts larger than reported assets. Ad hoc capital injections served to cover losses and liquidity shortfalls, a typical SBC sustaining mechanism. This is the kind of issu" which was tackled by ntroduceing UEFA FFP.

As long as the Bosman jurisprudence prevails, it will be extremely hard to combat those causes of SBC on its expenditure side, such as wage and transfer fee inflation on the one hand. While on the other hand, a re-regulation of the player transfer market does not seem juridically plausible in the post-Bosman context. Moreover, any salary cap adopted in a national football league would easily be circumvented by the best (most expensive) players through an even higher international mobility towards non-capped leagues.

Hard to Check Ex Post League Softening the Budget Constraint with TV Rights Revenues

The so-called financial crisis in European football leagues coincided with the increasing amount of income entering the game (Lago et al., 2006), in particular significant increases in TV rights revenues, the latter becoming the major source of league and club finance (Andreff & Staudohar, 2000); this massive increase in TV rights revenues triggered an even greater increase in spending on players. Tested on the French football league (Andreff, 2007b), a kind of vicious circle ensues. A league, as a monopoly on the market for its own TV rights, bargains for the highest possible TV rights in order ex post to raise the finance that will cover rampant payroll inflation and the escalating costs of superstar recruitment. When this strategy is successful, it will sustain league finances, which will be able to bail out football clubs that are in the red – guaranteeing an ex post rescue for the clubs, a typical scheme of SBC.

However, in many football leagues, like the French league, the recruitment strategy financed by TV revenues does not translate into sufficient team improvement to produce success in European competitions, as required to achieve substantial gain in revenues. Weak sport performance, sanctioned with lower revenues, often does not trigger a proportional downward adjustment of the clubs' expenditures due to the SBC. With the clubs unable to recoup their recruitment expenditures, the league has to revert to the broadcasters in an effort to negotiate an even higher price for the TV rights and so on. The econometrically tested causality (with instrumental variables, Andreff, 2014c) in the relationship between TV revenues and payroll runs from the former to the latter, meaning that the league softens its clubs' budget constraints with redistributing TV revenues in view to enable them ex post to cover their recruitment expenditures. As long as the TV rights accruing to football is on the rise, it will be hard to put a halt on this specific kind of bailing out by the league and associated club SBC.

Hard to Change the League System

Dietl et al. (2008) refer football clubs' financial problems back to the open league (promotion–relegation) system; highly uneven distribution of league revenue, including between top and lower divisions and additional prize money from participating in international club competitions (for example, UEFA's Champions League). All this creates strong incentives to overspend on players. Therefore, it is sometimes suggested to change the open league for a closed league system. Even in the best managed European football league, the *Bundesliga*, insolvency appears, at a frequency comparable to the English and French leagues, according to Szymanski & Weimar (2019). Insolvency is primarily attributable to deviations of actual team performance from expected performance, in particular when such deviations translate into a relegation to a lower tier of competition, which generates lower match attendance and revenues. The latter circumstance cannot be changed in an open league system, which boils down to saying that the SBC is partly linked to or worsened by such a league system. Therefore, it is sometimes suggested to change the open league for a closed league system.

Notice that, with different forms, the SBC syndrome is witnessed in some North American closed leagues (Andreff, 2015; Storm & Nielsen, 2015) so that changing the league system might not help to cure the SBC disease. Moreover, a closed league system has its own self-consistency (Andreff, 2019a), and it would not be efficient to change only a part of the open league system by importing into it one specific rule or regulation (the most often suggested being a salary cap) from the closed league system to improve efficiency and undermine the SBC. With a closed league, in addition to a salary cap, clubs get an enlarged profit-sharing and revenue redistribution scheme (not restricted to TV rights revenues), player recruitment through a reverse-order-of-finish rookie draft, a luxury tax, roster limits, collective bargaining and final offer salary arbitration. It would be extremely hard to convince most European football clubs and leagues to change the current open league for such an over-regulated league system. To some extent, a closed league, with all its rules and regulations, compares to a socialist centrally planned economy (Povich, 1951; Surdam, 2002; Andreff, 2007c, 2012). The latter would not be acceptable from the standpoint of the Bosman jurisprudence and of the EU full competition policy. Next we will look at the macro-dimension of the SBC.

HARDENING THE SOFT BUDGET CONSTRAINT AND TEAM SPORTS LEAGUES' MACRO-ENVIRONMENT

The macro-dimension of SBCs becomes crystal clear when the financial situation of domestic professional football arises as a governmental concern or the matter for a parliamentary report calling, as did for example a French Senate report in 2004, for a brake to be put on drifting financial charges in domestic football and on clubs' debts growing at an unsustainable pace (Andreff, 2007a). While public subsidisation in North American team sports leagues proceeds through local politicians' public spending on construction or replacement of stadiums that benefit franchise owners rather than direct lump-sum payments (Siegfried & Zimbalist, 2000; Hakes & Clapp, 2006), in European football those money streams that facilitate the management or rescue of clubs flow through different channels.

The two aforementioned examples underline that the macro-dimension of SBC heavily depends on domestic institutions, rules and regulations and public policies. Moreover, in particular for EU member countries, some institutions, rules and policies are aligned on an international (European) institutional and policy framework that European football cannot escape. The whole range of such issues is much too wide to be contained within the scope of this chapter. Only three examples are taken on board: the implications on football SBC of tax and fiscal policy; the rule of law enforcement in football with the case of bankruptcy law at national level and then at international level, the impact of a change in law enforcement with the football player market deregulation.

Hard to Enforce Tax and Fiscal Discipline

It is rare that the state (at central government level), just as in former socialist countries, steps in to cover or resolve professional sports financial dire straits. More often other governmental practices sustain the SBC syndrome. A number of clubs are not paying their debt to the state, which appears in their accounts as tax arrears and social contribution arrears; such arrears represent the most significant share of the French football league's total liabilities since 1999 (Andreff, 2014c), with the same observation applying to a number of other European soccer leagues. In Portugal, an inadequate state policy has prevailed in recent years, inducing the football clubs to behave as rent-seekers looking to public funds for their survival and being embroiled in tax debts that are never settled (Barros, 2006). In English soccer, often a claim is made by tax authorities (Inland Revenue, Customs and Excise) for unpaid taxes, which cause a club's entry in to administration.

In 2005, Lazio's Rome managers negotiated with Italian tax authorities regarding the rescheduling over 23 years of a €140 million tax liability to avoid an immediate collapse of the club (Storm & Nielsen, 2012, pp. 193–4), with the support of Rome's mayor. In Italy the SBC syndrome was even institutionalised by a *Salva Calcio* decree issued by the Italian government and adopted by parliament in 2002. The decree softened the requirements of financial reporting by football clubs, of licensing preconditions and regulations enforcement (Hamil et al., 2010) which, de facto, reduced the losses reported by football clubs (Baroncelli & Lago, 2006).

A French 75% tax rate law targeting all incomes over €1 million per year – and not directly aimed at the richest football superstar players – enforced in 2014 was a flop eventually (Terrien et al., 2016). First the tax was paid by the clubs concerned (having recruited the most expensive players) and not by the richest players, which is bad news as regards the probability of handling clubs' costs and SBC. Eventually the taxation was lifted for professional players. This shows that a domestic (national) legislation may both affect the SBC but also miss its target if not fine-tuned.

On the side of fiscal policy, local governments often agree to subsidise the local professional football club, namely in the form of providing the use of the local stadium for free or renting it at below the market price. Since fans and local communities take pride in a club's values and performances, the clubs are heavily backed by their respective regions, i.e., their governments and financial institutions (Barajas & Rodriguez, 2010); to support the local club, they sometimes buy their stocks. However, local governments have been more reluctant to support failing football clubs in the past two decades. This is one step on the path towards hardening clubs' SBC, but it remains a long way off until local governments, under the threat of not being re-elected, would resist to the pressure of clubs' stakeholders (their voters) for spending on football.

Hard to Enforce the Rule of Law: The Bankruptcy Law

A payment failure situation – or insolvency – is when a club's net debt cannot be repaid or reimbursed even by selling the club's total assets (and the net debt is defined as total liabilities being greater than total assets). Consequently, a final way out from insolvency is always a legal response: either an insolvency proceeding or the enforcement of bankruptcy law. The difference is that a club can survive the insolvency proceeding (Scelles et al., 2018) while, in any other industry than professional sport, a bankrupt company disappears from the industry's business and market. After insolvency proceedings, a club may or may not improve its financial performance – i.e., harden its SBC. In the latter case, the insolvency proceeding has no disciplinary or sanction effect over the mismanaged club and the SBC is long-lived. In the former case, where financial accounts are cleaned from net debt – which is rarer in an open league system where often insolvency's sanction is a relegation to a lower tier – bad management only incurs a temporary sanction of the SBC which may re-emerge some years later (Szymanski, 2014; Scelles et al., 2018).

On the other hand, with a bankruptcy law enforcement, the SBC definitively vanishes since the mismanaged company is thrown out of business: the company is liquidated, all its assets are sold, creditors receive their share of what is raised and the business no longer exists. Not only is the financial situation – of both the company and industry – cleared but also the sanction is exemplary and appears as a threat to other mismanaged companies in the industry. If bankruptcy were to be applied to professional team sports, the potential for future SBC would be lowered by the threat of bankruptcy while the actual current SBC would be phased out in bankrupt clubs. Therefore, it will be extremely hard to harden the SBC in European professional team sports as long as they are exempted, legally or de facto, from strict bankruptcy law enforcement.

Under English law, a club that is not able to pay its creditors can choose or be forced into administration. Entering administration was rare before the end of the 1990s. From 1999 to 2004, a quarter of all English professional football clubs experienced administration. This increased frequency of administrations signals that more clubs are in financial dire straits and are unable to harden their SBC-style management. Moreover, in English football, the current practices relating to insolvency leave scope for free-riding behaviour. For instance, Leicester City's rival clubs complained that the administration process (October 2001 to February 2003), when a consortium established a successful takeover bid, was unduly long and that during this period Leicester did not pay its creditors.

In Spanish football, local banks and economic forces allowed football clubs to borrow such large amounts of money to cover the expenditures on player acquisition which rose significantly after an increase in revenues. Club owners know that Catalonian or Castilian banks will always assist in covering losses in FC Barcelona and Real Madrid, because these clubs are national institutions (Ascari & Gagnepain, 2006). In these cases, bankruptcy is simply not an option. Under Belgian law, it is impossible for a non-profit organisation to go bankrupt (Dejonghe & Vandeweghe, 2006).

Changing the legal status of professional football clubs – transforming them from a non-profit company into a stockholding corporation – may become compulsory through passing a new law on the parliament, as was done in France and Spain. So far, this has changed neither the weak financial performance, nor the SBC behaviour in football clubs, even when shares are floated on the stock exchange (Olympique Lyonnais) or more generally in the whole Spanish league (Sanchez et al., 2017).

Transforming all clubs into specific 'sporting stockholding companies' as has been done in French football is not a solution: these companies are not allowed to pay dividends, and residual claimants have no incentive to make profits that would harden the SBC. When such a company has been floated on the stock exchange, as happened in the case of Olympique Lyonnais, the share value swiftly dropped and the fans-shareholders lost money.

Table 3.3   *Transfer fees in the Big Five, top seven spending clubs, 2014–2018*

English PL	Fees (million €)	Spanish LL	Fees (million €)	German BL	Fees (million €)
Manchester City	951.4	FC Barcelona	778.0	Bayern Munich	390.9
Manchester United	777.9	Atletico Madrid	479.6	Borussia Dortmund	368.7
Chelsea	749.2	Real Madrid	457.5	Wolfsburg	308.1
Liverpool	582.9	Valencia	308.5	Bayer Leverkusen	230.5
Tottenham Hotspur	446.5	Sevilla	253.0	Leipzig	191.0
Arsenal	420.6	Villareal	183.9	Schalke 04	155.8
Everton	410.2	Real Sociedad	83.1	Borussia Mönchengladbach	134.2
Total	4338.6	Total	2543.6	Total	1779.1
Italian SA	Fees	French L1	Fees		
Juventus	592.7	Paris Saint-Germain	678.0		
Inter Milan	432.7	Olympique Marseille	191.1		
AS Roma	428.7	Olympique Lyon	139.2		
AC Milan	368.5	Lille OSC	108.4		
Napoli	344.3	Rennes	92.00		
Fiorentina	186.5	Saint-Etienne	67.2		
Sampdoria	167.8	Bordeaux	63.8		
Total	2521.2	Total	1339.6		

Source: Transfermarkt (2018).

Hard to Hedge Against Superstar Players' Greater Contractual Power after Labour Market Deregulation

For years the Treaty of Rome was not enforced in the sports and football industry as regards its article warranting free labour mobility on a European unified labour market. The Bosman case boiled down to enforcing the Treaty in the labour market for football player talent. Since then, the Bosman ruling and the ensuing liberalisation of the player market have intensified the interleague competition for players, especially for superstars, and have then fuelled the necessity of overbidding for clubs to acquire the best players. This major source of SBC could not vanish unless a new international restrictive regulation of international player transfers were to be adopted and enforced, which is not foreseeable at the EU level; therefore, the SBC will survive in the foreseeable future.

The Bosman ruling transformed the global player labour market from monopsonistic to competitive on the demand side and to monopolistic on the supply side in the case of superstars; this monopoly situation has increased players' contractual power, in particular for superstars. Since it is not possible to legally nullify Bosman jurisprudence on the one hand and, on the other hand, it is hard to circumvent the rule of law in this respect, it has become harder and harder for clubs to countervail superstar players' (and their agents') contractual power and, thus, to avoid paying higher prices, i.e., higher individual wages and higher transfer fees. The strong contractual power of superstar players compels all the clubs to trade off between overspending on player talents, thus fuelling the SBC, or giving up superstar recruitment which translates into a low probability of winning on the pitch, lower attendance and TV rights and, finally, lower revenues that make it even harder to break even, therefore eventually nurturing an SBC survival as well.

Since football clubs cannot resist the superstar players' monopoly power, they have only a choice between paying them or playing them (in opponent teams), a choice eventually limited to a handful of wealthy European soccer clubs that can afford to pay skyrocketing transfer fees and do concentrate the major part of superstar transfers (Table 3.3). Thus, superstars' monopoly power fuels the 'investment thirst' of player recruitment which, at the end of the day, reproduces the SBC again and again. Following the literature on rent-seeking and hold-up in labour markets (Malcomson, 1997), then applied to German soccer (Feess et al., 2015), it has been suggested that monopolist, rent-seeking, superstar professional players actually hold up soccer clubs and impose on them an increasing wage cost inflation (Bastien, 2018). If it were to be so, superstar players' strategy is a major determinant of club overspending and a major fuel of the expenditure side of SBC. Held-up clubs have no other way out than paying a skyrocketing price for acquiring superstars and digging an ever-deeper deficit – then long lives SBC!

CONCLUSION

The conclusion arising out of the above analysis is that it is neither likely nor predictable that micro, meso and macro sources of the SBC would vanish or be eradicated in team sports (football) leagues and clubs in the foreseeable future. As a consequence, the SBC remains an attractive avenue for further research in sports economics. By the same token, the SBC will go on being a serious economic concern in the actual development of professional team sports, in particular in European football.

NOTES

1. The reference pertains to the French translation: J. Kornai (2014), *A la force de la pensée: Autobiographie irrégulière*, Paris: L'Harmattan.
2. A net debt occurs when a club's liabilities exceed its assets. A net debt accumulation is not sustainable after some time.
3. The French football league auditing body (*Direction Nationale de Contrôle de Gestion* – DNCG) required the publication and anyone's open access to clubs' financial accounts in 2003, though some reluctant clubs postponed this new rule enforcement until 2005 or 2006 (accepting to pay a fine in between).
4. When that paper was in the process of being written, in 2010, according to UEFA data, 41 national top division leagues (out of 54) were in the red and all UEFA member leagues together exhibited a €336 million aggregate loss, while 60% of all top division clubs had a net debt.
5. This is the wording initially adopted by Malinvaud (1977) and Benassy (1982) to coin this kind of model that can never reach Walrasian equilibrium.
6. The first reference to a dual market for football players is in Bourg (1983).
7. Excess demand in European football may be approximated by the number of inhabitants per team in the top league; in the Big Five football leagues, it is on average 3 million inhabitants per team (Andreff, 2019a). North American professional team sports leagues organise a more severe shortage of games with 10 million inhabitants per team on average.
8. At this point, Korna explicitly refers to the Barro–Grossman (1974) model and its suppressed inflation regime.
9. While consumers, being on the long side (excess demand) of the market for goods, endeavour an HBC in a socialist economy.
10. It was contended that Kornai (1980) is an attempt at rooting shortages into – not really micro (at the level of each agent's behaviour) – infra-microeconomic foundations, at the level of each decision (buying, producing, selling, investing, recruiting) made by each decision maker at each time *t* (Andreff, 1986). This infra-micro-dimension is not taken on board in this chapter.
11. In Soviet-style planned economies, the intensity of shortage in a given industry was highly dependent on its ranking in the pecking order adopted by central planners (Andreff, 1993).
12. Mesoeconomic or industrial input shortages generate forced substitutions of those missing products, a process through which shortages spill over, step by step, to the whole economy, then founding a (macro) shortage economy.
13. Kornai's SBC triggered a number of interpretations but few criticisms. A possibly mistaken, critical Chinese assessment has not yet surfaced internationally; it simply denies the very existence of SBCs with the following statement 'that a hard budget constraint exists for each specific problem' (Luo, 2014).
14. Since in the following we consider, by the same token, micro, meso and macro determinants of the SBC, we do not opt for the exogenous or endogenous explanation of the SBC. Since Kornai (1998), the SBC is said to be exogenous when determined by exogenous reasons such as state paternalism, government's aims for job creation or to gain political support. The SBC is said to be endogenous when arising from a commitment and time-inconsistency problem as with the Dewatripont–Maskin model or an accountability problem – the state is accounta-

   ble for state-owned firms' losses, policy burdens and plan failures (Lin and Tan, 1999); see also Vahabi (2001).

15. For instance, in German equestrian sports, non-profit organisations perform better in terms of price structure and social aspects while profit organisations outperform as regard financial performance and quality (Nowy et al., 2015).

16. Ex post means here when the club's financial deficit is surfacing which also means 'too late' in terms of good management.

17. It has been shown that fans wish their favourite team to win at least two-thirds of its games (Buraimo & Simmons, 2008; Rascher & Solmes, 2007).

18. For instance, in French football, it has been compulsory for clubs to publish their financial accounts since 2004 (Andreff, 2007a), which has neither hardened the SBC nor alleviated the fans' spending pressure on managers.

19. A number of money streams associated with tax evasion were unveiled by Football Leaks, which is a leak of 18.6 million documents about tax evasion in the football business that were obtained by *Der Spiegel* from the European Investigative Collaborations (a group of European media) and publicised in December 2016.

20. Since Fenerbahçe and Trabzonspor board members, managers, coaches and players were involved in a huge match fixing scandal in 2011 encompassing the payment of opponent teams' players and chairmen (Andreff, 2019b), some doubt may be raised against their accounting transparency and effectively 'clean' profit-making.

21. Note that performance-based and media-based revenue redistribution already distorts sporting competition and benefits to the wealthiest clubs, and thus deepens interclub economic inequality.

22. Creative accounting is also used to inflate assets and hide liabilities (Dietl & Franck, 2007). Note that cooking the books was the very first tool of state-owned companies run under an SBC for providing fake statistics (showing a false 100% fulfilment of their plan) in centrally planned economies (Andreff, 1993).

23. In September 2017, again a new UEFA inquiry was opened against PSG. Due to its purchase of Neymar and Kylian M'Bappé, PSG breached the FFP rules with a €74 million deficit over the previous three years (instead of the €30 million allowed). Again, an amicable arrangement was agreed by PSG with UEFA: the club would not be sanctioned but it must accept a 37% devaluation of its QTA sponsorship contracts and sell some players, which is what it did. PSG financial accounts are still under the CFCB examination at the time of writing.

REFERENCES

Aglietta, M., Andreff, W. & Drut, B. (2008). Bourse et football. *Revue d'Economie Politique*, 118(2), 255–96.

Andreff, W. (1986). Compte rendu de J. Kornai, 'Socialisme et économie de la pénurie' (Comment on *Economics of Shortage*). *Revue d'Economie Politique*, 96(1), 68–73.

Andreff, W. (1993). *La crise des économies socialistes: La rupture d'un système*, Grenoble: Presses Universitaires de Grenoble.

Andreff, W. (2000). Financing Modern Sport in the Face of a Sporting Ethic. *European Journal for Sport Management*, 7(1), 5–30.

Andreff, W. (2005). The Financial Crisis in French Soccer: About a French Senate Report, *7th IASE Conference*, Ottawa, 18–19 June.

Andreff, W. (2006). Dérives financières: une remise en cause de l'organisation du sport. *Finance et Bien Commun*, 26, 27–35.

Andreff, W. (2007a). French Football: A Financial Crisis Rooted in Weak Governance. *Journal of Sports Economics*, 8(6), 652–61.

Andreff, W. (2007b). Governance Issues in French Professional Football. In Rodríguez, P., Késenne, S. & Garcia, J. (Eds), *Governance and Competition in Professional Sports Leagues*, Oviedo: Ediciones de la Universidad de Oviedo, 47–78.

Andreff, W. (2007c). Régulation et institutions en économie du sport. *Revue de la Régulation: Capitalisme, Institutions, Pouvoirs*, 1, juin, varia.

Andreff, W. (2009). Equilibre compétitif et contrainte budgétaire dans une ligue de sport professionnel. *Revue Economique*, 60(2), 591–634.

Andreff, W. (2011). Some Comparative Economics of the Organization of Sports: Competition and Regulation in North American vs. European Professional Team Sports Leagues. *European Journal of Comparative Economics*, 8(1), 3–27.

Andreff, W. (2012). *Mondialisation économique du sport. Manuel européen d'Economie du sport*, Bruxelles: De Boeck.

Andreff, W. (2014a). Le réalisme économique de János Kornai: évolutif et éclectique. *Economies et Sociétés*, série Histoire de la pensée économique, 50(6), 1039–62.

Andreff, W. (2014b). Building Blocks for a Disequilibrium Model of a European Team Sports League. *International Journal of Sport Finance*, 9(1), 20–38.

Andreff, W. (2014c). French Professional Football: How Much Different? In Goddard, J. & Sloane, P. (Eds), *Handbook on the Economics of Professional Football*, Cheltenham: Edward Elgar Publishing, 298–321.

Andreff, W. (2015). Governance of Professional Team Sports Clubs: Agency Problem and Soft Budget Constraint. In Andreff, W. (Ed.), *Disequilibrium Sports Economics: Competitive Imbalance and Budget Constraints*, Cheltenham: Edward Elgar Publishing, 175–227.

Andreff, W. (2018). Financial and Sporting Performance in French Football Ligue 1: Influence on the Players' Market. *International Journal of Financial Studies*, 6(4), 55–71. https://doi.org/10.3390/ijfs6040091.

Andreff, W. (2019a). Origins and Developments of Sports Systems. In Downward, P., Frick, B., Humphreys, B.R., Pawlowski, T., Ruseski, J.E. & Soebbing, B.P. (Eds), *The SAGE Handbook of Sports Economics*, London: Sage.

Andreff, W. (2019b). *An Economic Roadmap to the Dark Side of Sport*, Pivot in Sports Economics, Cham: Palgrave Macmillan.

Andreff, W. & Bourg, J.-F. (2006). Broadcasting Rights and Competition in European Football. In Jeanrenaud, C. & Késenne S (Eds), *The Economics of Sport and the Media*, Cheltenham: Edward Elgar Publishing, 37–70.

Andreff, W. & Scelles, N. (2015). Walter C. Neale 50 Years After: Beyond Competitive Balance, the League Standing Effect Tested with French Football Data. *Journal of Sports Economics*, 16(8), 819–34.

Andreff, W. & Staudohar, P. (2000). The Evolving European Model of Professional Sports Finance. *Journal of Sports Economics*, 1(3), 257–76.

Ascari, G. & Gagnepain, P. (2006). Spanish Football. *Journal of Sports Economics*, 7(1), 76–89.

Barajas, A. & Rodriguez, P. (2010). Spanish Football Clubs' Finances: Crisis and Player Salaries. *International Journal of Sport Finance*, 5(1), 52–66.

Barajas, A. & Rodriguez, P. (2014). Spanish Football in Need of Financial Therapy: Cut Expenses and Inject Capital. *International Journal of Sport Finance*, 9(1), 73–90.

Baroncelli, A. & Lago, U. (2006). Italian Football. *Journal of Sports Economics*, 7(1), 13–28.

Barro, R.J. & Grossman, H.I. (1971). A General Disequilibrium Model of Income and Unemployment. *American Economic Review*, 61(1), 82–93.

Barro, R.J. & Grossman, H.I. (1974). Suppressed Inflation and the Supply Multiplier. *Review of Economic Studies*, 41(1), 87–104.

Barros, C.P. (2006). Portuguese Football. *Journal of Sports Economics*, 7(1), 96–104.

Barros, C.P. & Leach, S. (2006). Performance Evaluation of the English Premier Football League with Data Envelopment Analysis. *Applied Economics*, 38(12), 1449–58.

Barros, C.P. & Lucas, J. (2001). Sports Managers and Subsidies. *European Sport Management Quarterly*, 1(2), 112–23.

Barros, C.P., Garcia del Barrio, P. & Leach, S. (2009). Analysing the Technical Efficiency of the Spanish Football League First Division with a Random Frontier Model. *Applied Economics*, 41(25), 3239–47.

Bastien, J. (2018). Une analyse économique des contrats de travail dans l'industrie du sport professionnel: *Hold-up* en football. *Economie et institutions*, 27. https://doi:10.4000/ei.6189.

Benassy, J.-P. (1982). *The Economics of Market Disequilibrium*, New York: Academic Press.

Berglöf, E. & Roland, G. (1998). Soft Budget Constraints and Banking in Transition Economies, *Journal of Comparative Economics*, 26(1), 18–40.

Bourg, J.F. (1983). *Salaire, travail et emploi dans le football professionnel français*, Centre de Droit et d'Economie du Sport, Université de Limoges.

Buchholz, F. & Lopatta, K. (2017). Stakeholder Salience of Economic Investors on Professional Football Clubs in Europe. *European Sport Management Quarterly*, 17(4), 506–30.

Budzinski, O. (2018). Financial Regulation as an Anticompetitive Institution. In Breuer, M. & Forrest, D. (Eds), *The Palgrave Handbook on the Economic of Manipulation in Sport*, Cham: Palgrave Macmillan, 159–79.

Buraimo, B. & Simmons, R. (2008). Do Sports Fans Really Value Uncertainty of Outcome? Evidence from the English Premier League. *International Journal of Sport Finance*, 3(3), 146–55.

Buraimo, B., Simmons, R. & Szymanski, S. (2006). English Football. *Journal of Sports Economics*, 7(1), 29–46.

Clower, R. (1965). The Keynesian Counter-Revolution: A Theoretical Appraisal. In Hahn, F.H. & Brechling, F.P.R. (Eds), *The Theory of Interest Rates*, London: Macmillan, 103–25.

Collier, T., Johnson, A.L. & Ruggiero, J. (2011). Measuring Technical Efficiency in Sports. *Journal of Sports Economics*, 12(6), 579–98.

De Barros, C., Barros, C.P. & Correia, A. (2007). Governance in Sports Clubs: Evidence for the Island of Madeira. *European Sport Management Quarterly*, 7(2), 123–39.

Dejonghe, T. & Vandeweghe, H. (2006). Belgian Football. *Journal of Sports Economics*, 7(1), 105–13.

Dewatripont, M. & Maskin, E. (1995). Credit and Efficiency in Centralized and Decentralized Economies. *Review of Economic Studies*, 62(4), 541–55.

Dietl, H.M. & Franck, E. (2007). Governance Failure and Financial Crisis in German Football. *Journal of Sports Economics*, 8(6), 662–9.

Dietl, H.M., Franck, E. & Lang, M. (2008). Overinvestment in Team Sports Leagues. A Contest Theory Model. *Scottish Journal of Political Economy*, 55(3), 353–68.

Dimitropoulos, P. (2011). Corporate Governance and Earnings Management in the European Football Industry. *European Sport Management Quarterly*, 11(5), 495–523.

Dimitropoulos, P. & Tsagkanos, A. (2012). Financial Performance and Corporate Governance in the European Football Industry. *International Journal of Sport Finance*, 7(4), 280–308.

Dimitropoulos, P., Leventis, S. & Dedoulis, E. (2016). Managing the European Football Industry: UEFA's Regulatory Intervention and the Impact of Accounting Quality. *European Sport Management Quarterly*, 16(4), 459–86.

Drut, B. & Raballand, G. (2012). Why Does Financial Regulation Matter for European Professional Football Clubs. *International Journal of Sport Management and Marketing*, 11(1), 73–88.

Einolf, K.W. (2004). Is Winning Everything? A Data Envelopment Analysis of Major League Baseball and the National Football League. *Journal of Sports Economics*, 5(2), 127–51.

Feess, E., Gerfin, M. & Muehlheusser, G. (2015). Contracts as Rent-seeking Devices: Evidence from German Soccer. *Economic Inquiry*, 53(1), 714–30.

Fort, R. & Quirk, J. (1995). Cross-subsidization, Incentives and Outcomes in Professional Team Sports Leagues. *Journal of Economic Literature*, 33(3), 1265–99.

Franck, E. (2014). Financial Fair Play in European Club Football – What is it All About? *International Journal of Sport Finance*, 9(1), 193–217.

Franck, E. (2015). Regulation in Leagues with Clubs' Soft Budget Constraints: The Effect of the New UEFA Club Licensing and Financial Fair Play Regulations on Managerial Incentive and Suspense. In Andreff, W. (Ed.), *Disequilibrium Sports Economics: Competitive Imbalance and Budget Constraints*, Cheltenham: Edward Elgar Publishing, 228–49.

Frick, B. & Prinz, J. (2006). Crisis? What Crisis? Football in Germany. *Journal of Sports Economics*, 7(1), 60–75.

Goldfeld, S.M. & Quandt, R.E. (1988). Budget Constraints, Bailouts and the Firm under Central Planning. *Journal of Comparative Economics*, 12(4), 502–20.

Goldfeld, S.M. & Quandt, R.E. (1993). Uncertainty, Bailouts, and the Kornai Effect. *Economics Letters*, 41(2), 113–19.

Gomulka, S. (1985). Kornai's Soft Budget Constraint and the Shortage Phenomenon: A Criticism and Restatement. *Economics of Planning*, 19(1), 1–11.

Gudasic, D. (2018). Croatian Club Football and the Transition from Former Yugoslavia to Croatia, MESGO Master thesis, Nyon.

Guzman, I. (2006). Measuring Efficiency and Sustainable Growth in Spanish Football Teams. *European Sport Management Quarterly*, 6(3), 267–87.

Guzman, I. & Morrow, S. (2007). Measuring Efficiency and Productivity in Professional Football Teams: Evidence from the English Premier League. *Central European Journal of Operations Research*, 15(4), 309–28.

Haas, D.J., Kocher, G.M. & Sutter, M. (2004). Measuring Efficiency of German Football Teams by Data Envelopment Analysis. *Central European Journal of Operations Research*, 12(3), 251–68.

Hakes, J.K. & Clapp, C.M. (2006). The Edifice Complex: The Economics of Public Subsidization of Major League Baseball Facilities. *International Journal of Sport Finance*, 1(2), 77–95.

Hamil, S. & Walters, G. (2010). Financial Performance in English Professional Football: 'An Inconvenient Truth'. *Soccer & Society*, 11(4), 354–72.

Hamil, S., Morrow, S., Idle, C., Rossi, G. & Faccendini, S. (2010). The Governance and Regulation of Italian Football. *Soccer & Society*, 11(4), 373–413.

Havran, Z. & Andras, K. (2016). Understanding Soft Budget Constraint in Western European and Central-Eastern-European Professional Football, Corvinus University Budapest.

Hersch, P.L. & Pelkowski, J.E. (2019). The Consequences (and Nonconsequences) of Ownership Change: The Case of Major League Baseball. *Journal of Sports Economics*, 20(1), 72–90.

Késenne, S. (1996). League Management in Professional Team Sports with Win Maximizing Clubs. *European Journal of Sport Management*, 2(2), 14–22.

Kornai, J. (1958). Kell-e korrigàlni a nyereségrészesedést? (Is the Profit-sharing Practice to be Corrected?). *Közgazdasàgi Szemle*, 5(7), 720–34.

Kornai, J. (1971). *Anti-Equilibrium. On Economic Systems Theory and the Tasks of Research*, Amsterdam: North Holland.

Kornai, J. (1972). *Rush versus Harmonic Growth*, Amsterdam: North Holland.

Kornai, J. (1979). Resource-Constrained versus Demand-Constrained Systems. *Econometrica*, 47(4), 801–19.

Kornai, J. (1980). *Economics of Shortage*, Amsterdam: North Holland.

Kornai, J. (1986). The Soft Budget Constraint. *Kyklos*, 39(1), 3–30.

Kornai, J. (1992). *The Socialist System. The Political Economy of Communism*, Oxford: Clarendon Press.

Kornai, J. (2005). *A gondola erejével, Rendhagyoönéletrajz (By Force of Thought: Irregular Memoirs of an Intellectual Journey)*, Cambridge, MA: The MIT Press, 2008.

Kornai, J., Maskin, E. & Roland, G. (2003). Understanding the Soft Budget Constraint. *Journal of Economic Literature*, 41(4), 1095–1136.

Lago, U., Simmons, R. & Szymanski, S. (2006). The Financial Crisis in European Football: An Introduction. *Journal of Sports Economics*, 7(1), 3–12.

Leach, S. & Szymanski, S. (2015). Making Money out of Football. *Scottish Journal of Political Economy*, 62(1), 25–50.

Lin, J. Y. & Tan, G. (1999). Policy Burdens, Accountability, and the Soft Budget Constraint. *American Economic Review*, 89(2), 426–31.

Luo, C. (2014). Questioning the Soft Budget Constraint. *Annals of Economics and Finance*, 15(1), 251–60.

Malcomson, J.M. (1997). Contracts, Hold-up, and Labor Markets. *Journal of Economic Literature*, 35(4), 1916–57.

Malinvaud, E. (1977). *The Theory of Unemployment Reconsidered*, Oxford: Basil Blackwell.

Maskin, E. & Xu, C. (2001). Soft Budget Constraint Theories: From Centralization to the Market. *Economics of Transition*, 9(1), 1–27.

Michie, J. & Oughton, C. (2005). The Corporate Governance of Professional Football Clubs in England. *Corporate Governance: An International Review*, 13(4), 517–31.

Miningou, E.W. & Vierstraete, V. (2012). Efficience des clubs français de football des Ligues 1 et 2. *Revue d'Economie Politique*, 122(1), 37–66.

Morrow, S. (2006). Scottish Football: It's a Funny Old Business. *Journal of Sports Economics*, 7(1), 90–5.

Morrow, S. (2013). Football Club Financial Reporting: Time for a New Model? *Sport, Business and Management: An International Journal*, 4, 297–311.

Müller, C., Lammert, J. & Hovemann, G. (2012). The Financial Fair Play Regulations of UEFA: An Adequate Concept to Ensure the Long-term Viability and Sustainability of European Club Football? *International Journal of Sport Finance*, 7(2), 117–40.

Nielsen, K. (2017). Profit Maximization, Win Optimization and Soft Budget Constraints in Professional Team Sports, Birkbeck, University of London, mimeo draft.

Nowy, T., Wicker, P., Feiler, S. & Breuer, C. (2015). Organisational Performance of Non-profit and For-profit Sport Organisations. *European Sport Management Quarterly*, 15(2), 155–75.

Piore, P.B. & Doeringer, M.J. (1971). *Internal Labor Markets and Manpower Analysis*, New York: Lexington Heath.

Poli, R. (2007). Transferts de footballeurs: la dérive de la marchandisation. *Finance & Bien Commun*, 26, 40–47.

Povich, S. (1951). He Sighs over Foes' TV Take. *Baseball Digest*, August.

Qian, Y. (1994). A Theory of Shortage in Socialist Economies Based Upon the 'Soft Budget Constraint'. *American Economic Review*, 84(1), 145–56.

Rascher, D.A. & Solmes, J.P.G. (2007). Do Fans Want Close Contests? A Test of the Uncertainty of Outcome Hypothesis in the National Basketball Association. *International Journal of Sport Finance*, 2(3), 130–41.

Robinson, J.A. & Torvik, R. (2009). A Political Economy Theory of the Soft Budget Constraint. *European Economic Review*, 53(7), 786–98.

Sanchez, L.C., Barajas, A. & Sanchez-Fernandez, P. (2017). Does the Agency Theory Play Football? *Universia Business Review*, 14(1). https://doi:10.3232/UBR.2017.V14.N1.01.

Sanchez, L.C., Sanchez-Fernandez, P. & Barajas, A. (2016). Estructuras de propriedad y rentabilidad financiera en el futboll europeo. *Journal of Sports Economics y Management*, 6(1), 5–17.

Scelles, N., Szymanski, S. & Dermit-Richard, N. (2018). Insolvency in French Soccer: The Case of Payment Failure. *Journal of Sports Economics*, 19(5), 603–24.

Scelles, N., Durand, C., Bonnal, L., Goyeau, D. & Andreff, W. (2013). Competitive Balance versus Competitive Intensity Before a Match: Is One of these Concepts More Relevant in Explaining Attendance? The Case of the French Football Ligue 1 over the Period 2008–2011. *Applied Economics*, 45(29), 4184–92.

Schaffer, M.E. (1998). Do Firms in Transition Economies Have Soft Budget Constraints? A Reconsideration of Concepts and Evidence. *Journal of Comparative Economics*, 26(1), 80–103.

Schubert, M. (2014). Potential Agency Problems in European Club Football? The Case of UEFA Financial Fair Play. *Sport, Business and Management: An International Journal*, 4(4), 336–50.

Schubert, M. & Hamil, S. (2018). Financial Doping and Financial Fair Play in European Club Football Competitions. In Breuer, M. & Forrest D. (Eds), *The Palgrave Handbook on the Economics of Manipulation in Sport*, Cham: Palgrave Macmillan, 135–57.

Siegfried, J. & Zimbalist, A. (2000). The Economics of Sport Facilities and their Communities. *Journal of Economic Perspectives*, 14(3), 95–114.

Storm, R.K. (2010). Professional Team Sports Clubs: Cases of Soft Budget Constraints in Capitalist Economies? Danish Institute for Sport Studies, Syddansk Universitet working paper.

Storm, R.K. & Nielsen, K. (2012). Soft Budget Constraints in Professional Football. *European Sport Management Quarterly*, 12(2), 183–201.

Storm, R.K. & Nielsen, K. (2015). Soft Budget Constraints in European and US Leagues: Similarities and Differences. In Andreff, W. (Ed), *Disequilibrium Sports*

Economics: Competitive Imbalance and Budget Constraints, Cheltenham: Edward Elgar Publishing, 151–74.

Surdam, D. (2002). The American 'Not So Socialist' League in the Post-war Era. The Limitations of Gate Sharing in Reducing Revenue Disparity in Baseball. *Journal of Sports Economics*, 3(3), 264–90.

Szymanski, S. (2014). Insolvency in English football. In Goddard, J. & Sloane, P. (Eds), *Handbook on the Economics of Professional Football*, Cheltenham: Edward Elgar Publishing, 100–16.

Szymanski, S. & Weimar, D. (2019). Insolvencies in Professional Football: A German Sonderweg? *International Journal of Sport Finance*, 14(1), 54–68.

Terrien, M. & Andreff, W. (2020). Organisational Efficiency of National Football Leagues in Europe. *European Sport Management Quarterly*, 20(2), 205–24. https://doi:10.1080/16184742.2019.1598455.

Terrien, M., Scelles, N. & Durand, C. (2016). French 75% Tax Rate: An Opportunity to Optimize the Attractiveness of the French Soccer League. *International Journal of Sport Finance*, 11(3), 183–203.

Transfermarkt (2014–2018). https//www.transfermarkt.com.

Turner, G. (2016). Measuring the United Kingdom's 'Offshore Game'. In *Global Corruption Report: Sport*, Transparency International, Copyright material provided by Taylor & Francis, London, 106–8.

UEFA (2019). *The European Club Footballing Landscape: Club Licensing Benchmark Report, Financial Year 2017*, Nyon: UEFA.

Vahabi, M. (2001). The Soft Budget Constraint: A Theoretical Clarification. *Recherches Economiques de Louvain, Louvain Economic Review*, 67(2), 157–95.

Vahabi, M. (2014). Soft Budget Constraint Reconsidered. *Bulletin of Economic Research*, 66(1), 1–19.

Verschuuren, P. & Kalb, C. (2013). *Money Laundering: The Latest Threat to Sports Betting?* Paris: IRIS (Institut de Relations Internationales et Stratégiques) Editions.

Wilson, R., Ramchandani, G. & Plumley, D. (2018). Parachute Payments in English Football: Softening the Landing or Distorting the Balance? *Journal of Global Sport Management*. https://doi: 10.1080/24704067.2018.1441740.

Woo, W.T. (2017). China's Soft Budget Constraint on the Demand-side Undermines its Supply-side Structural Reforms. *China Economic Review*. https://doi.org/10.1016/j.chieco.2017.09.010.

Zambom-Ferraresi, F., Garcia-Cebrian, L.I., Lera-Lopez, F. & Iraizoz, B. (2017). Performance Evaluation in the UEFA Champions League. *Journal of Sports Economics*, 18(5), 448–70.

4. Budget constraints in French professional football: contrasting situations

Nadine Dermit-Richard and Aurélien François

INTRODUCTION

Recent studies in sports economics agree that the professional team sports clubs competing in Europe operate within soft budget constraints (SBCs), and this is especially so for football (Andreff, 2007, 2009, 2015; Storm & Nielsen, 2012, 2015; Franck, 2014). Within the framework of the European open leagues, which are based on the promotion of the strongest clubs and the relegation of the weakest, the club objective is to maximize performance (Sloane, 1971; Ascari & Gagnepain, 2006; Késenne, 1996, 2007). However, the results depend on talent recruitment, and pressure is intense to recruit the best possible players to gain a competitive advantage (Szymanski & Kuypers, 1999; Hall et al., 2002). Authors have described this strategy as being like an 'arms race', with clubs recruiting beyond their needs (Rosen & Sanderson, 2001; Ascari & Gagnepain, 2006; Solberg & Haugen, 2010). In a competitive market, this strategy generates an excessive demand for players, which then drives up salaries (Andreff, 2018; Staudohar, 2004) and ultimately causes recurring financial difficulties for the European football clubs. The Union of European Football Associations (UEFA) thus noted a record cumulative deficit of €1,675 million over the 2010–2011 season for the 679 football clubs making up the first-tier division of the 53 UEFA domestic leagues (UEFA, 2013, p. 105).

In a traditional market economy, this accumulation of deficits would lead to bankruptcy. However, the clubs regularly find external financing to compensate, thus remaining solvent and avoiding bankruptcy. This situation characterizes the clubs that operate under an SBC. For example, in the case of the French Ligue 1, Andreff (2018) showed that the league operates within an SBC, given the recurring and generalized deficits that can be explained by high club payrolls yet very few bankruptcies.

Some French, English and German football clubs have nevertheless gone bankrupt (Carin, 2019; Scelles et al., 2018; Szymanski, 2017; Szymanski & Weimar, 2019) which raises questions about the limits of applying the SBC approach. A large part of these contributions establishes a link between bankruptcies and the ranking level of the clubs concerned. We thus assumed that the level of budget constraint imposed on clubs is not uniform and that, although some clubs operate within an SBC, others are subject to a hard budget constraint (HBC). Consistently with the aforementioned work, our main hypothesis is that the level of budget constraint varies according to the sporting level of the club. To test it, we carried out analyses at the club level rather than the leagues as a whole, thereby selecting the French professional football that was able to provide the necessary financial data for a significant period of analysis. This chapter is thus structured in four parts. We first present a brief literature review on SBC in professional football. Then we display our results after having described the methodological design of the study. In the discussion part, we offer a typology of the degree of budgetary constraints which clubs should face according to their financial profiles.

BRIEF LITERATURE REVIEW

This contribution relies on the soft budget constraint (SBC) approach. Developed by Kornai (1980) within the framework of planned socialist economies, it has been transposed into market economies where the organizational objective is the maximization of production rather than profit (Kornai, Maskin & Roland, 2003). This is the case of the open team sports leagues (Andreff, 2015) since the promotion/relegation system pushes clubs to maximize their production/performance in order to avoid relegation and the significant drop in revenue that ensues (Morrow, 2006; Vrooman, 2007). SBC has not only been applied to socialist systems. Recently, this research line has interested authors whose studies put the focus on liberal market economies. As argued by Kornai et al. (2003, p. 1095), the SBC approach is increasingly acknowledged to be pertinent well beyond the realm of socialist and transition economies and is now encountered in various national business systems and situations (Kornai, 2014).

European Football as a Fertile Ground for Applying the SBC 'Theory'

It is widely acknowledged that the business of professional team sports is peculiar (Neale, 1964). In Europe, it is even more peculiar given the predominant logic of sporting results over financial ones (Andreff, 2015). Theoretically, the pursuit of 'win maximization' is limited by a break-even constraint required by the national bodies in charge of controlling the club's financial account and by other control mechanisms, such as Financial Fair Play, for the most successful clubs in Europe. In practice, this is not always the case. Thus, Storm & Nielsen (2015) have attempted to apply the SBC concept to the European football by postulating the existence of a 'softness' with regards to the club's budget constraints. Based on Kornai's assumptions, they identified six types of softness (S-conditions):

- Soft administrative pricing (S1) illustrated by the acquisition by a club of a stadium or other facilities at a below-market interest rate or, conversely, the sale of the stadium naming rights to the public authorities at an above-market price.
- Soft taxing (S2) designing all kinds of tax exemptions granted by the public authorities and allowed by the law or some political decisions in favour of the clubs.
- Soft subsidies (S3) in all its forms, whether hidden or not, and in a broader sense, including all supports from clubs' shareholders and investors.
- Soft credit conditions (S4), referring to the banking institution largesse when granting a loan and knowing that rich tycoons or other wealthy investors behind the clubs can reimburse the debt.
- Soft investments (S5), particularly in the sport facilities, seldomly funded by the private sector alone and for which the public sphere participates, sometimes in a large extent, to public–private partnerships.
- Soft accounting (S6) taking the form of a softness of accounting and reporting criteria as shown by the reduction of financial information retrieved from the financial books.

In European football, much evidence supports the existence of softness mechanisms as shown by these few examples retrieved from the Big Five. In Spain, a large number of clubs benefited from both bank support for the most popular of them and state largesse as well (Ascari & Gagnepain, 2006; Barajas & Rodríguez, 2010). Twice, in 1985 and 1991, the government intervened to facilitate debt forgiveness and refinancing, without any lasting effect on the clubs' financial situation. A law was even introduced in Spain, known as the '*Concursal*' Law, which allowed Spanish clubs to gain 50% debt remissions and clearance plans while avoiding relegation. Twenty-one clubs benefited from it for the 2010–2011 season (Barajas & Rodríguez, 2014). In England, Buraimo et al. (2006) asserted a long tradition of wealthy owners rescuing first-tier divisions clubs from bankruptcies during the 20th century. Although the German model is the most balanced in terms of stream of revenues among the Big Five, Frick & Prinz (2006) have nevertheless shown cases of clubs on the verge of bankruptcy, such as Schalke 04 and Borussia Dortmund, finally saved by public bailouts. In Italy, Baroncelli & Lago (2006) underlined that clubs have benefited from partial or total write-offs of their debts to the state and others social bodies. As a consequence, the *Salva Calcio* was enacted in order to reduce the debt of Serie A clubs from €1318m to €400m for the 2003–2004 season. To close this long list, French football is interesting to study. Although relatively spared from serious financial crises (Gouguet & Primault, 2006) unlike their European counterparts, a few clubs went bankrupt in the 1990s, necessitating the French government to frame their public funding in the early 2000s.

'Too Big to Fail': A High Survival Rate Despite Large Deficits

Storm & Nielsen (2012) demonstrated that these mechanisms of softness were particularly relevant when applying the SBC approach to European football. The rationale under this assumption would be that many European football clubs benefit from these mechanisms of softness because they are seen as 'too big to fail' by their external stakeholders. As stated by these authors, 'In the classical SBC case, the organizations have important societal assignments that serve or affect a larger number of people. This has the effect that the supporter considers the organization as "too big to fail" which translates into expectations of ex post support' (Storm & Nielsen, 2012, p. 190). The relevance of applying the SBC approach to professional football leagues is asserted by the observation of chronic deficits in European clubs that, in turn, result in surprisingly few bankruptcies. Storm & Nielsen (2012) have thus questioned the small proportion of professional football clubs having filed for bankruptcy in Europe and the persistent losses and growing debts in the sector. According to them, the large presence of football clubs in the social sphere makes it relatively easy for them to find enough financial support to avoid bankruptcy. This result, stated in the literature under the principle of 'too big to fail' (Andreff, 2015; Storm & Nielsen, 2012; Nielsen & Storm, 2017), is still relevant today. Few recent works have shown such a phenomenon. In the UK, Szymanski (2017) thus noted that, of the 67 bankruptcies recorded between 1982 and 2010 out of the four top tiers, only one occurred in the Premier League. In France, several studies have been recently led on the French football clubs' bankruptcies (Carin, 2019; Scelles et al., 2018). For instance, Scelles et al. (2018) identified 69 bankruptcies between 1981 and 2014 of the three top tiers in French football, of which only five were in the first division. Finally, in Germany, Szymanski & Weimar (2019) identified 119 football club insolvencies across the top five tiers (including 36 cases where a club was liquidated) from 1994–1995 to 2016–2017, stating that 'The focus on the financial stability of clubs currently playing in the top two tiers of football appears to have created biased perceptions about the financial health of clubs in the German football pyramid as a whole' (Szymanski & Weimar, 2019, p. 54).

This high survival rate of European football clubs has been illustrated by all the aforementioned contributions, especially within the top leagues in Europe (Big Five) where the financial debts are the largest. Among the different S-conditions mentioned above, S3 constitutes one of the main mechanisms of softness in budget constraints observed in Europe. A tradition of wealthy owners or rich tycoons rescuing some historical clubs emerged at the end of the 20th century. Interestingly, support from the clubs' shareholders is still in vogue nowadays. It is such a phenomenon that the term 'sugar daddy' is commonly accepted in the literature (Lang et al., 2011). Bailing out some over-indebted clubs, many of them were unable to recover the money invested in them but continue to do so (Hamil & Walters, 2010; Grant, 2007). Continuing to invest despite the accumulation of debts and deficits appears irrational in a market economy. It can be justified by a football club meeting the fans' social and emotional expectations and that of the investors and communities, a conclusion reached by some researchers such as Frick & Prinz (2006).

Still today, many historical and high-level clubs are the subject of keen interest from external investors without any guarantee of profitability. Such a phenomenon was at the origin of the inception of Financial Fair Play (FFP) in 2010. FFP was designed to regulate the financial behaviour of clubs competing in UEFA club competitions (Peeters & Szymanski, 2014). As officially posited by UEFA (2018, p. 2), the main objective was first to encourage clubs to operate on the basis of their own revenues through the break-even rule acting as a constraint to balance 'relevant' income and 'relevant' expenses calculated on a three-year period and subject to an acceptable deviation of €5m up to €30m if such excess is entirely covered by contributions from equity participants and/or related parties. Even though some contributions have recently questioned the effectiveness of FFP (Franck, 2018; Peeters & Szymanski, 2014), the introduction of such a tool by UEFA bears witness to the abuses observed in Europe and described above. In doing so, UEFA also wished to regulate the sector by controlling the injection of money by wealthy shareholders in the richest and well-known clubs in the world – in other words – those that are 'too big to fail'.

METHODOLOGY

In this section, we successively present the overall methodological design of our research. We first introduce our research rationale by detailing the research objectives and associated hypotheses. Then we present the data sample we collected. Finally, we detail the indicators selected as well as the way we proceeded to analyse them in order to address the hypotheses raised.

Research Rationale

Traditionally, the academic contributions on the SBC approach put the lens of their analysis at a league level. However, they mask some disparities in clubs' financial behaviour, especially that of the smallest. To fill this void, we aim to examine the budget constraints at clubs' level. The research rationale here is that the level of a club's budget constraint varies according to its sporting level. Through this rationale, a set of two hypotheses is postulated, intrinsically linked to each other:

- The better a club performs from a sporting standpoint, the more it operates under an SBC.
- Conversely, the worse a club performs from a sporting standpoint, the harder its budget constraint becomes.

Consistently with the principle of 'too big to fail', we precisely assumed that some clubs benefit from a strong support of external stakeholders and their shareholders, in particular. Thus, this contribution focuses on the S3 condition according to which soft subsidies are sometimes granted when a club is struggling to meet the budgetary constraints imposed by regulatory bodies. Considering the large financial debts observed in the European football, we thus postulate that clubs' losses are compensated, first and foremost, by their main shareholders. Although French football has been an exception in the early 2000s, its financial health has worsened this last decade, as shown by the most recent financial annual report indicating some large and recurrent financial losses these last years.[1] This is one of the reasons why French football constitutes an interesting case study that we will depict.

Data Collection

French football has already been investigated with regards to the SBC approach as shown by the contribution of Andreff (2007). In a study carried out in the first top-tier division over the 1995–2005 period, he showed that the clubs' excessive pursuit of talent led to higher cost growth than revenue, despite strong rise in television rights, thus generating recurring deficits. To avoid bankruptcy, the shareholders then globally recapitalized their clubs, often at the behest of the *Direction Nationale du Contrôle de Gestion* (DNCG), the French official financial control body in charge of controlling the clubs' financial accounts. The financial support thus provided by public and/or private actors (tycoons, television networks, sponsors) is characteristic of the S3 condition (cf. *soft subsidies*) in Storm & Nielsen (2015)'s classification.

In a more recent study within the Ligue 1 (L1) and Ligue 2 (L2) over the 1999–2017 period, Andreff (2018) reached similar conclusions.

All these aforementioned conclusions have been raised through the analysis of the DNCG financial reports. From 2009 onward, this body has published annually the individual accounts of clubs for which it guarantees their reliability and consistency. From 2009–2010 to 2017–2018, the latest year for which data were available, we selected the clubs that participated successively to the nine seasons of L1 and/or L2 over the study period. Although 59 different clubs have competed at least once in one of these two competitions, only 25 of them have remained in the first and/or second division since 2009. It is thus noted that among the 34 clubs having not played successively in L1 and/or L2, 12 clubs went bankrupt over the period, confirming the worrying financial health of French football raised in the DNCG report. Table 4.1 displays the main characteristics of our sample. From a sporting perspective, the 25 clubs selected represent a total of 225 participations between 2009 and 2018 in the two first-tier divisions, of which two-thirds are in L1 and one-third in L2. Considering that the 59 clubs competed at least once in these two competitions, this figure represents approximatively 63% of the total number of participations in these two first divisions over the period (225/360). From an economic perspective, their cumulative income (including trading activity) reached nearly €15 billion over the period weighting for more than 87% of the comparable total of all the 59 clubs (14,781/16,969). The size of our sample and its financial weight led us to conclude that the financial and sporting indicators, depicted below, would be representative of the functioning of the professional championship as a whole.

Table 4.1   The sample

Clubs	Acronym	Participation in the French League		Average annual
		L1	L2	income (in €m)
AC Ajaccio	ACA	3	6	13.326
Angers SCO	ASCO	3	6	21.622
AJ Auxerre	AJA	3	6	23.286
AS Monaco	ASM	7	2	141.920
AS Nancy-Lorraine	ASNL	5	4	28.391
AS St Etienne	ASSE	9	0	69.017
Clermont Foot Auvergne	CFA	0	9	8.745
Dijon FC	DFCO	3	6	19.558
FC Lorient	FCL	8	1	41.019
FC Nantes	FCN	5	4	32.668
FC Sochaux-Montbelliard	FCSM	5	4	31.019
Girondins de Bordeaux	GB	9	0	79.453
Le Havre AC	HAC	0	9	18.461
Lille OSC	LOSC	9	0	96.857
Montpellier Hérault FC	MHSC	9	0	56.301
OGC Nice	OGCN	9	0	51.607
Olympique Lyonnais	OL	9	0	167.734
Olympique de Marseille	OM	9	0	139.892
Paris St Germain	PSG	9	0	395.777
RC Lens	RCL	3	6	31.762
Stade Brestois	SB29	3	6	19.342
SM Caen	SMC	6	3	33.039
Stade Rennais	SR	9	0	50.654
Toulouse FC	TFC	9	0	46.569
Valenciennes FC	VAFC	5	4	24.367
Total (2009–2018)	-	149	76	14.781
Mean	-	5.96	3.04	65.695

Source: Annual DNCG reports and official league website.

Indicator Setting and Statistical Processing

To address the hypotheses previously laid out, we set four financial indicators (FIs) that led us to build two linked financial ratios (FRs), in order to categorize all the 25 clubs of our sample as follows:

- FI1: **NAR Cum** is the cumulative result over the entire period, i.e., the addition of the annual **net accounting results** (NARs). The cumulative amount was determined for the entire period, with annual profits compensating for annual losses (NAR Cum). The net amount of the deficit generated by a club over the period could then be determined.
- FI2: **SC** is the amount of **shareholder contributions** over the period, which can take three forms:

- the 'capital contributions from shareholders', referring to the amount of money brought by the shareholder in the clubs' share capital;
- the 'net contributions to current accounts', referring to the loans from shareholders to their clubs which can therefore be reimbursed;
- the 'abandonments of current accounts net of recovery', referring to the waiver of claims held by the club on their shareholders, which constitutes exceptional profits for the club. Under French law, under certain predefined conditions (exceptional profit for the club), these subsidies can be cancelled. The amounts returned to the shareholders therefore constituting an exceptional charge. The total amount of capital contributions had to be reconstituted on the basis of changes in the annual net situations, which was the only information available. We estimated the current account waiver per club from aggre-gated data from the DNCG, individual club data and secondary data (press information). For example, the net amount of waiver represented €125m for the 2013–2014 season (€66m the previous season). The high level of waiver meant that they had to be taken into account in the analysis. The amounts were nevertheless undervalued because only the abandonments that could reasonably be reconstituted were included in the data analysis. This prudent approach undervalued the shareholders' contributions and therefore may have underestimated our results. The same procedure was followed to assess the reversals of current account abandons made in the context of the application of better-fortune clauses.[2]
- FI3: **CovL** is the amount of shareholder contributions described above, used to **cover losses**: the lesser of two values, in absolute value, between negative NAR Cum and the total SC. We expected that this indicator would make it possible to evaluate the behaviour of shareholders who act as 'sugar daddies' in the French clubs and to check the S3 condition consistently with our research hypotheses.

From these three indicators, we have constructed a first financial ratio (FR1) corresponding to the ratio CovL/NAR Cum that works as follows:

- If FR1 = 0% then either the club is profitable for the whole period, or the shareholders have not contributed in any way to cover the losses.
- If FR1 = 100% then all losses are covered by the shareholders' contribution.
- If 0% < FR1 < 100%, then the shareholders partially finance the club's losses.

Based on Kornai et al.'s (2003) assumptions, Storm & Nielsen (2012, p. 187) consider that the budget constraint is soft, especially when 'The firm cannot receive any free state or other grants to cover current expenses.' As such, the more the shareholder finances the losses (i.e., FR1 tends towards 100%), the softer the budgetary constraint gets. They also consider an SBC when the same firm cannot receive any money from anywhere to 'finance investment' (Storm & Nielsen, 2012, p. 187). This is the reason why we also wanted to analyse the contribution of shareholders to the financing of their clubs' investments, and in particular to the most significant of them, namely the one corresponding to transfer fees. To do so, we have defined the financial indicator INV and the financial ratio FR2 below.

• FI4: **INV** is the net **investment** in player transfer fees over the period (INV < 0 corresponding to a disbursement), or the net disinvestment (INV > 0 corresponding to an incoming payment). Insofar as player capital reflects the sporting level of a club, disinvestment, i.e., player sales, indicated a club's intention to limit its financial commitments by reducing its ability to acquire top players and therefore accepting the possibility of lower competitiveness.

From this financial indicator, we constructed a second financial ratio (FR2) corresponding to the ratio in absolute value (SC – CovL)/INV. This indicator assesses the share of shareholders' contributions not used to cover losses and dedicated to financing investments, in particular in transfer fees for recruited players. It is therefore calculated for clubs which make a net investment over the period (INV < 0) and for which the amount of the shareholder contributions are greater than the amount of losses covered, i.e., (SC - CovL) > 0. This ratio can be of 0% in the case where the shareholders' contribution is less than the amount of the investment. In other cases, it measures the shareholders' contribution over the period that was used to finance the investments and sometimes beyond. When the club has disinvested over the period, it has been written 'disinvestment' in the results table. Coupled with RF1, this indicator allows us to identify clubs that benefit from shareholders' contributions to finance both losses and investments, which is characteristic of an SBC.Moreover, it is acknowledged that financial support is linked to the club's ability to establish itself as an institution in its locality. As such, it is considered by some researchers as a common flagship of reference and branding within its community and, consequently, benefits from the support of shareholders and local authorities in particular (Nielsen & Storm, 2017). With a few exceptions, a club's ability to benefit from this financial support increases if it is successful on the pitch.[3] Thus, a causal link between the sporting level of the club, its reputation and therefore its ability to refinance its losses in financial difficulty has been shown in the literature (Storm & Nielsen, 2012; Andreff, 2015). As a consequence, we finally introduced two sporting indicators relating to the classification of the clubs. Indeed, the concept of SBC is based on the principle of maximizing sports performance and the idea that a club has weight in society that is highly unlikely to disappear. Reputation depends greatly on a club's ability to perform at the highest level of competition. For this reason, we chose to integrate variables representing the clubs' levels of sporting performance. Therefore, we collected two types of data to develop two indicators.

- SI1: **CR** is the cumulative sum of the individual **club rankings** over the period. We chose a classification from 1 to 20 for the clubs in L1 and from 21 to 40 for the clubs in L2. The highest performing club was therefore the one with the lowest number of points.
- SI2: **P-UEFA** is the **total UEFA points** obtained by a club over the period, i.e., from the 2009–2010 to 2017–2018 seasons.[4] This indicator is equal to zero for clubs that did not participate in a European competition during this period. It is used to classify clubs according to their sporting level.

We then selected five of these indicators (NAR Cum, SC, CovL, INV, CR) corresponding to the raw data, to carry out statistical inference tests. We used Spearman's test to highlight the correlations among these variables, whose distributions did not meet the normality assumption. We then classified the clubs into three groups based on their total UEFA points: group A with P-UEFA higher than the average (UEFA average), group B with P-UEFA between 1 and the average UEFA, and group C with P-UEFA less than 1. Kruskal–Wallis and Wilcoxon tests assessed the differences between groups regarding financial indicators 1 to 4. The results of these tests would enable us to consider that the clubs within these groups have distinct financial profiles, or not, in order to validate or invalidate our hypothesis of variation of the BC according to the sporting level of the clubs.

RESULTS

We first introduced the descriptive statistics gained through the data collection stage. From this, we calculated correlation tests between the indicators to make sure of their reliability. Consistently with our research hypotheses, we finally carried out comparative tests of the 25 clubs previously classified on the basis of their sports results in order to verify the concordance between this classification and the financial profile of the clubs.

Descriptive Statistics at a Glance: The Weak Financial Health of French Football

Table 4.2 presents successively each of the financial and sporting indicators. For the 25 clubs in the sample, the cumulative net accounting results showed an overall deficit of more than €1 billion, including €222m for LOSC alone. A deeper look into these figures shows that 18 out of 25 clubs had a negative NAR Cum for the nine seasons for a total of €1,145m, representing 7.7%

Table 4.2   *Financial and sporting indicators calculated per club*

	Financial indicators (FIs)				Sporting indicators (SIs)	
	NAR Cum	SC	CovL	INV	CR	P-UEFA
ACA	-5.695	1.707	1.707	0.000	236	0
ASCO	19.708	-3.339	0.000	5.967	194	0
AJA	-35.955	27.780	27.780	9.458	222	7
ASM	-2.071	334.576	2.071	-169.217	86	63
ASNL	-12.820	-0.998	0.000	10.709	180	7
ASSE	2.339	-3.155	0.000	-5.346	69	46.5
CFA	2.607	0.2	0.000	-0.183	263	0
DFCO	7.822	1.293	0.000	-5.445	197	0
FCL	20.486	-4.147	0.000	6.930	127	0
FCN	-36.438	32.904	32.904	-2.625	177	0
FCSM	-38.532	39.852	38.532	7.286	196	0.5
GB	-90.634	128.374	90.634	-11.557	61	59.5
HAC	-4.576	5.842	4.576	-0.983	252	0
LOSC	-222.135	57.169	57.169	-50.358	58	46.5
MHSC	15.902	5.631	0.000	-7.977	88	7
OGCN	-8.931	33.240	8.931	-23.064	92	12
OL	-137.211	226.295	137.211	-9.947	28	150.5
OM	-206.159	227.918	206.159	-39.478	47	107
PSG	-204.384	748.006	204.384	-379.539	26	172
RCL	-71.494	116.636	71.494	9.739	220	0
SB29	-3.119	5.364	3.119	0.058	206	0
SMC	6.447	2.942	0.000	-1.475	154	0
SR	-41.303	74.623	41.303	-22.596	77	10
TFC	-2.990	-3.299	0.000	0.963	114	6
VAFC	-20.737	16.016	16.016	9.560	199	0
Total	-1069.873	2071.232	943.990	-688.24	3569	391
Mean	-42.795	82.849	37.760	-27.530	142.760	19.550
Min.	-222.135	-4.147	0	-379.539	26	0
Max.	20.486	748.006	206.159	10.709	263	172
Median	- 8.931	16.016	4.576	-1.475	154	0
Stand. Dev.	72.951	164.176	61.057	81.855	75	44.595

Note: Data in €m for the financial indicators.

of the total budget of the 25 clubs (including trading activity). Thus, nearly three-quarters of the clubs (72%) were structurally indebted. The other seven clubs were generally in balance since their cumulative profits (€75m) represented only 0.5% of the overall budget. As such, a large part of the shareholders' contributions is used to cover losses totalling almost €1 billion over the period. The remainder is allocated to intangible investments, mainly in the players' trading activity. From a sporting perspective, the situation is logically more contrasted and shows a polarization between the top-clubs that are successful in strengthening their positions on the top of the tables and the others.

Correlation Tests

The results of the statistical tests are presented in Table 4.3. The correlation tests were carried out by crossing the variables two by two. The significance threshold for all inference tests was fixed at $p < 0.05$.

Table 4.3   *Spearman's test results*

	Spearman's test				
	NAR Cum	SC	CovL	INV	CR
NAR Cum		-0.78308	-0.92782	0.28385	0.38769
		.0000**	.0000**	0.169	0.056
SC			0.88450	-0.57077	-0.47000
			.0000**	0.003*	0.018*
CovL				-0.36861	-0.39381
				0.070	0.051
INV					0.72385
					.0000**
CR					

Note: *p < 0.05; **p < 0.01.

Spearman's rank correlation coefficients between these indicators were significant in six out of 10 cases ($p < 0.05$). This therefore indicates that the cumulative result (NAR Cum) was correlated with shareholders' contribution (SC) (78%) and the amount devoted to covering losses (CovL) (93%). In addition, there was a strong correlation (88%) between the shareholder contributions and the amount spent to cover losses. These correlations indicate that clubs' losses were covered by the shareholders' contributions. With the exception of Nancy (ASNL) and Toulouse (TFC), all clubs with deficits used shareholder contributions to cover their debts, for a total of €944m representing 82% of the losses. For French football, it therefore seems that it is mainly the shareholders who finance the shortfall in cash resulting from deficits. However, this made up only 46% of the contributions, which means that 54% of the shareholder financing, or more than €1.12 billion, was used for club development such as investment in players' trading activity. The correlation between the amount of shareholder contributions (SC) and investments in player transfer fees (INV) thus confirmed that these contributions were used particularly to finance player investment. It should be recalled that when the INV indicator is negative, this means that the club has invested. Therefore, this negative correlation of 57% clearly showed the connection between shareholder contributions and player investment. Similarly, the negative correlation of 47% between shareholder contributions (SC) and the club ranking (CR) shows that the greater the shareholder funding, the better the club performance. Last, the positive correlation (72%) between INV and CR showed that the more a club invests in its players, the better it performs. The relationship between financial and sporting results has been regularly demonstrated in the academic literature (cf. Szymanski & Kuypers, 1999), and it has also been shown that clubs with the highest transfer expenses achieve better sporting performance (Matesanz et al., 2018). Our results also show the link between shareholder contributions and performance.

Comparative Tests and Clubs' Financial Status Based on Sporting Results

Despite similarities between clubs, it is worth noting that several types of clubs appear in our sample. First, although the initial results show a majority of structurally loss-making clubs, some of them have managed to generate profits. Then, for the large portion of clubs that recorded losses between 2009 and 2018, much-contrasted situations are revealed. For instance, the clubs ASNL and TFC, previously cited, are characterized by losses that did not have shareholder support to finance their deficits whereas five others have only been partially funded (AC Ajaccio, AJ Auxerre, FC Nantes, Lille OSC, Valenciennes FC). The remaining loss-making clubs are (unfortunately) in a more classic situation where the shareholders finance both losses and substantial investments in players' trading activity. In addition, very substantial differences in performance were noted between the clubs that regularly played in the European competitions and, in contrast, the others, which tended to play in the second division. Consistently both with the principle of 'too big too fall' and our research hypotheses, it is assumed that some clubs would receive substantial support from their shareholders, enabling them to reach high performance levels while still showing deficits, whereas others would seek to maximize their performance results under budget constraints. To test this, we classified the clubs into three distinct groups according to their performances in European competitions measured by the accumulation of UEFA points (P-UEFA) as shown in Table 4.4.

Table 4.4   *Typology of clubs based on the accumulation of UEFA points between 2009 and 2018*

Group	Criteria for classing[a]	N	Clubs
A	Ind UEFA > Mean	7	ASM, ASSE, GB, LOSC, OL, OM, PSG
B	1 < Ind UEFA < Mean	6	AJA, ASNL, MHSP, OGCN, SR, TFC
C	Ind UEFA < 1	12	ACA, ASCO, CFA, DFCO, FCL, FCN, FCSM, HAC, RCL, SB29, SMC, VAFC

Note: [a] The threshold of 0 could have been chosen instead of 1, as one of the clubs in our sample (FCSM) had won 0.5 UEFA points over the study period after having drawn the first leg of the Europa Cup qualifying round in 2011 before losing the second leg. In fact, the profile of this club is more similar to those in group C, which had never played in a European cup during the period.

To check the reliability of the constitution of the groups of clubs, we conducted several statistical comparative tests. Kruskal–Wallis tests ($p < 0.05$) were first carried out to determine the intergroup differences for the following indicators: NAR Cum, SC, CovL and INV. It was not carried out for CR, which is a national performance indicator to determine participation in UEFA competitions. If this test proved conclusive, the Wilcoxon test was then performed to compare the groups two by two. Results are presented in Table 4.5.

Table 4.5   *P-values of Kruskal–Wallis and Wilcoxon tests*

			A	B	C
NAR Cum		Mean	-122.894	-14.350	-10.293
	KW Tests			$P_{total} = 0.046*$	
		A		$P_{AB} = 0.138$	
		B			$P_{BC} = 0.553$
		C	$P_{AC} = 0.017*$		
SC		Mean	245.598	22.830	17.923
	KW Tests			$P_{total} = 0.014*$	
		A		$P_{AB} = 0.035*$	
		B			$P_{BC} = 0.682$
		C	$P_{AC} = 0.007**$		
CovL		Mean	99.661	13.002	14.029
	KW Tests			$P_{total} = 0.049*$	
		A		$P_{AB} = 0.055$	
		B			$P_{BC} = 0.986$
		C	$P_{AC} = 0.028*$		
Inv		Mean	-95.063	-5.418	2.402
	KW Tests			$P_{total} = 0.000**$	
		A		$P_{AB} = 0.051$	
		B			$P_{BC} = 0.553$
		C	$P_{AC} = 0.000**$		

Notes: Data in €m for the financial indicators. *$p < 0.05$; **$p < 0.01$. P-values are displayed in brackets.

These results indicate that groups A and C are significantly different for the four indicators, whereas groups B and C never are. Groups A and B are different on the SC indicator, meaning shareholder financing. Group A includes seven clubs showing, on average, slightly more than €122m in losses, with an average of €99m covered. However, the average shareholder contributions of almost €245m enabled them to invest an average of €95m in players over the period and to rank within the top six in the championships (CR/9 seasons),[5] thus ensuring that they regularly qualified for the European competitions. Group B comprises six clubs with an average deficit of €14m, almost entirely covered by the €13m in contributions from their shareholders (90%). The additional contributions were used to finance an average investment of €5m over the period. These clubs are on average in the middle of the Ligue 1 classification (ranked 11th). Finally, the 12 clubs in group C show an average loss of €10m, fully covered by their shareholders, but they are considered talent 'selling' clubs (INV > 0), which did not position them to perform well since they generally played in the second division (22nd on average). The Wilcoxon test results show strong differences between groups A and C on the four financial indicators (NAR Cum, SC, CovL, INV). Group B differs from group A only in the amount of the shareholders' contribution, which is 10 times less. Finally, groups B and C are not statistically different on the four remaining indicators.

It is possible to observe very different shareholders' behaviours between groups with regard to the two financial ratios developed above. Table 4.6 concludes this section on the results and provides a basis for discussion on the existence of very contrasting situations between clubs. Sporting results thus appear to be a key variable that creates distinct budgetary constraints between the best performing clubs and the others.

In group A, ASSE is an atypical case in the sense that it is a beneficiary and its shareholders have drawn dividends over the period. The other six clubs in this group are loss-making, and for five of them the shareholders have contributed to cover both the accumulated deficits and more than the amount of the players' investments (FR2 > 100%). Only the LOSC shareholder limited its contributions to an amount lower than the club's accumulated losses (FR1 = 55%). However, in this case, it can be noted that €183m of the €222m cumulative losses of the club over the period result from the last two seasons (2016–2018) when the club was bought out in January 2017 by a new investor.

Group B gathers clubs with three different profiles. Two clubs (SR and OGCN) make losses that are 100% covered by their shareholders who also participate in the financing of their players' investments (FR2 > 100%). For the other three indebted clubs (AJA, ASNL, TFC), only AJA benefited from a contribution from their shareholders but all three had to sell players (INV > 0) to guarantee their solvency, at the risk of reducing their sporting perfor-

*Table 4.6   Financial profile of clubs by group according to UEFA
points*

		P-UEFA	Nar Cum	FR1 CovL/NAR Cum	FR2 (SC-CovL)/Inv
A	OL	150.50	Losses	100%	896%
	GB	59.50	Losses	100%	327%
	ASM	63.00	Losses	100%	196%
	PSG	172.00	Losses	100%	143%
	OM	107.00	Losses	100%	55%
	LOSC	46.50	Losses	26%	0%
	ASSE	46.50	Profits	0%	0%
B	SR	10.00	Losses	100%	147%
	OGCN	12.00	Losses	100%	105%
	AJA	7.00	Losses	77%	Disinvestment
	ASNL	7.00	Losses	0%	Disinvestment
	MHSC	7.00	Profits	0%	71%
	TFC	6.00	Losses	0%	Disinvestment
C	HAC	-	Losses	100%	129%
	FCSM	0.50	Losses	100%	Disinvestment
	RCL	-	Losses	100%	Disinvestment
	SB29	-	Losses	100%	Disinvestment
	FCN	-	Losses	90%	0%
	VAFC	-	Losses	77%	Disinvestment
	ACA	-	Losses	30%	0%
	ASCO	-	Profits	0%	Disinvestment
	CFA	-	Profits	0%	1%
	DFCO	-	Profits	0%	24%
	FCL	-	Profits	0%	Disinvestment
	SMC	-	Profits	0%	199%

mance. The last identifiable club profile is that of MHSC, which appears to have made an overall profit over the period, but which also benefited from a contribution from its shareholders to finance part of the players' investments.

Finally, group C includes clubs that can be divided into two categories. The first comprises the seven loss-making clubs (HAC, FCSM, RCL, SB29, FCN, VAFC, ACA[6]) which have benefited from the support of their shareholders to finance all or part of their losses, but which have also had to sell players. HAC does not have this profile, but the amount of the club's net investment is less than €1m, which means that it can be considered to be in the same case as the others. The five other clubs in this group are beneficiaries. Three of them (CFA, DFCO, SMC) have benefited from contributions from their share-holders to participate in the financing of their player investments. However, it should be noted that the amount of these investments is between €0.2m and €5.44m, i.e., relatively small amounts in nine years. Finally, the two other clubs in this sub-group had to sell players to finance their losses (INV > 0).

CONTRIBUTIONS, LIMITATIONS AND RESEARCH PERSPECTIVES

In this concluding section, we sum up our results by delivering two main contributions of the present study. The first is the confirmation of the existence of an SBC, particularly relevant for the most successful clubs. The second pre-sents a typology of the degree of budgetary constraints that clubs should face according to their financial profiles. We conclude this chapter with a discus-sion on the limitations that could be overcome through new research avenues.

Double Confirmation: A Budgetary Constraint Softened by Sporting Performance

Despite the financial control operated by the DNCG, we found that French clubs were no exception among the European leagues, being predominantly and structurally in deficit. We showed that 18 out of 25 clubs had a negative NAR Cum for the nine seasons for a total of €1,145m, representing 7.7% of the total budget of the 25 clubs (including trading activity). This finding is consistent with previous works (Gouguet & Primault, 2006; Andreff, 2007; Dermit-Richard et al., 2019). However, the persistence of these deficits does not indicate the ineffectiveness of the DNCG's control. In fact, the objective of this body is not to ensure club profitability but rather club solvency for the coming season by requiring the shareholders to recapitalize the clubs (Dermit-Richard, 2004). This is indeed the case, as 82% of the losses (€944m) were compensated by shareholders' contributions, thus letting clubs benefit from the soft subsidies characteristic of the SBC approach (Storm & Nielsen, 2012, 2015; Nielsen & Storm, 2017). The additional contribution of €1,127m from shareholders was primarily used to finance club investments.

Nevertheless, when we examined the performance indicator at the level of each club and not globally at the league level, striking contrasts emerged. Our theoretical framework is based on the principle that the best performing clubs are considered 'too big to fail'. We have therefore classified the clubs into three groups based on their performance in European competitions. The KW tests coupled with those of Wilcoxon made it possible to clearly distinguish the financial profile of the clubs in group A, which regularly participate in European competitions, from that of the clubs in group C, which hardly ever take part in them. The clubs in the intermediate group B have a financial profile that is not statistically different from that of the clubs in group C and group A, except for the shareholders' contribution. These results therefore show that not all clubs have the same financial profile. As examples, PSG, which has the highest UEFA League 1 index, with a shareholders' contribution of €748m to finance more than the cumulative deficit of €204m and player investments of €379m, clearly presents the financial profile of a club playing under an SBC. Conversely, Angers (ASCO), which never took part in any European competitions, and which has to sell players to finance its deficit in the absence of shareholder contributions, is clearly operating under a hard budget constraint (HBC). These results therefore confirm our hypothesis. The better a club performs from a sporting standpoint, the more it operates under a SBC and vice versa.

The Refinement of the SBC Model: Proposal for a Scale to Measure Budget Constraint

Our results also show differences in financial profiles within groups and sometimes blurred boundaries between groups. This is the reason why we deliver a scale for assessing the level of budget constraint. This scale was constructed from the indicators characterizing the SBC in the literature, namely the existence or not of a deficit and the contribution of shareholders to this deficit and/ or to the financing of investments. To do so, we therefore used NAR Cum as an indicator of profitability, FR1 to measure the contribution of shareholders to the financing of deficits and FR2 to measure their contribution to the financing of investments. Combining these indicators enables us to define different financial profiles, each corresponding to a level of budgetary constraint. These profiles are presented in Table 4.7.

This typology is structured in three main levels. The first corresponds to an SBC in which loss-making clubs have the support of their shareholders to finance at least part of their losses and at most all of their player investments. The three conditions for an SBC mentioned in the literature are therefore fulfilled. The second corresponds to a budgetary constraint qualified as 'medium' when one of the conditions of the SBC is relaxed, so that the clubs are profitable or are obliged to disinvest.[7] The budgetary constraint becomes hard when two conditions are no longer met. Within these three levels, it is possible to identify different sub-levels within each level. On the SBC level, we identified three sub-levels as follows:

- SBC1 corresponds to clubs in deficit whose shareholders finance more than the total of losses (FR1 = 100%) and player investments (FR2 > 100%). This is the case for OL, GB, ASM, PSG, SR, OGCN and HAC.

- SBC2 corresponds to clubs in deficit whose shareholders finance the losses and part of the investments (FR2 between 0% and 100%). This is the case of OM.
- SBC3 corresponds to clubs whose deficit is partially covered by the shareholders, who therefore do not participate in the financing of investments (FR2 = 0%). This is the case of LOSC and FCN.

Table 4.7 *Typology of the degree of clubs' budget constraints according to their financial profiles*

	Soft budget constraint			Medium budget constraint				Hard budget constraint			
	SBC1	SBC2	SBC3	MBC1	MBC2	MBC3	MBC4	HBC1	HBC2	HBC3	HBC4
RNC Cum<0	X	X	X	X	X				X		
RNC Cum>0						X	X	X		X	
FR1=100 %	X	X		X							
0%<FR1<100%			X		X						
FR1=0%									X		
FR2>100%	X					X					
0%<FR2<100%		X					X				
FR2=0 %			X					X			
DISINV				X	X				X	X	
Bankrupt clubs											X

Thus, these clubs are loss-making, and the shareholders participate in their financing. These elements are characteristic of a CBL where the degree of softness is determined by the degree of financing of clubs' losses and investments. The second level corresponds to a medium budget constraint (MBC) that displays four different sub-levels such as follows:

- MBC1 corresponds to clubs whose deficit is entirely financed by shareholders but which still have to sell players (disinvestment), which handicaps the club in sporting terms. This is the case of FCSM, RCL, SB29.
- MBC2 corresponds to clubs whose deficit was partially covered by their shareholders, but which also had to sell players. This is the case for AJA, VAFC, ACA.
- MBC3 corresponds to clubs that have benefited from a contribution from their shareholders for more than the amount of their player investments (FR2 > 100%). This is the case of SMC.

- MBC4 corresponds to clubs that have benefited from a contribution from their shareholders to finance only part of their player investments (FR2 between 0% and 100%). This is the case for MHSP, CFA and DFCO.

Finally, a third level is broken down into four different sub-levels of HBC, so far as the clubs concerned do not benefit from any support from their shareholders to finance any deficit or investments:

- HBC1 is a group of profit-making clubs, which do not benefit from any support from their shareholders but retain their investment capacity (FR2 = 0%). This is the case of ASSE.
- HBC2 has the profile of a loss-making club, not supported by its shareholder and which must therefore sell players. This is the case of ASNL, TFC, ASCO, FCL.
- HBC3 is a profitable club but has had to sell players. No club in our sample has this profile.
- HBC4 is a group of clubs that have gone bankrupt and therefore have the hardest BC. Scelles et al. (2018) had examined insolvencies in French football over the 1970–2014 period and we updated this work by incorporating the 2015–2018 seasons. It enabled us to identify 12 bankruptcies between 2009 and 2018, corresponding to more than 20% of the clubs having participated at least once in the professional championship over this period.[8]

The positioning of the clubs on this scale does not correspond exactly to the categorization of groups A, B and C previously defined. Indeed, HAC, resident club of Ligue 2, has the financial profile of an SBC1 but it was previously noted that the amounts involved in this case are small and therefore its inclusion in this group is not very significant. ASSE is another exception, which appears in our classification as subject to an HBC even though it participates relatively regularly in European competitions (P-UEFA = 46.5). On the other hand, two clubs previously ranked in group B (SR and OGCN) are considered to have an SBC1 consistent with their aspirations to join the top group. We also note that a very significant number of clubs (n = 10) are considered to have a financial profile that falls under the MBC, whereas they were previously classified in groups B and C in our classification. Finally, there are two types of clubs in HBC. On the one hand, we identify five clubs whose shareholders have systematically withheld dividends (SC < 0). On the other hand, we identify the 12 professional clubs which went bankrupt during the period studied.

These differences illustrate the permeability of our three-group classification, which was already perceptible with the results of the Wilcoxon tests, which did not show very significant differences between groups A and B on the one hand, and between groups B and C on the other. However, this typology confirms that, overall, the top-ranked clubs are those with the softer budget constraint and vice versa. It also shows that the situations are not as contrasted as shown by our classification and that there is rather a continuum between SBC and HBC along which the clubs are distributed.

Limits and Future Research Avenues

This typology proposes for the first time an attempt to objectively scale the budget constraint imposed on clubs. As with any scale, it can be discussed in terms of the number of levels of classification and possibly their prioritization. For example, we have considered the MBC1 as being 'softer' than the MBC4. However, the question of the hierarchy of the level of hardness/softness within this category could be debatable. Is the budgetary constraint for a club 'harder' when it has to have a profitable NAR Cum or when it has to sell players? This question could be further investigated through further research. On the other hand, it is also necessary to consider that a club's membership at one level may vary over time and in particular depending on the strategy of the shareholders, the deficits made by the clubs and the level of constraint imposed by the DNCG. For example, SR, which participated in the European League in 2018–2019, and OGCN have a profile of SBC1 but have been included in group B on the study period. This limitation is reinforced by the use of aggregative data which is tailored to the objectives of the study but masks the dynamics of clubs' strategies.

To overcome these limitations, a first proposal would be to conduct further investigations in a more qualitative manner in order to observe these dynamics. However, if such studies cannot be carried out, a second proposal could be to retain statistical tests carried out for this study and apply them to a larger sample. The selection of clubs in our sample could thus be extended by adding those from the other 'Big Five' championships for which it would appear possible to collect data that would enable the financial indicators and ratios developed in this chapter to be calculated. This would make it possible to try to empirically validate the typology of the degree of SBC according to the financial profile of the clubs. Finally, with a view to generalizing our results, a final option could be to study the financial behaviour of clubs in other sports disciplines in order to increase the external validity of our study presented here.

NOTES

1. For instance, a net accounting loss of €176m has been reported for the 2017–2018 season following a loss of more than €100m for the previous season (DNCG, 2018).
2. Only one resumption of an abandoned current account was identified: AS Monaco for the 2017/2018 season for €78m.

3.   This is the case in our sample with Le Havre (Ligue 2) which shows that some-times there is local support for clubs that do not perform. As the first football club created in France, Le Havre is strongly supported by public authorities and was saved from bankruptcy in 2015 with the arrival of a new shareholder, an international businessman with family ties to the club's region. This club has thus a financial profile in our results that is close to that of the more successful clubs from a sporting standpoint.
4.   Data collected from the following site: https://kassiesa.net/uefa/.
5.   The average club rankings of the three groups are as follows: 53,500 for the first group, 128,800 for the second and 201,700 for the third.
6.   We have included the very special case of the ACA which, cumulatively over the entire study period, has neither invested nor disinvested in sporting talent (see Table 4.2).
7.   As a reminder, for a club, disinvestment corresponds to an incoming payment from another club that would like to acquire a player. As such, it indicates that a club is more into selling rather than buying players (cf. financial ratio 4 in methodology).
8.   Scelles et al. (2018) have identified the clubs of Grenoble, Strasbourg, Gueugnon, Besançon, Sedan, Le Mans, Rouen, Vannes having gone bankrupt between 2009 and 2014. Additionally, we revealed four more club bankruptcies since: Arles-Avignon (2014), Evian-Thonon Gaillard (2016), Istres (2017) and Bastia (2018).

BIBLIOGRAPHY

Acero, I., Serrano, R. & Dimitropoulos, P. (2017). Ownership structure and financial performance in European football. *Corporate Governance: The International Journal of Business in Society*, 17(3), 511–523. https://doi.org/10.1108/CG-07-2016-0146.

Andreff, W. (2007). French football: A financial crisis rooted in weak governance. *Journal of Sports Economics*, 8(6), 652–661. https://doi.org/10.1177/1527002506297021.

Andreff, W. (2009). Équilibre compétitif et contrainte budgétaire dans une ligue de sport professionnel. *Revue Economique*, 60(2), 591–633. https://doi.org/10.3917/reco.603.0591.

Andreff, W. (2015). *Disequilibrium sports economics: Competitive imbalance and budget constraints*. Cheltenham (UK): Edward Elgar Publishing.

Andreff, W. (2018). Financial and sporting performance in French football Ligue 1: Influence on the players' market. *International Journal of Financial Studies*, 6(4), 91. https://doi.org/10.3390/ijfs6040091.

Ascari, G. & Gagnepain, P. (2006). Spanish football. *Journal of Sports Economics*, 7(1), 76–89. https://doi.org/10.1177/1527002505282869.

Barajas, A. & Rodríguez, P. (2010). Spanish football clubs' finances: Crisis and player salaries. *International Journal of Sport Finance*, 5(1), 52–66.

Barajas, A. & Rodríguez, P. (2014). Spanish football in need of financial therapy: Cut expenses and inject capital. *International Journal of Sport Finance*, 9(1), 73–90.

Baroncelli, A. & Lago, U. (2006). Italian football. *Journal of Sports Economics*, 7(1), 3–12. https://doi.org/10.1177/1527002505282863.

Buraimo, B., Simmons, R. & Szymanski, S. (2006). English football. *Journal of Sports Economics*, 7(1), 29–46. https://doi.org/ 10.1177/1527002505282911.

Carin, Y. (2019). A prediction model for bankruptcy of football clubs: The French case. *International Journal of Sport Finance*, 14(4), 233–248. https://doi.org/10.32731/IJSF/144.112019.03.

Dermit-Richard, N. (2004). *La légitimité de la régulation financière des championnats professionnels de sports collectifs: le cas du championnat professionnel de football en France* [*The legitimacy of the financial regulation of professional team sports championships: the case of the professional football championship in France*], PhD Dissertation, University of Rouen.

Dermit-Richard, N. (2012). Football professionnel en Europe: un modèle original de régulation financière sectorielle [Professional football in Europe: An original model of sector-based financial regulation]. *Management et Avenir*, 7(57), 78–94. https://doi.org/10.3917/mav.057.0079.

Dermit-Richard, N., Scelles, N. & Evrard, B. (2019). Gouvernance des clubs de football professionnels: Entre régulation et contrainte budgétaire [Governance of professional football clubs: Between regulation and budgetary constraint]. *Revue Française de Gestion*, 45(279), 53–72. https://doi.org/10.3166/rfg.2019.00315.

DNCG (2018). *French professional football financial report*. Paris: Ligue de football professionnel.

Downward, P. & Dawson, A. (2000). *The economics of professional team sports*. London: Routledge.

Franck, E. (2014). *Financial fair play in European club football – What is it all about?* UZH Business Working Paper Series (ISSN 2296-0422). https://papers.ssrn.com/sol3/papers.cfm?abstract_id=2284615.

Franck, E. (2018). European club football after 'five treatments' with Financial Fair Play – Time for an assessment. *International Journal of Financial Studies*, 6(4), 16–34. https://doi.org/10.3390/ijfs6040097.

Frick, B. & Prinz, J. (2006). Crisis? What crisis? Football in Germany. *Journal of Sports Economics*, 7(1), 60–75. https://doi.org/10.1177/1527002505282868.

Gouguet, J. J. & Primault, D. (2006). The French exception. *Journal of Sports Economics*, 7(1), 47–59. https://doi.org/10.1177/1527002505282912.

Grant, W. (2007). An analytical framework for a political economy of Football. *British Politics*, 2, 69–90. https://doi.org/10.1057/palgrave.bp.4200036.

Hall, S., Szymanski, S. & Zimbalist, A. S. (2002). Testing causality between team performance and payroll: The cases of Major League Baseball and English Soccer. *Journal of Sports Economics*, 3(2), 149–168. https://doi.org/10.1177/152700250200300204.

Hamil, S. & Walters, G. (2010). Financial performance in English professional football: 'An inconvenient truth'. *Soccer & Society*, 11(4), 354–372. https://doi.org/10.1080/14660971003780214.

Késenne, S. (1996). League management in professional team sports within win maximizing clubs. *European Journal of Sport Management*, 2, 14–22.

Késenne, S. (2007). The peculiar international economics of professional football in Europe. *Scottish Journal of Political Economy*, 54(3), 388–399. https://doi.org/10.1111/j.1467-9485.2007.00421.x.

Kornai, J. (1980). *Economics of shortage*. Amsterdam: North Holland Publishing.

Kornai, J. (2014). The soft budget constraint. An introductory study to volume IV of the life's work series. *Acta Oeconomica*, 64(S1), 25–79. https://doi.org/10.1556/AOecon.64.2014.S1.2.

Kornai, J., Maskin, E. & Roland, G. (2003). Understanding the soft budget constraint. *Journal of Economic Literature*, 41(4), 1095–1136. https://doi.org/10.1257/002205103771799999.

Lang, M., Grossmann, M. & Theiler, P. (2011). The sugar daddy's game: How wealthy investors change competition in professional team sports. *Journal of Institutional and Theoretical Economics*, 167(4), 557–577.

Matesanz, D., Holzmayer, F., Torgler, B., Schmidt, S. L. & Ortega, G. J. (2018). Transfer market activities and sportive performance in European first football leagues: A dynamic network approach. *PLoS One*. https://doi.org/10.1371/journal.pone.0209362

Morrow, S. (2006). Scottish Football: It's a funny old business. *Journal of Sports Economics*, 7(1), 90–95. https://doi.org/10.1177/1527002505282867.

Neale, W. C. (1964). The peculiar economics of professional sports. *The Quarterly Journal of Economics*, 78(1), 1–14. https://doi.org/10.2307/1880543.

Nielsen, K. & Storm, R. K. (2017). Profit maximization, win optimization and soft budget constraints in professional team sports. In U. Wagner, R. K. Storm & K. Nielsen (Eds), *When sport meets business: Capabilities, challenges, critiques* (pp. 153–166). London: Sage Publications.

Peeters, T. & Szymanski, S. (2014). Financial fair play in European football. *Economic Policy*, 29(78), 343–390. https://doi.org/10.1111/1468-0327.12031

Rosen, S. & Sanderson, A. (2001). Labour markets in professional sports. *The Economic Journal*, 111(469), 47–68. https://doi.org/10.3386/w7573.

Scelles, N., Szymanski, S. & Dermit-Richard, N. (2018). Insolvency in French soccer: The case of payment failure. *Journal of Sports Economics*, 19(5), 603–624. https://doi.org/10.1177/1527002516674510.

Sloane, P. J. (1971). The economics of professional football: The football club as a utility maximizer. *Scottish Journal of Political Economy*, 18(2), 121–146. https://doi.org/10.1111/j.1467-9485.1971.tb00979.x.

Solberg H. A. & Haugen, K. K. (2010). European club football: Why enormous revenues are not enough? *Sport in Society*, 13(2), 329–343. https://doi.org/10.1080/17430430903523036.

Staudohar, P. D. (2004). The European and U.S. sports labor markets. In R. D. Fort, & J. Fizel (Eds), *International sports economics comparisons* (pp. 63–74). Westport (UK): Praeger Publishers.

Storm, R. K. & Nielsen, K. (2012). Soft budget constraints in professional football. *European Sport Management Quarterly*, 12(2), 183–201. https://doi.org/10.1080/16184742.2012.670660.

Storm, R. K. & Nielsen, K. (2015). Soft budget constraints in European and US leagues: Similarities and differences. In W. Andreff (Ed.), *Disequilibrium sports economics: Competitive imbalance and budget constraints* (pp. 151–174). Cheltenham (UK): Edward Elgar Publishing.

Szymanski, S. (2017). Entry into exit: Insolvency in English professional football. *Scottish Journal of Political Economy*, 64(4), 419–444. https://doi.org/10.1111/sjpe.12134.

Szymanski, S. & Kuypers, T. (1999). *Winners and losers: The business strategy of football*. London: Viking.

Szymanski, S. & Weimar D. (2019). Insolvencies in professional football: A German Sonderweg? *International Journal of Sport Finance*, 14, 54–68. https://doi.org/10.32731/IJSF.141.022019.05.

UEFA (2013). *The European club licensing benchmarking report. Financial year 2011*. Nyon, Switzerland: UEFA.

UEFA (2015). *The European club footballing landscape. Club licensing benchmarking report. Financial year 2014*. Nyon, Switzerland: UEFA.

UEFA (2018). *UEFA club licensing and financial fair play regulations*. Nyon, Switzerland: UEFA

Vrooman, J. (2007). Theory of the beautiful game: The unification of European football. *Scottish Journal of Political Economy*, 54(3), 314–354. https://doi.org/10.1111/j.1467-9485.2007.00418.x.

5. Heterogeneity of budget constraints in Hungarian and Polish football

Karolina Nessel, Zsolt Havran and Tünde Máté

INTRODUCTION

Thirty years after the change of political and economic regimes in Hungary and Poland, the transition of the sport systems in both countries is not completed yet. The sport organisations, despite their growing commercialisation and professionalisation, are still to a varying degree dependent on regular as well as ad hoc public aid. Actually, the public support is also awaited in the most market-oriented sport organisations in both countries – in professional football clubs. These expectations grow especially in the times of financial hardship, which seem to be a pertinent state for many of the clubs.

According to Kornai (2009), the expectations of managers that their organisations will be rescued by an external agent in case of a financial distress impact their decisions and behaviours ex ante and create a syndrome of soft budget constraint (SBC). In fact, SBC is first of all a mental phenomenon which subsequently translates into actions:

> Soft budget constraint (…) is present in the mind, thinking and understanding of the decision-maker. It is a particular expectation (…) Anyone's budgetary limit is soft if the person (either with good reason or wrongly) expects that he will surely be rescued if he gets into trouble. He then adjusts his actions to this expectation. (Kornai, 2009, p. 8)

The rescue of unprofitable companies during the period of socialism in Hungary and Poland was granted, as virtually no bankruptcies of state enterprises were allowed, with quasi totality of companies in industry and services being state owned. This orthodoxy was overturned in 1990 when the economic reforms were introduced with the aim of transformation towards a liberal market economy. And although both countries have chosen a different transformation strategy (shock therapy in Poland vs. a more gradual approach in

Hungary), the hardening of the budget constraint for public entities and privatisation of state ownership were very high on both agendas (Balcerowicz, 1994; Kornai, 2001). The introduction of new bankruptcy laws was accompanied by the belief that market selection would enforce adaptation of the firms to a new economic environment. Effectively, already by the second half of the 1990s more than 65% of GDP was produced in the private sector in both countries (EBRD, 1999). And even if the state has retained (or regained) control over a few sectors of economy, the public aid today is limited not only by constraints on the central and local public budgets but also by the need to comply with EU competition rules.

Professional football clubs were among many organisations having to adapt to abruptly changing rules of the game during the economic transition. Actually, 30 years since the beginning of the economic transition in both countries have seen dramatic twists in the history of many clubs, bankruptcies included. Numerous clubs have been registering considerable budget deficits and growing debts for many years. Clearly, they find ways to regularly soften their budgetary limits. In fact, public support for professional clubs has not been eradicated, rather it has been reinvented to fit the new reality. It is not, however, equally accessible for all clubs. In addition, with economic and technological development in both countries the clubs have gained new potential rescue providers: sponsors and fans.

In view of these phenomena, this chapter explores the softness of the budgetary limits in the professional football clubs in Hungary and Poland. In this context, we aim to investigate the scale, determinants and heterogeneity of the rescue options expected by the clubs, with a particular focus on public aid. The study follows Kornai's idea of degrees of softness of budget constraint (Kornai, 2001). Namely, the degrees of softness reflect managers' subjective probabilities that their organisations will be helped when in financial distress. The research to date has proceeded in different ways to observe and quantify these subjective probabilities (e.g., Bignebat & Gouret, 2006; Josselin, Padovano, & Rocaboy, 2013; Pettersson-Lidbom, 2010). In this respect, our approach follows Anderson, Korsun, & Murrell (2000), who used a questionnaire with a direct question to the managers of Mongolian enterprises about the probability of a rescue by the state authorities. However, we extend the question to cover other potential rescue providers. In addition, we are the first to ask this question to the managers of professional football clubs. This way, we contribute to the progress of empirical research in SBC literature, as advocated by Kornai (2014), and to the limited literature on the transition of the football system in post-socialist countries.

In the next part of the chapter, an overview of socialism, transition and the current state of professional football in Hungary and Poland is offered. It is followed by a presentation of the research material and methods, as well as the research results. The final part of the chapter discusses the findings in a broader context of relationships between professional football and public authorities in both countries. It also presents research limitations and a possible further research agenda.

FROM SOCIALISM TO A FREE MARKET ECONOMY IN POLISH AND HUNGARIAN FOOTBALL

The Role of Professional Football under Socialism

During socialism, sport had a special role in Central and Eastern European countries. It was supposed to lend legitimacy to the political system, improve the public feeling towards the authorities and demonstrate the supremacy of the system over capitalism (András, 2003; Duke, Gammelsaeter, & Senaux, 2011). Moreover, it was meant to play an important state-building role, with a clear propaganda and education mission:

> Poland should be a country of healthy and strong people, enjoying their life. Education and sport should strengthen their will, self-control and courage, hardship endurance, capability of common life and effort, as well as readiness to work for the socialist homeland and to defend its border if needed.
> Mass sport education in People's Republic of Poland should multiply the forces of people constructing the socialist country. It is one of the education means in the spirit of international solidarity of progressive forces, it is a tool of a struggle for permanent and democratic peace. (Polish United Workers Party, 1949)

Sport was therefore just a tool of politics in the hands of the ruling party and its organisation was completely subordinate to the state. It applied both to the numerous sport organisations created during the socialist period, and to the entities of a longer, pre-war history. The latter had to adjust to new rules in terms of organisational and legal form, hierarchical subordination to the state, sources of financing, nationalisation of their properties (stadiums) and even changes to their names (Rajkiewicz, 2019). In many cases the leadership of the football clubs was handed over to high-ranking party leaders. This way, the regime assured the right ideological operation of all the major football teams (Molnar, 2007) and 'football became both the part of, and a reflection of, the socialist state' (Duke et al., 2011, p. 241).

The new football clubs created during socialism were attached to various organisations, of which the main were the army and the police (Ministry of Army, Ministry of Interior) and industrial companies (e.g., mines, metallurgy, railways, etc.) (Szerovay et al., 2017). Also, the older clubs were given pro-tectors (mostly from industry). As a result of this attachment to the ministries or state companies, the financial, and thus the sporting, stance of the clubs was directly dependent on the financial prosperity of their protectors and the rivalries between them. Generally, the clubs attached to coal mines or the army were in a better situation (Woźniak, 2013). The army clubs also had an advantage in the race for footballing talent – national service was obligatory and players were forced to join the army clubs during their service. Interestingly, as elite sport was officially amateur, the football players were employed directly by state companies and institutions and in this way enjoyed a better standard of living than the rest of the population.

The financing of sport at that time was like in other sectors of the economy, and clubs operated with clearly soft budget limits (András, 2003). The funding was to be arranged with people in power. Therefore, the main task of the club administrators was to keep good relations with their protectors, national and local committees of the socialist party and central and local governments. Football clubs' own economic activity was very limited and mostly focused on spending the money they had secured from their protectors and through tax allowances (Szerovay et al., 2017). It was up to the state to finance the clubs, construct new stadiums and build a strong national team to represent the country (Molnar, 2007).

The model of football development based on state control and funding, as well as the ban on international player transfers, brought real success in international championships to the clubs of the region, especially during the 1950s and 1960s. Later, however, the economic condition of the state companies and state institutions in Central and Eastern European countries deteriorated. Moreover, the political significance of football for the central state authorities also decreased. On the other hand, the West European clubs reinvented their business models with a greater emphasis on acquiring international fans, selling TV rights and signing foreign players. These phenomena led to a fall in the financial and sporting competitiveness of the clubs from socialist countries (András & Havran, 2016; Molnar, 2007).

Painful Transition

The year 1989 marked a shift in political and economic regimes in both Hungary and Poland. In economic terms, it meant a sudden hardening of the budget constraints for central and local authorities, as well as for state companies. The latter were privatised, underwent reconstruction or went bankrupt. Consequently, public financing of football clubs suddenly came to a stop. Moreover, rising unemployment, during the first years of the transition, meant a fall in match attendance. The football clubs completely lost their financial stability. The generation of new sources of income was extremely difficult as there were no potential sponsors, no international fans and no developed football products for television or online media (contrary to Western countries).

Unsurprisingly, the best players migrated to Western Europe in search of higher salaries. On the bright side, the clubs were released from the ideological burden of the past and regained their autonomy from patronising institutions (Kobiela, 2011).

The football clubs tried to adapt to the new reality with the tenacity of the clubs' activists and fans. The survival of the clubs required their transformation across multiple dimensions: symbolic and material (return to previous names, sometimes getting back their proprieties), organisational (change in legal forms, very often into public companies) and financial (inventing new sources of financing). The latter was the most challenging, and many clubs faced bankruptcy.

In Poland the most common rescue came from local governments – in the form of either a direct takeover or constant subsidies. Still, the burden of this solution was too great for many localities, and many sport clubs were put up for sale to commercial companies or individual investors (Lenartowicz & Karwacki, 2005). Frequently, the new investors turned out to be incapable of developing the club or even keeping it alive, which led to ownership changes and dramatic turns in the history of many clubs (Mieżejwski, 2016). Clubs bought by a prosperous local government or a credible and long-planning private investor hit the jackpot. In this respect, the 1990s were the most turbulent. Later, the processes of the commercialisation and professionalisation of sport (and football in particular) progressively set in. They were, however, obstructed by sport administrators from the socialist era who were slow to adapt to the new conditions. In fact, the lack of business orientation, as well as of professional business knowledge and competence has been daunting to many clubs up to the present day (Nessel & Drewniak, 2020). Nevertheless, football clubs have been at the vanguard of sport transformation in Poland. Their transition into a free market model of operation has been additionally supported by the professionalisation and rising market orientation of the national football federation and the top leagues' governing bodies, which have accelerated since 2012.

In Hungary, in contrast, the pathway of the football system transformation has been evidently more marked by the central state authorities. In fact, since the second half the 1990s, the state has rescued many clubs directly via tax debt release or the possibility of issuing restructuring bonds with the guarantee of the league (and thus indirectly of the state) (András, 2003). These measures revived the paternalism and over-politicisation of football, and sport in general (Földesi & Egressy, 2005). Moreover, in 2010, sport in Hungary was declared a strategic industry, as the current government makes use of it to reinvent a strong nation and national identity (Molnar & Whigham, 2019; Sárközy, 2017). Consequently, the size of direct and indirect subsidies is significant, and sport organisations (professional football clubs included) may expect a bailout by the state. Football clubs enjoying the personal support of important politicians passionate about football are in a particularly advantageous situation. The political relationships allow them to secure necessary funding and outbid other clubs in the players' market, even when they are uncompetitive in terms of number of fans or sponsors. Unsurprisingly, under these conditions, the increased modernisation and professionalisation of Hungarian football has been relatively slower than that in Poland (Havran & András, 2019).

The Current Situation

Nowadays, professional football clubs from both countries belong on the periphery of international football. Their unfinished transition towards full professionalisation and restricted budgets make them uncompetitive on the global playing field. Even the clubs with the greatest resources (in Poland: Legia Warszawa, with spending of c. €40m; in Hungary: Fehérvár FC – c. €30m) cannot count on regular participation in the UEFA European League.

At club level, the Polish sporting results are superior, although the recent dynamic is clearly better in Hungary (Figure 5.1). In the 2019/2020 season, the Polish first division ranked 29th and the Hungarian one 33rd in Europe, according to UEFA (2020). At the level of individual clubs, in the last 10 years, both countries have had only two clubs among the best 200 in the UEFA rankings (Poland: Legia Warszawa – 91st, Lech Poznan – 162nd; Hungary: Fehérvár FC – 122nd, Ferencváros – 135th). Moreover, only one Polish club has participated in the group stage of the Champions League (Legia Warszawa in 2016/2017), and only three other teams have played in the European League's group stage (Poland: Lech Poznan in 2015/2016; Hungary: Fehérvár FC in 2018/2019 and Ferencváros in 2019/2020). Regarding the results of the national teams, the dominance of Polish football is even more clear: as of 2019/2020, the Polish team ranks 19th, while the Hungarian team ranks 52nd (FIFA, 2020). Actually, nine players from the Polish national team, but only three from the Hungarian team, play for clubs in the Big Five leagues (Transfermarkt, 2020c, 2020d).

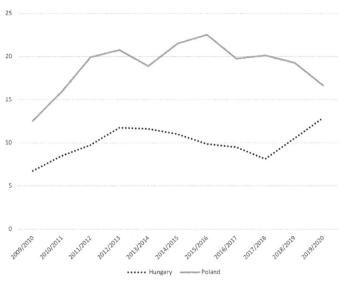

Source: Based on uefa.com.

Figure 5.1   *Cumulated UEFA association club coefficients for Hungary and Poland, 2009/2010–2019/2020*

Also, the current business situation of the majority of the clubs in both countries is poor (Table 5.1). According to the latest available data, only one Hungarian and three Polish clubs have clearly positive financial results (with return on assets ratio higher than 0.2). And the situation has been like this for many years. Consequently, more than 80% of clubs run high levels of debt (their debt-to-equity ratio is higher than 0.5).

Table 5.1   *Financial situation of the football clubs in the Hungarian and Polish first divisions, 2018 (share of all clubs)*

Liabilities/ assets	Hungary	Poland	Financial result/ assets	Hungary	Poland
Small (<=0.5)	17%	19%	Negative (< = -0.2)	42%	44%
Big (0.5,1)	58%	25%	Neutral (-0.2, 0.2)	50%	38%
Very big (>=1)	25%	56%	Positive (> = 0.2)	8%	19%

Source: Company register systems in Poland and Hungary.

Given the lack of international fans and international sponsors, the budget size of the clubs is dependent on the national markets. In this respect, the differences in the size of population between the two countries are reflected in match attendance figures and media rights. The average attendance in Poland for the first division clubs is c. 9,000 spectators, while it is under 3,000 in Hungary. In the second division, attendance is only about one-quarter of the first division level (Transfermarkt, 2020a, 2020b). The media rights for the first division are of about €32m Euro in Poland and €12m Euro in Hungary.

In terms of ownerships structures, differences in the transition pathways in Hungary and Poland have led to some dissimilarities between both countries (Table 5.2). The most striking one is the greater role of associations and foundations in Hungary – especially in the first division. In contrast, the particularity of Poland is the greater share of local authorities in both top divisions. Additionally, local authorities often have minority ownerships in clubs of all divisions, both in Hungary and in Poland (which is not seen in the data in Table 5.2). In general, however, the majority ownership of the clubs in both countries is in the hands of private capital (predominantly of national origin). In fact, only one club in Poland currently belongs to a state-owned company.

Table 5.2   *Ownership structure of the Hungarian and Polish first and second divisions, 2019/2020 (percentage of the number of the clubs, according to the majority owner)*

	Hungary		Poland	
	First division	Second division	First division	Second division
Association/foundation	42%	21%	0%	33%
Private individual	0%	26%	33%	17%
Private company	58%	37%	28%	11%
Foreign company	0%	5%	11%	0%
State-owned company	0%	0%	6%	0%
Local authorities	0%	11%	22%	39%

Source: Company register systems in Poland and Hungary.

METHOD

Data Collection and Participants

In this study, the primary data were collected using an online survey addressed to the football clubs in the two highest divisions, both in Hungary and Poland. The surveying was carried out in January and February 2020. The process of data collection involved multiple phone and mail contacts with clubs' representatives in order to explain the research idea and to remind them about the survey. The survey collection had to be stopped at the beginning of March 2020 due to the COVID-19 pandemic and the sudden break in sporting competition, which would certainly influence the answers given in the questionnaire. Finally, it was possible to obtain complete surveys from 31% of Hungarian clubs and 50% of Polish clubs, 28 clubs in total (Table 5.3). Although the survey was directed to the top management, almost half of the answers come from other managers, with many of them being the club spokesmen (Table 5.4). After consideration, these answers were included in the dataset, given the difficulty of reaching the clubs' top management, and the small size of administrative employment in clubs in the second division which makes all administrators engaged and well informed about all of the management issues in their club.

Table 5.3   Football clubs in the sample

	Hungary			Poland			Total		
	No of clubs in the division	No of clubs in the sample	Share of clubs in the sample	No of clubs in the division	No of clubs in the sample	Share of clubs in the sample	No of clubs in the division	No of clubs in the sample	Share of clubs in the sample
I division	12	5	42%	16	11	67%	28	16	57%
II division	20	6	30%	18	6	33%	38	12	32%
Total	32	11	34%	34	17	50%	66	28	42%

Table 5.4		*Characteristics of the respondents*

Variable	Share
AGE (years)	
20–30	14%
31–40	39%
41–50	32%
51–60	14%
SEX	
Male	93%
Female	7%
POSITION	
CEO	29%
CFO	14%
Board member	11%
Other	46%

The main survey questions were aiming to estimate: (1) the subjective probability of a set of proposed solutions in the case of hypothetical future sudden and serious financial problems of the club; (2) the frequency of such problems in the past five years and (3) the extent to which proposed solutions were used in comparable situations in the past. The respondents were also asked to evaluate the importance and state of the current financial and sporting results, as well as the contacts of the club with local authorities and state institutions. Answers to these questions were based on the 7-point item-specific scale (1: very low/absolutely not important/very bad/never–7: very high/absolutely important/very good/very often). The survey finished with a set of questions about the respondents (their role in the club, age, gender).

For the clubs in the sample, the dataset was completed with additional, secondary information on the clubs' financial and sporting results (objective measures), environment (size of the locality, countries), fans (their number in stadiums and on social media) and ownership (type of capital behind the main owner).

Table 5.5   Descriptive statistics of the data 1

Variable	Description	Number of observations	Median	Mean	SD
EXPECTATIONS	The probability (1–7) that the club will:				
E OWNER	get help from the owner*	28	6.0	5.8	1.3
E LAUTH	get help from the local authorities*	28	4.0	3.7	2.0
E STATE	get help from the state institutions*	28	2.0	2.1	1.3
E FED	get help from the federation or league governing body*	28	3.0	2.8	1.1
E ASPONS	get help from the actual sponsors*	28	4.0	4.1	1.5
E NSPONS	get help from the new sponsors*	28	3.0	3.3	1.4
E FANS	get help from the fans*	28	2.0	3.0	2.0
E FMARKETS	arrange financing in financial markets*	28	2.0	2.9	1.7
E PARREARS	increase payment arrears*	28	4.0	3.8	1.7
E SPLAYERS	sell players*	28	5.0	4.6	1.5
E SASSETS	sell other assets*	28	3.0	2.9	1.5
E RESTR	undergo restructuring*	28	4.5	4.3	1.9
E BANKR	go bankrupt*	28	2.0	2.4	1.7
PAST1	The degree to which clubs have registered sudden and financial problems in the last five years (1–7)	28	2.0	2.0	1.14
PAST EXPERIENCE	The degree (1–7) to which in the last five years the club has:				
P OWNER	got help from the owner*	16	6.0	5.8	1.6
P LAUTH	got help from the local authorities*	16	6.0	4.6	2.3
P STATE	got help from the state institutions*	16	1.0	1.5	0.9
P FEDER	got help from the federation or league governing body*	16	2.0	2.8	2.0
P ASPONS	got help from the actual sponsors*	16	2.5	3.0	1.7
P NSPONS	got help from the new sponsors*	16	1.5	2.2	1.9
P FANS	got help from the fans*	16	2.0	2.2	1.2
P FMARKETS	arranged financing in financial markets*	16	1.0	2.6	2.4
P PARREARS	increased payment arrears*	16	4.0	3.8	1.9
P SPLAYERS	sold players*	16	4.5	4.1	1.9
P SASSETS	sold other assets*	16	1.0	1.8	1.2
P RESTR	undergone restructuring*	16	3.0	3.6	2.1
P BANKR	gone bankrupt*	16	1.0	1.4	0.8
FINANCIAL RESULTS					

Variable	Description	Number of observations	Median	Mean	SD
DEBT	Ratio liabilities/assets***	28	1.1	2.0	2.2
ROA	Ratio financial result/assets***	28	-0.2	-0.6	0.9
BUDGET	Total costs (€m)***	28	3.8	5.6	7.1
SQUAD	Squad market value (€m)**	28	7.0	7.4	6.4
EVALFR	Subjective evaluation of state of financial results (1–7)*	28	5.0	4.7	1.5
IMPFR	Subjective evaluation of importance of financial results (1–7)*	28	6.5	6.3	0.8
SPORTING RESULTS					
EVALSR	Subjective evaluation of state of sporting results (1–7)*	28	5.0	5.0	1.3
IMPSR	Subjective evaluation of importance of financial results (1–7)*	28	7.0	6.4	0.8
SR-FR	IMP SR – IMP FR	28	0.0	0.1	1.0
RANK	Final rank in the two divisions combined**	28	10.0	11.3	6.9
ENVIRONMENT					
OFC	Number of other football clubs in I and II division in the locality	28	0.0	0.7	1.6
CONLOCAL	Evaluation of the contact with local authorities (1–7)*	28	6.0	5.4	1.8
CONSTATE	Evaluation of the contact with state institutions (1–7)*	28	4.0	4.8	1.4
RESIDENTS	Residents in the locality (thous., February 2020)	28	143.3	309.4	377.6
FANS					
ATTENDANCE	Average match attendance (thous.)**	28	3.6	4.5	4.6
FACEBOOK	Followers (thous., February 2020)	28	36.9	86.4	180.1
INSTAGRAM	Observers (thous., February 2020)	28	4.0	16.1	37.0

Sources: *survey, ** Transfermarkt (for the season 2018/2019), ***clubs' financial reports from the national company registers (accounting year ending in 2018).

Table 5.6   Descriptive statistics of the data 2

Variable	Number (% of the sample)	Description
COUNTRY		
HUN	11 (39.3%)	Hungary
POL	17 (60.7%)	Poland
DIVISION		In the season 2019/2020**
I	16 (57.1%)	
II	12 (42.9%)	
OWNERSHIP		The type of the main owner***
LC	8 (28.6%)	Local authorities
SC	1 (3.6%)	State institution or company owned by state
PC	16 (57.1%)	Private capital (companies, private individuals)
AF	3 (10.7%)	Associations and foundations
PAST2		Based on PAST1 (see Table 5.5)
Yes	16 (57.1%)	At least one case of sudden and serious financial problem in the past
No	12 (42.9%)	No cases of sudden and serious financial problem in the past
SOF		Based on IMPSR, IMPFER (see Table 5.5)
S	8 (28.6%)	Sporting results more important than financial ones
F	6 (21.4%)	Financial results more important than sporting ones
O	14 (50.0%)	Balance between importance of financial and sporting results

Sources: ** Transfermarkt (for the season 2018/2019), ***clubs' financial reports from the national company registers (accounting year ending in 2018).

Data Analysis

Given the limited sample size, answering the research questions involved two main statistical techniques: correlation analysis and segmentation followed by profiling of the clusters. The segmentation was done using the K-means technique (with maximisation of Euclidean distance between the clusters), with the number of clusters estimated both with Ward's method and the *k*-fold cross-validation technique. As most of the data from the survey were not normally distributed, the non-parametric tests were used in the analyses of correlation and variance.

RESULTS

The main direct result of the survey (Figure 5.2 and Table 5.5) indicates that the clubs evaluated the probability of their bankruptcy in the case of sudden and serious financial problems as low (median 2.0, SD 1.7), with the exception

of just two clubs (both of them in Poland, and both being put up for sale). The
generality of low expectations of bankruptcy is seen as the predominance of
answers in the left part of Figure 5.2 in the case of variable E BANKR.

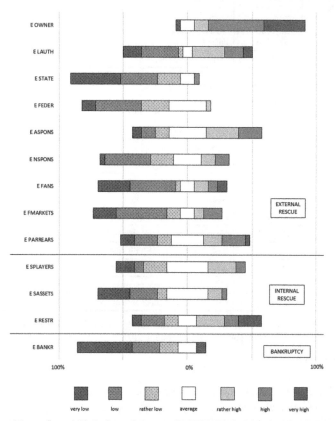

Note: (a) gets financial help from: the owner (E OWNER), local authorities (E LAUTH),
state institutions (E STATE), football federation/league governing body (E FEDER), actual
sponsors (E ASPONS), new sponsors (E NSPONS), fans (E FANS); (b) arranges financing
in financial markets (E FMARKETS); (c) increases arrears in payments (E PARREARS); (d)
sells players (E SPLAYERS); (e) sells other assets (E SASSETS); (f) undertakes an internal
restructuring (E RESTR); (h) goes bankrupt (E BANKR).

*Figure 5.2   Managers' subjective probability of different solutions in the
case of hypothetical financial problems of the club*

This optimism is correlated mainly to the expectations of an external rescue (Table 5.7). In this category, the most hope is placed in the owner (median 6.0, SD 1.3, high probability), irrespective of its type (Table 5.8). Moreover, data in Figure 5.2 and Table 5.5 indicate that the second source of the optimism is the expectation of a rescue from actual sponsors (with an average probability), followed closely by payment arrears and local authorities. Regarding the rescue by local authorities, it is clearly most expected by clubs with the local authority as the majority owner, and is least expected by those owned by private capital (Table 5.8). The other external rescue options are judged on average as rather not likely (Figure 5.2, Table 5.5). Among the internal rescue options, the sales of assets other than players are considered the least probable (which is surely due to the fact that most of the clubs' infrastructure in both countries is owned by local authorities and the clubs' main assets are their players and their brands).

Table 5.7   Expectations of bankruptcy vs. expectations of external and internal rescue (Kendall's tau correlation coefficient)

Variable	BANKRUPTCY	EXTm	INTm
BANKRUPTCY	1.00	-0.2934**	0.1533
EXTm	-0.2934**	1.00	0.01765
INTm	0.1533	0.01765	1.00

Notes: EXTm, INTm – value of the most probable rescue option among external and internal solutions; * p < 0.01, ** p < 0.05, *** p < 0.001.

Table 5.8   Expectations of a rescue by owner, local authorities and state institutions vs. ownership type

OWNER	E OWNER		E LAUTH		E STATE	
	<= median (6.0)	> median (6.0)	<= median (4.0)	> median (4.0)	<= median (2.0)	> median (2.0)
Local authorities	62.50%	37.50%	12.50%	87.50%	62.50%	37.50%
State-owned company	100.00%	0.00%	100.00%	0.00%	100.00%	0.00%
Private capital	62.50%	37.50%	68.75%	31.25%	62.50%	37.50%
Association/foundation	37.50%	62.50%	66.66%	33.33%	100.00%	0.00%
Total	69.19%	30.80%	53.57%	46.42%	67.85%	32.15%
Pearson's χ^2	2.2105		7.9811**		2.2105	

Notes: * p < 0.01, ** p < 0.05, *** p < 0.001.

In addition to these average observations, there is clearly a dose of heterogeneity in the rescue expectations among the clubs (as seen in the dispersion of answers in Figure 5.2). It seems worthwhile, therefore, to search for homogenous segments. In fact, based on external rescue options, both Ward's method and the *k*-fold cross-validation indicate the existence of two clusters (Figure 5.3). Cluster 1, which we label 'Realists', is the dominant one (68% of the sample). For the realist clubs, the most probable and practically the only expected source of external rescue is the club's owner. Hence, it is the relationship with the owner that determines their SBC mindset. In contrast, the clubs in the second cluster ('Optimists' – 32% of the sample) see some additional highly probable external rescue options in addition to the owner – from actual and new sponsors, as well as fans. They are also less pessimistic about potential state help. Thus, they have more reasons for SBC expectations, and consequently SBC decisions and acts. Considering the other, internal rescue solutions, or the probability of bankruptcy, there are no statistically significant differences between the clusters.

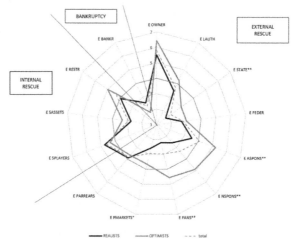

Notes: * p < 0.01, ** p < 0.05, *** p < 0.001.

Figure 5.3   *Subjective probability of different solutions to sudden and serious financial problems in two clusters of the clubs: Realists and Optimists (1: very low; 4: average; 7: very high)*

On the other hand, the clusters differ in terms of their past experience. There are relatively more clubs with no situation of sudden and serious financial problems during the last five years in the cluster of Optimists than in that of the Realists (67% vs. 32%, $\chi^2 = 3.0701$, p = 0.0797).

Table 5.9   Expectations of rescue options vs. past experience of rescue (Kendall's tau correlation coefficient)

Variable	E OWNER	E LAUTH	E STATE	E FEDER	E ASPONS	E NSPONS	E FANS	E FMAREKTS	E PARREARS	E SPLAYERS	E SASSETS	E RESTR	E BANKR
P OWNER	0.49**	0.36**	-0.23	0.19	-0.09	-0.02	-0.33*	0.34*	0.25	0.20	0.03	-0.23	-0.21
P LAUTH	-0.03	0.66***	0.17	-0.04	-0.15	0.04	0.18	0.07	0.12	0.24	-0.15	-0.15	0.10
P STATE	-0.27	0.03	0.67***	0.08	-0.21	0.07	0.41**	0.32*	-0.11	-0.06	-0.08	-0.35*	0.11
P FEDER	-0.05	0.10	0.15	-0.01	0.44**	0.33*	0.24	0.09	-0.01	-0.18	-0.33*	0.27	-0.18
P ASPONS	-0.10	0.13	0.19	0.15	0.36*	0.53**	0.31*	0.02	-0.20	-0.24	-0.16	0.32*	0.00
P NSPONS	-0.24	0.09	0.34*	0.03	0.17	0.50**	0.65***	-0.13	-0.04	-0.11	-0.27	0.06	0.09
P FANS	-0.11	-0.26	0.48**	0.41**	0.03	0.18	0.31*	0.35*	-0.14	-0.26	0.05	-0.06	0.09
P FMARKETS	0.27	0.03	0.33*	0.48**	-0.01	0.18	-0.06	0.56**	-0.02	-0.35*	0.00	-0.27	-0.23
P PARREARS	0.19	-0.06	0.06	0.08	0.01	0.30	0.12	0.24	0.50**	-0.02	-0.22	-0.01	-0.11
P SPLAYERS	0.17	0.12	0.05	0.25	-0.01	0.51**	0.11	-0.10	-0.18	0.39**	0.12	0.33*	-0.18
P SASSETS	-0.27	-0.08	0.28	-0.18	-0.27	-0.03	0.00	0.12	0.07	0.29	0.27	0.00	-0.12
P RESTR	0.04	0.02	-0.01	-0.15	0.46**	0.33*	0.29	-0.06	0.25	-0.01	-0.24	0.35*	-0.10
P BANKR	-0.36*	-0.37**	0.24	-0.07	-0.47**	-0.44**	0.03	0.16	0.03	-0.06	0.10	-0.39**	0.18

Notes: * p < 0.01, ** p < 0.05, *** p < 0.001.

The significance of past experience in the formation of expectations about the probability of rescue in the future is confirmed by the analysis of the correlation between the specific solutions in the past and the hypothetical future (Table 5.9). The correlation is particularly strong in the case of rescue coming from local authorities, state institutions and financial markets. This is indicative of the adaptive expectations of the managers, as well as the repetitiveness of the help from public institutions: the stronger the help in the past from a particular saviour, the more awaited it is in the future (and the softer the budgetary constraint in the present thinking and acting). This correlation is somewhat less strong, but still statistically significant (at $p < 0.05$), in the case of the owner, new sponsors, payment areas and sale of players.

In something of a surprise, profiling the clusters with variables representing the ownership structure, financial and sporting situation (its state and importance), number of fans, relations with environment and home countries results in no statistically significant differences between Realists and Optimists (data available on request). In contrast, some of these variables correlate with individual rescue options (Table 5.10). In particular, a higher risk of bankruptcy is related to a worse evaluation of the financial situation (both in subjective and objective measures) and hence to a primacy of financial results over sporting ones, as well as to a lower evaluation of contacts with local authorities and state institutions. On the other hand, trust in fans goes with an increased debt and importance of financial results, as well as higher value of the squad, bigger fan community, and larger localities. It is stronger in Poland than Hungary (58.2% vs. 9.1% over the median 2.0, $\chi^2 = 6.9253$, $p = 0.0085$). Moreover, the expectations of help from the local authorities are linked to good evaluations of the contacts with them, in addition to positive subjective evaluations of financial and sporting results. Finally, the dependence on the owner goes along not only with satisfaction with the financial and sporting results, but also with the presence of other clubs in the locality.

Taken together, the data lead to several conclusions. First, in general, the clubs evaluate the probability of their bankruptcy in the case of sudden and serious financial problems as low (with the exception of only two Polish clubs). This optimism is correlated mainly to the expectations of an external rescue. On the other hand, it decreases with the number of past financial problems and past events of bankruptcy. Consequently, the subjective risk of bankruptcy is higher, the worse the clubs' objective and subjective financial situation is. When the financial situation is critical, the financial results dominate over the sporting ones (the evaluation of which is, by the way, also rather bad in those situations). The clubs with a lower subjective risk of bankruptcy evaluate their contacts with local authorities and state institutions as better.

Second, among external rescue options, most hope is placed in the owner, irrespective of its type, the characteristics of the club or its objective financial

Table 5.10   Expectations of rescue options vs. characteristics of the clubs (Kendall's tau correlation coefficient)

Variable	E OWNER	E LAUTH	E STATE	E FEDER	E ASPONS	E NSPONS	E FANS	E FMARKETS	E PARREARS	E SPLAYERS	E SASSETS	E RESTR	E BANKR
DEBT	-0.10	-0.09	-0.27**	0.05	-0.11	-0.19	0.30**	-0.04	0.25*	0.08	-0.05	0.30**	0.36**
ROA	-0.03	0.04	0.23*	-0.02	0.10	0.09	-0.17	-0.08	-0.28**	0.01	0.22	0.02	-0.24*
BUDGET	0.03	0.12	-0.11	0.37**	0.01	-0.06	0.25*	0.23*	0.12	0.26**	0.09	0.32**	0.20
SQUAD	0.02	0.03	-0.05	0.30**	0.10	-0.03	0.31**	0.23*	-0.07	0.01	0.07	0.12	0.05
EVALSR	0.28**	0.51***	0.05	-0.05	0.14	0.07	0.19	0.12	0.00	0.19	0.09	0.25*	-0.28**
EVALFR	0.41**	0.43**	0.19	0.01	0.40**	0.16	0.07	0.23*	-0.04	-0.11	0.00	0.29**	-0.50***
IMPSR	0.18	0.27**	-0.10	-0.10	0.36**	0.19	0.11	0.11	-0.01	0.16	0.03	0.41**	-0.31**
IMPFR	0.07	0.18	-0.04	-0.31**	0.17	0.19	0.30**	0.23*	0.21	0.31**	-0.06	0.20	0.21
SR-FR	0.12	0.03	-0.08	0.19	0.15	-0.04	-0.17	0.27**	-0.11	-0.11	0.08	0.12	-0.42**
RANK	-0.01	0.01	0.02	0.36**	-0.04	-0.02	0.22*	-0.12	0.09	0.02	-0.02	0.02	0.17
OFC	0.31*	-0.20	-0.15	0.18	0.08	0.04	-0.22	0.06	0.20	-0.05	-0.07	-0.03	-0.01
CONLOCAL	0.10	0.56***	0.25*	-0.13	0.08	0.06	0.03	0.14	-0.13	0.07	-0.05	0.08	-0.29**
CONSTATE	0.05	0.10	0.11	0.24*	0.00	0.04	-0.12	0.31**	-0.06	-0.07	-0.27**	-0.15	-0.27**
RESIDENTS	-0.01	-0.02	-0.16	0.00	0.17	0.04	0.38**	0.09	0.12	0.16	0.13	0.35**	0.19
ATTENDANCE	-0.04	0.06	-0.07	0.09	0.12	-0.03	0.38**	0.05	0.01	0.09	0.17	0.33**	0.22
FACEBOOK	-0.03	0.00	-0.25*	0.13	0.11	-0.11	0.24*	0.17	0.15	0.18	0.06	0.39**	0.19
INSTAGRAM	0.00	-0.06	-0.10	0.42**	-0.02	-0.13	0.41**	0.27**	0.18	0.17	0.13	0.30**	0.26*

Notes: * p < 0.01, ** p < 0.05, *** p < 0.001.

and sporting results (in contrast, there is a weak positive correlation with the subjective evaluation of sporting and financial results). This is backed by the experience of previous help from the owner. The owner is regarded as the main and practically the only rescue provider for the majority of the clubs (cluster of Realists – 68%). The other 32% of the clubs (cluster of Optimists) report some additional positive probability of a rescue by sponsors and fans.

Third, rescue by public money is judged as probable by 46% of the clubs in the sample. These expectations rely mainly on money from the local authorities. In fact, only one Hungarian club estimates the probability of the rescue by state institutions as high (as it does for the rescue by local authorities). The expectations of state help show a strong positive correlation with such help in the past. On the other hand, the expectations of rescue by the local authorities have the largest variation among all the rescue options. They are stronger among clubs owned by local authorities than privately owned clubs. Moreover, they correlate positively with such help in the past and better financial and sporting results, although only in subjective terms.

Fourth, the clubs hoping for financial help from sponsors make up 46% of the sample. The remaining rescue options are not considered very likely. In fact, only clubs in Poland count on their fans' help in the case of problems; especially those from bigger localities, with more fans and, last but not least, with more debt. Only 21% of the clubs report the possibility of financing from financial markets as a probable rescue option. This probability correlates with past experience of this kind (and only weakly with the size of the budget, but not with the size of the debt or the current financial result). With the exception of only one Hungarian club, help from the federation or league governing bodies is not considered to be probable.

Finally, considering the determinants of subjective probabilities of rescue from different sources, the strongest one is past experience. In addition, the objective characteristics of the clubs' financial or sporting standing do not show strong correlations with the expectations of a rescue – in contrast to the subjective evaluations, which rise with higher optimism about possible help.

DISCUSSION

Kornai, Maskin, & Roland (2003) insist that the soft budget constraint phenomenon is a syndrome, and as such consists of manifestations and settings giving rise to it. And the SBC mindset of an organisation's managers is one of the key circumstances leading to SBC behaviour: only if managers anticipate a bailout ex ante and adjust their actions accordingly, does the SBC syndrome set in (Kornai et al., 2003). Consequently, our study set out to explore empirically the football managers' ex ante expectations of a rescue of their club in the case of a financial distress.

The results of the study show, first of all, a high level of optimism about survival in the case of serious and sudden financial problems, which is indicative of a high level of budgetary softness in the minds of football clubs' managers. Especially so as the optimism is based principally on trust in the owner. This conclusion seems general despite the differences in the ownership structure across clubs, divisions and countries – and despite the absence of typical sugar daddies in both countries, who are often considered as one of the sources of the softness in English or French football (Andreff, 2007; Lang & Grossmann, 2011; Nielsen & Storm, 2017; Szymanski, 2010). In fact, most of the owners do support their clubs regularly (as seen in the past experiences of the clubs in the sample) and keep nourishing the softness of the budgetary constraint in the minds of the clubs' managers (and raising the debt of the clubs, as the rescue often comes in the form of liability, not equity). Consequently, for the survival of the club, the support of the owner seems more important than the current financial situation of the club, which corresponds to the results of other research showing an irrelevance of the financial situation for the bankruptcy of the clubs (Barajas & Rodríguez, 2010) or their managers' attention (Perechuda, 2020). Actually, in our sample, there are a few clubs with both high indebtedness and negative current returns on assets, but only two of them estimate their risk of bankruptcy as high in the hypothetical worsening of the financial situation. Both clubs are currently on sale. Moreover, there are also clubs outside our sample that have big financial problems and are also desperately looking for new owners. In fact, the risk of bankruptcy becomes real when the clubs' owners have no more possibility or willingness to support them. And the bankruptcies do happen in both countries (in the last 10 years, it has been the case for three clubs from the I division and five from the II division in Poland and, respectively, five and two clubs in Hungary). And although there is life after bankruptcy, as most of these bankrupt clubs have re-emerged in sporting competitions under other legal forms, its price is very high.

Regarding the expectations of rescue by public money, the study shows mainly a dependence on local authorities. The relationship is particularly evident in Poland, where the local authorities are very often owners of the clubs, if not majority then at least minority owner, especially in the II division. In fact, for some clubs, local authorities have played the role of the owner of last resort and have bought clubs on the brink of insolvency from their private owners. Under pressure from fans, the community, electoral stakes, a region's brand image issues and, not least, administrators' personal relations and passion for their local club, many local governments regularly shield their clubs from bankruptcies. This is also widely seen in other European countries (e.g., in Spain, Italy or France) for the same reasons – clubs are considered socially too big to fall (Senaux, 2008; Storm & Nielsen, 2012). In Poland, the local government help is often accorded even to clubs with majority private capital. In 2018, the financial support from local authorities for the I division clubs only amounted to c. €16m (Grabowski, 2019). Śląsk Wrocław received the biggest share – (€3m) (equivalent to 160% of the club's media income and 464% of its match day revenues - Deloitte, 2019). However, the exact size of local government support is difficult to evaluate as the direct subsidies are only part of it. Other forms include, inter alia, soft pricing (e.g., infrastructure lease below market price), soft credits (with preferential interest rates and postponed repayment), other soft subsidies (e.g., support for clubs' youth academies, sport scholarships for the football players).[1] By way of an example, there are clubs (such as Radomiak Radom in the Polish II division) where the scholarships for the football players pay c. 80% of their salaries (Rzemiński, 2020). This kind of public local funding, both on a regular and (repeatedly) ad hoc basis, not only softens the budget limits and leads to inefficiencies in the management – in extreme cases it turns into money laundering or fictitious employment (Grabowski, 2019).

The expectations of direct ad hoc state help for the clubs, on the other hand, are not significant according to the results of our survey. While this result is plausible for the Polish clubs, it does not seem to align with general observations of the football system in Hungary. However, in Hungary, the state help is not always granted directly to a club itself. Instead, it is quite often arranged by the majority owner of a club, who happens to be an association or foundation with a prominent politician on the board. Alternatively, the public money is supplied by sponsors, which are often state-owned companies, or private companies dependent on public procurement. In fact, the most significant private sponsors usually come from the typically government-to-business building industry, which is contrary to general European trends, where the construction and real estate industry comprise only 5% of total sponsorship revenues (UEFA, 2020, p. 44).

The emergence of online crowdsourcing facilities and innovative forms of direct communication between clubs and fans create new opportunities for fans' support for their clubs (Kopera, 2016). Yet, according to the results of our study, these possibilities are considered only by a minority of the clubs. This is surprising as fans are important stakeholders, whose loyalty may be turned to an economic advantage for the clubs (Theysohn et al., 2009). In Poland, some clubs have even been saved from bankruptcy by their loyal individual and corporate fans (e.g., Wisła Kraków). The reason for the relatively limited trust in fans may lie in a high degree of faith in the owner or the public authorities. Additionally, it may be restricted by the small fan base of many clubs, especially in Hungary (where only Ferencváros has a significant number of fans), and in the limited disposable income in both countries (compared to Western Europe). Finally, it may also be due to insufficient competencies in clubs in terms of developing and managing their relationship with the fans.

This latter reason may also be responsible for the relatively low expectations of help from the sponsors, as nourishing sponsors' commitment and building a lasting business network around a club demands professionalism, resources and a long-term perspective (Chadwick & Thwaites, 2006; Junghagen, 2018).

In sum, each of the external rescue options was seen as at least rather probable by at least one of the clubs. It confirms Storm & Nielsen's (2012) idea about the multitude of stakeholders considered by football club managers when expecting a bailout, and the horizontal relationships between clubs and their expected saviours. However, it is the dependence on the owner that is the strongest and most homogenous and that seems mainly responsible for the prevalence of the SBC in both countries under study. This hierarchical dependence on the owner corresponds to the hierarchical relationships between state organisations and state authorities observed by Kornai in socialist countries and reported also in case of the football clubs of this period (directly subordinated to protector institutions). The softness of budget constraints in contemporary football in Hungary and Poland may therefore be considered both as a residual factor of socialism (the reliance on the protector transformed into the reliance on the owner) and as an outcome of institutional changes over the last 30 years in the sport sector (the diversification of horizontal relationships).

Apart from these general observations, the study also shows heterogeneity in terms of the sources of an expected rescue. Except for the prevailing trust in the owner and the prevailing distrust in state and sport governing bodies, the expectations with regard to all other stakeholders are quite varied. The clubs in the minority Optimists' cluster are those with more diversified potential rescue options (in particular, sponsors, fans and local authorities), which may be indicative of their better management of external relations. At the national level, football clubs in Hungary are more dependent on central state institutions, while those in Poland rely rather on local authorities. The post-socialist transition has clearly contributed to the divergence of football's budgetary constraints in the region.

Regarding the determinants of rescue expectations, they rely mainly on the past experience of the clubs. This is a clear confirmation of Kornai's consideration of the SBC as a self-generating process, in which after every bailout an organisation starts over again with the expectation of yet another rescue in the future (Kornai, 2009). Even worse, such a bailout for one organisation may give rise to expectations of the same rescue for others in the same sector of the economy (Kornai et al., 2003). Our results show, however, that in case of football clubs in Hungary and Poland, the expectations are largely contingent on the organisation's own past experience in terms of the source of the rescue. This is particularly apparent in case of public aid – both at the state and local levels. Evidently, some football clubs enjoy more privileged relationships with public stakeholders and profit more often than others from such relationships, which explains a part of the observed heterogeneity. The situation is especially striking in Hungary, where the financial paternalism of the state (directly or through networks of sponsors and associations) concerns mainly clubs from smaller localities (and leads to their superior sporting performance compared to rivals from big cities). Manifestly, in terms of football financing, the state authorities in Hungary and the local authorities in both countries are unable to commit themselves not to prolong their help in the future, which is the problem of dynamic commitment (Kornai et al., 2003). In the absence of institutional changes introducing barriers to future support with taxpayers' money, the vested interests of some public stakeholders effectively soften the budget constraints of some fortunate football clubs.

CONCLUSION

Our study makes an empirical contribution to the understanding of the constituents of SBCs in professional football in the particular setting of post-socialist countries in Central Europe. The focus on managers' subjective probabilities of different rescue sources has allowed us to determine the main source of the SBC mindset: the dependence on the club owner's repeated ad hoc help. However, besides this hierarchical relationship, some of the clubs have also established additional horizontal rescue relationships (mainly with local authorities, sponsors and fans) that impact their decisions and behaviours ex ante and lead to the SBC syndrome. The 30 years of institutional changes for post-socialist football has thus led to not only the transformation but also the diversification and divergence of the SBC phenomenon in the football clubs of the region.

Regarding these contributions, at least two main limitations are to be noted. First, the COVID-19 pandemic forced us to stop collecting the data and restricted the sample size. Second, there is some time discrepancy in our data, as the latest available financial statements cover the financial year ending in 2018, while in the survey the managers were asked about their evaluations of the current situation at the beginning of 2020. When the new, post-pandemic normalisation sets in, it would be worth continuing this exploration with a bigger sample (covering more countries) that would allow us to explore with more precision the determinants of the observed heterogeneity in the football clubs' budget constraints.

NOTE

1.   For more examples of possible mechanisms softening the budget constraint, see Nielsen & Storm (2017).

REFERENCES

Anderson, J. H., Korsun, G., & Murrell, P. (2000). Which Enterprises (Believe They) Have Soft Budgets? Evidence on the Effects of Ownership and Decentralization in Mongolia. *Journal of Comparative Economics*, 28(2), 219–246.

András, K. (2003). *Business Elements in Sports, Through Example of Football* [Budapest University of Economics Sciences and Public Administration]. http://phd .lib.uni-corvinus.hu/150/2/andras_krisztina_en.pdf (accessed 21 March 2020).

András, K., & Havran, Z. (2016). Examination of Central and Eastern European Professional Football Clubs' Sport Success, Financial Position and Business Strategy in International Environment. In P. Trąpczyński, Ł. Puślecki, & M. Jarosiński (Eds), *Competitiveness of CEE Economies and Businesses: Multidisciplinary Perspectives on Challenges and Opportunities* (pp. 197–210). Springer.

Andreff, W. (2007). French Football: A Financial Crisis Rooted in Weak Governance. *Journal of Sports Economics*, 8(6), 652–661.

Balcerowicz, L. (1994). Economic transition in Central and Eastern Europe: Comparisons and Lessons. *Australian Economic Review*, 27(1), 47–59.

Barajas, Á., & Rodríguez, P. (2010). Spanish Football Clubs' Finances: Crisis and Player Salaries. *International Journal of Sport Finance*, 5(1), 52–66.

Bignebat, C., & Gouret, F. (2006). Which Firms Have a Soft Loan? Managers' Believes in a Cross-Country Survey in Transition Economies. In *Working Paper* (03/2006).

Chadwick, S., & Thwaites, D. (2006). Distinguishing Between Short-term and Long-term Commitment in Football Shirt Sponsorship Programmes: Towards a Matrix of Management Implications. *International Journal of Sports Marketing and Sponsorship*, 7(3), 11–27.

Deloitte. (2019). *Pieniądze leżą na boisku – Ranking przychodów klubów piłkarskich, Raport 'Piłkarska liga finansowa – rok 2018'.* https://www2.deloitte.com/content/ dam/Deloitte/pl/Documents/Reports/PL__Liga_finansowa_2018.pdf (accessed 21 March 2022).

Duke, V., Gammelsaeter, H., & Senaux, B. (2011). From Bohemian Rhapsody to a New World: The Organisation of Football in the Czech Republic. In *The Organisation and Governance of Top Football Across Europe: An Institutional Perspective* (pp. 238–252). Routledge.

EBRD (1999). *Transition Report 1999. Ten Years of Transition.* https://doi.org/10 .1016/j.jpowsour.2010.04.050 (accessed 21 March 2020).

FIFA (2020): https://www.fifa.com/fifa-world-ranking/ranking-table/men/ (accessed 21 March 2020).

Földesi, G. S., & Egressy, J. (2005). Post-transformational Trends in Hungarian Sport (1995–2004). *European Journal for Sport and Society*, 2(2), 85–96.

Grabowski, P. (2019, 20 August). Anatomia piłkarskiego nieszczęścia. *Onet. Sport.* https://sport.onet.pl/pilka-nozna/ekstraklasa/finansowanie-polskiej-pilki-noznej -przez-samorzady-i-problemy-klubow/5xbl1es (accessed 21 March 2020).

Havran, Z., & András, K. (2019). *Understanding Soft Budget Constraint in Western-European and Central Eastern-European Professional Football.* In *Working Paper* of Corvinus University of Budapest. http://unipub.lib.uni-corvinus .hu/4205/ (accessed 21 March 2020).

Josselin, J.-M., Padovano, F., & Rocaboy, Y. (2013). Grant Legislation vs. Political Factors as Determinants of Soft Budget Spending Behaviors. Comparison between

Italian and French Regions. *The European Journal of Comparative Economics*, *10*(3), 317–354.

Junghagen, S. (2018). Football Clubs as Mediators in Sponsor-Stakeholder Relations. *Sport, Business and Management: An International Journal*, *8*(4), 335–353.

Kobiela, F. (2011). From State Socialism to Free Society: Sport in Poland from 1945 until Present Day. In S. G. Folesine & T. Doczi (Eds), *The Interaction of Sport and Society in the V4 Countries*. Hungarian Society of Sport Science.

Kopera, S. (2016). Social Media Challenges. In T. Byers (Ed.), *Contemporary Issues in Sport Management: A Critical Introduction* (pp. 349–362). Sage.

Kornai, J. (2001). Hardening the Budget Constraint: The Experience of the Post-socialist Countries. *European Economic Review*, *45*(9), 1573–1599.

Kornai, J. (2009). The Soft Budget Constraint Syndrome in the Hospital Sector. *Society and Economy*, *31*(1), 5–31.

Kornai, J. (2014). The Soft Budget Constraint: An Introductory Study to Volume IV of the Life's Work Series. *Acta Oeconomica*, *64*, 25–79.

Kornai, J., Maskin, E., & Roland, G. (2003). Understanding the Soft Budget Constraint. *Journal of Economic Literature*, *41*(4), 1095–1136.

Lang, M., & Grossmann, M. (2011). The Sugar Daddy Game: How Wealthy Investors Change Competition in Professional Team Sports. *Journal of Institutional and Theoretical Economics*, *167*(4), 557–577.

Lenartowicz, M., & Karwacki, A. (2005). An Overview of Social Conflicts in the History of Polish Club Football. *European Journal for Sport and Society*, *2*(2), 97–107.

Mieżejwski, J. (2016, 16 August). Szemrani prezesi Ekstraklasy. *RetroFutbal.Pl*. https://rfbl.pl/szemrani-prezesi-ekstraklasy/ (accessed 21 March 2020).

Molnar, G. (2007). Hungarian Football: A Socio-historical Overview. *Sport in History*, *27*(2), 293–317.

Molnar, G., & Whigham, S. (2019). Radical Right Populist Politics in Hungary: Reinventing the Magyars through Sport. *International Review for the Sociology of Sport*, *56*(1), 133–148.

Nessel, K., & Drewniak, D. (2020). Motivation (For) and Outcomes Of a Continuing Professional Education in Football Management: An Exploratory Study. *Polish Journal of Sport and Tourism*, *27*(2), 3–7.

Nielsen, K., & Storm, R. K. (2017). Profit Maximization, Win Optimization and Soft Budget Constraints in Professional Team Sports. In K. Nielsen, U. Wagner, & R. K. Storm (Eds), *When Sport Meets Business: Capabilities, Challenges, Critiques* (pp. 153–166). Sage.

Perechuda, I. (2020). Utility of Financial Information in Managing Football Business Model: Case from Central Eastern Europe. *Journal of Physical Education and Sport*, *20*(2), 1257–1264.

Pettersson-Lidbom, P. (2010). Dynamic Commitment and the Soft Budget Constraint: An Empirical Test. *American Economic Journal: Economic Policy*, *2*(3), 154–179.

Rajkiewicz, M. (2019, 18 October). Kluby resortowe, czyli jak władze komunistyczne wpływały na polskie kluby piłkarskie. *RetroFutbal.Pl*. https://rfbl.pl/kluby-resortowe-czyli-jak-wladze-komunistyczne-wplywaly-na-polskie-kluby-pilkarskie/ (accessed 21 March 2020).

Rzemiński, B. (2020, 12 April). Kolejny polski klub na skraju bankructwa. Miał walczyć o awans do ekstraklasy. *Sport.Pl*. https://www.sport.pl/pilka/7,65044,25864038,kolejny-polski-klub-staje-na-skraju-bankructwa-mial-walczyc.html (accessed 21 March 2020).

Sárközy, T. (2017). A sport mint nemzetstratégiai ágazat. Előnyök és hátrányok, hosszú távú kilátások. *Polgári Szemle: Gazdasági És Társadalmi Folyóirat, 13*(4–6), 143–159.

Senaux, B. (2008). A Stakeholder Approach to Football Club Governance. *International Journal of Sport Management and Marketing, 4*(1), 4–17.

Storm, R. K., & Nielsen, K. (2012). Soft Budget Constraints in Professional Football. *European Sport Management Quarterly, 12*(2), 183–201.

Szerovay, M., Itkonen, H., & Vehmas, H. (2017). 'Glocal' Processes in Peripheral Football Countries: A Figurational Sociological Comparison of Finland and Hungary. *Soccer & Society, 18*(4), 497–515.

Szymanski, S. (2010). The Financial Crisis and English Football: The Dog That Will Not Bark. *International Journal of Sport Finance, 5*(1), 28–40.

Theysohn, S., Hinz, O., Nosworthy, S., & Kirchner, M. (2009). Official Supporters Clubs: The Untapped Potential of Fan Loyalty. *International Journal of Sports Marketing and Sponsorship, 10*(4), 302–324.

Transfermarkt (2020a). https://www.transfermarkt.com/1-liga/besucherzahlen/ wettbewerb/PL2/saison_id/2018 (accessed 21 March 2020).

Transfermarkt (2020b). https://www.transfermarkt.co.uk/nemzeti-bajnoksag-ii-/ besucherzahlen/wettbewerb/UN2/saison_id/2018/plus/ (accessed 21 March 2020).

Transfermarkt (2020c). https://www.transfermarkt.de/polen/startseite/verein/3442 (accessed 21 March 2020).

Transfermarkt (2020d). https://www.transfermarkt.de/ungarn/startseite/verein/3468 (accessed 21 March 2020).

Uchwała Biura Politycznego Komitetu Centralnego PZPR 'w sprawie kultury fizycznej i sportu' (1949). (Testimony of Biuro Polityczne KC PZPR).

UEFA (2020): https://www.uefa.com/memberassociations/uefarankings/country/#/yr/ 2020 (accessed 21 March 2020).

Woźniak, W. (2013). Zawodowe amatorstwo? Futbol w okresie PRL w relacjach polskich piłkarzy. In M. Kazimierczak & J. Kosiewicz (Eds), *Sport i turystyka. Uwarunkowania historyczne i wyzwania współczesności* (pp. 537–551). Akademia Wychowania Fizycznego im. Eugeniusza Piaseckiego w Poznaniu.

6. The soft budget constraint syndrome in Hungarian professional football from a Central and Eastern European perspective

Zsolt Havran and Krisztina András

INTRODUCTION

In European professional football, sporting performance is mostly prioritized over financial performance (Frick, 2007). This feature of professional football gives rise to special financial challenges for football clubs. These challenges include mainly the presence of so-called 'sugar daddies' and irresponsible spending on the transfer market (Andreff, 2018; Franck, 2014; Storm & Nielsen, 2017). In connection with these challenges, several sport economists (e.g., Storm & Nielsen, 2012) have applied the soft budget constraint theory (hereinafter SBC theory) of the renowned economist János Kornai (1986). However, these applications have focused only on Western European leagues. In contrast, in Central and Eastern Europe (hereinafter CEE), weakening competitiveness, a decreasing number of domestic consumers and recurring public funding are the main problems (András & Havran, 2016). Our aim is to expand the research on SBC in professional football with understanding of the characteristics of the operation of professional CEE football. Despite the possibility that the economic operation of CEE football clubs may strongly differ from that of their Western European counterparts, few publications have addressed this area. Using Kornai's theoretical model, we analyse the extreme case of Hungary.

Hence, the application of SBC theory to Eastern European sport can be viewed as a completely new field, thus rendering this study a significant contribution. For the international academic literature, this region deserves interest for two main reasons. On the one hand, for being an important market in terms of consumer numbers, and on the other, since several outstanding players in the best leagues and clubs come from CEE leagues. Accordingly, some CEE teams are fairly successful in international national team tournaments.[1]

To reveal the specificities of CEE football, we have conducted a thorough analysis of the sporting and financial performance of nine nations (Bulgaria, Croatia, Czech Republic, Hungary, Poland, Romania, Serbia, Slovakia and Slovenia), revealing significant differences in the structure and role of public funding. The analysis shows that Hungarian football provides a striking example of being characterized by the combination of huge financial contributions and minimal sporting success. For this reason, we apply the SBC theory primarily to contemporary Hungarian professional football. Our main question is to what extent the peculiar operation of professional Hungarian football clubs can be described by using the SBC theory. Our analysis shows that the structure of budget constraints in contemporary Hungarian football is very similar to those under operation in the former socialist regime.

The chapter is structured as follows. First, we analyse the efficiency of professional football leagues operating in the CEE region. This is followed by the presentation of the concept of SBC in general, and then in football under socialism and in capitalism. In the third section, we describe the data collection and research processes, and present our findings. The final part concludes that Hungarian professional football is an illustrative example of how SBCs work in practice.

THE CHARACTERISTICS OF PROFESSIONAL FOOTBALL IN CEE AND IN HUNGARY

Professional football is increasingly business-oriented worldwide; however, to date it is questionable how business-based the operation of professional football clubs can be considered, as sporting performance often overrides financial performance (Garcia-del-Barrio & Szymanski, 2009). Regardless, in the second half of the 20th century, the earlier association model gradually transformed into a corporate model in capitalist countries. In socialist countries, the state dominated the professional sports field, but following the regime change, clubs gradually transformed into a more corporate operational form as well (András, 2003).

Economic features are similar throughout the region. After the regime change, football clubs had a limited number of consumers and low profits from TV royalties and were unable to provide high-quality service. Due to these hindrances the clubs were in constant need of (extra) support from the government (public funding), while their international sport professional competitiveness decreased considerably. These trends were experienced in the Czech Republic (Procházka, 2012), Poland (Lenartowicz & Karwacki, 2005), Hungary (András, 2003; Vincze et al., 2008), Bulgaria (Girginov & Sandanski, 2008), Croatia (Hodges & Stubbs, 2013) and Romania (Buhaş et al., 2017; Roşca, 2017). During the socialist regime, even during the 1980s, clubs in the region were still fairly successful. For example, in 1986, the Romanian Steaua Bucharest won the European Champion Clubs Cup (ECC), the forerunner of today's Champions League – beating Barcelona in the final. There was also the victory of the Serbian Crvena Zvezda Club in 1991. Nowadays, reaching the group stage of the Champions League (the best 32 teams) by a club from the region is exceptional. Success in both sporting performance and financial results in the region is concentrated in very few clubs in a handful of countries. This is a trend which, incidentally, is present also in Western Europe. Clubs have continuously been struggling with financial difficulties, accumulating sizable losses and debts (András, 2003; Havran & András, 2014; András & Havran, 2016).

During the years of the regime change, other industries were facing similar problems, i.e., strong European competition, limited local demand, lack of capital and weak markets. However, in professional football, the disadvantages of being a CEE club were especially severe. In Western Europe, football clubs that were used to functioning in a capitalist environment managed to increase the number of their international consumers and supporters thanks to the increasing use of television, and later, the internet. In the early 1990s, the most important leagues (e.g., the English Premier League) and cup tournaments (Champions League) were founded and started to be widely broadcast on television. In the same period, many previously successful football clubs of post-socialist countries found themselves in a difficult economic situation, as without the state companies that had supported them earlier they fell behind their competitors for international consumers (András et al., 2012). The liberalization of the players' market also played a major role in the growing differences between regions (Szymanski, 2014). On the one hand, after the Iron Curtain had come down, talented Eastern European players could sign with Western clubs more easily, where they received much better payment and circumstances. On the other hand, the regulations of the players' market also moved the market towards a higher player-trade rate. One of these regulations was the Bosman ruling, an important element of which is that players sign for a club only for a determined period of time, and when that period is over, they can transfer to another club with no compensation fee required (Sárközy et al., 2000; Lembo, 2011).

These are the factors that have contributed to the limited international success of CEE clubs since the 1990s, although they had always been among the best before. Besides public funding, earlier successes in the region were also due to talented coaches and players with considerable know-how. Modern football has developed significantly; now, even for small-scale success, both international sport professional knowledge and club leadership skills are essential. Only clubs with personal contacts, i.e., with former players and coaches, which follow innovations and are open to new ideas, can keep up with the best leagues and clubs. Our hypothesis is that only clubs that are forced to fundamentally rely on market resources based on consumer demand are capable of all this, especially those who rely on their youth training systems and create the major part of the necessary resources based on their transfer incomes.

There are two ways left for clubs in CEE leagues: they may turn towards market-based operation to an larger extent, increasing the number of their consumers or improving their youth training system in order to procure more income and thus enhance their competitiveness; the other way is in channelling public funding, which is prohibited both by the Union of European Football Associations (UEFA) and the European Union, but is still practised in some countries of the region, as well as in Western Europe (Storm & Nielsen, 2017).

Hungary's background is very similar to that of other CEE countries, but despite significant state subsidies, the Hungarian national football team and local clubs are not very successful. We describe the special operation of Hungarian football to understand how SBC obstructs the development of football.

THE CONCEPT OF SOFT BUDGET CONSTRAINTS (SBC) IN FOOTBALL

The Original Meaning of SBC in Socialism and its Interpretation in Football

One of the first economic descriptions of the operation of Hungarian football (András, 2004) focused on the question of whether it was worthwhile – purely from a financial perspective – to invest in a first-class league team. The results showed that owners of football clubs in that period could not realize financial profits. According to András (2004), for the sake of efficiency, some specialization was needed (Smith, 1992, cited by Chikán, 2017); thus, specialization of organizations and facilities occurred, and athletes became professionals (for details, see András (2003) based on Brasher (1986)). However, specialization necessitates coordination (Douma & Schreuder, 1991, cited by Chikán, 2017). The interpretation of these coordination mechanisms is generally based on Kornai (1986), both in the social context and its subsystems, including the broader economy and sports. The coordination mechanisms can be either bureaucratic/organizational or market-oriented, of which market coordination became dominant in the 20th century, a phenomenon observable in the economy in general and also in sports (Chikán, 2017).

There are several descriptions to define types of public funding in the economic sense (Meyer & Peng, 2016). The main ones are the following:

1. Planned economy: the bureaucratic/state-coordinating mechanism is exclusive, controlling all coordinating mechanisms.
2. Liberal market economy: the market-coordinating mechanism is dominant, characterized by the freedom of entrepreneurial activity, the protection of private property and minimal government interference.
3. Social market economy: it also has mixed coordination, but the main purpose of government interference is to create social well-being.
4. State capitalism: the operation of a market economy is based on the relationship between the government and the business world. This means controlling 'the wealth that markets generate by allowing the government to play a dominant role through public-sector companies and politically loyal corporations' (Bremmer, 2014, p. 2).

The operation of professional football in a country largely depends on the general role the state takes in the economy. Hungary today can be characterized by state capitalism.

In the process of football becoming a business, the organizational framework of clubs has still not transformed completely into corporations; for details about this and the concept of football companies, see András (2003). In their operational model, we see a mix of business-operated, state-operated and non-profit models (András, 2004). When defining the business-based operation it is crucial to determine if football companies' expenditures are covered by revenue coming from the professional football markets. There are three other aspects to consider (András, 2003, p. 29):

1. the size of investments,
2. the organizational form of the clubs, and
3. the presence of consumers.

In the case of a mixed or a state-operated model, according to Kornai & Matits (1987), we can expect that budget constraints start to soften. Before the regime change, the softening of budget constraints was probably especially significant in Hungarian sport, thus in Hungarian football, and this was also typical of all other socialist countries. The danger of this operational model comes from the fact that the state as a macroeconomic player typically spends income produced by other actors, therefore the market mechanism is distorted, and hard budget constraints do not prevail (Friedman et al., 1998). According to Kornai

(2014, pp. 852–853), the softening of budget constraints is accompanied by the following phenomena:

1. it promotes a tendency for wanton spending,
2. it reduces decision-makers' sensitivity to price and cost, and
3. it alters the outlook of leaders who are in charge of organizations applying for rescue or subsidies, and also the allocation of their attention and activity (they will pay less attention to the quality and improvement of the original function, and more to establishing relationships with potential rescuers and to gaining patrons and serving them faithfully).

Points 1–3 jointly reduce the efficiency of the organization,

4. it is destructive to the morals of society: the consequent redistribution is widely considered as unfair and dishonourable.

During the transition period, in connection with the need for bailout, Kornai (2014, p. 845) remarks: 'One or two cases of bailout will not automatically mean creating a soft budget constraint syndrome, it evolves if bailouts become an expectation.' An example to illustrate this is the extent of public dues accumulated by 2000 (social insurance and tax dues, which were remitted by the state ministry responsible for sport) following the 1999 debt consolidation. This had a strong demoralizing effect: citizens who had been conscientiously paying their dues were suddenly at a disadvantage.

   Both in socialist and capitalist regimes, the economic policy providing the state with the direct power to exert its influence often determines priorities, and thus has the potential to treat sport as a strategic sector. This happened in the period of capitalism in Hungary between 1998 and 2002, and the same has applied since 2010 (during the government of Viktor Orbán). This affects various fields, and has a markedly strong impact on sports, especially football.

The Emergence of SBC in Capitalism and in Football Today

Kornai's theory (1986) can also be used for capitalist economies built on market coordination mechanisms. Behind the bailout of an organization, there are usually the intentions of the prevention of a bigger problem. Kornai himself marvels at the use of the concept in the field of international football (2014, p. 860).

   Storm (2012) provides us with a glimpse into the soft budget constraints appearing in football. He considers the FFP (Financial Fair Play) ruling as an important countermeasure. Soft budget constraints take political, cultural and emotional attachment into consideration in order to provide an explanation for the operation of football clubs. Andreff (2015) focuses on the governance and management of clubs and gives recommendations on how football clubs can harden their budget constraints. Storm & Nielsen (2012) use the concept of soft budget constraints to explain how it is possible for professional European football clubs to continuously operate on the verge of insolvency without going bankrupt. They also argue that clubs focus on winning because of the social attachment related to the specific emotional logic of sport. Clubs build identity in their own community and region for people of the same interests, loyalties and enthusiasms. Being part of European football brings significant prestige; for example, Russian oil industry billionaire Roman Abramovich invested £1.5 billion into Chelsea Football Club (Altukov et al., 2020).

According to Rohde & Breuer (2016), the emergence of soft budget constraints in European football clubs has happened due to the appearance of sugar daddy owners, loose taxation, soft or interest-free loans, and infrastructure subsidies. In addition, the low level of care, the moral risk of leaders taking wrong decisions, and the weak incentives to innovate are seen as additional reasons (Franck, 2014). Based on Kornai et al. (2003), D'Andrea & Masciandaro (2016) emphasize low efficiency. Storm & Nielsen (2017) complement the 'soft' factors identified by Kornai (1986) related to football, citing individual cases in Western European leagues (Spanish, Italian, Danish, English, and French). State subsidies, cancellation of debts, centralized prices, tax benefits, soft investments, and so-called 'soft accounting' are all aimed at softening the budget and the operation of football clubs.

METHODOLOGY

Our research question is the following: To what extent is the operation of professional Hungarian football clubs characterized by soft budget constraints? To answer this question, we examine the efficiency of Hungarian professional football in terms of sporting performance, which we examine by benchmarking analysis, that is, by comparing it to the efficiency of other regional football leagues. Furthermore, we describe anomalies typical of the operation of Hungarian football.

Among the most recent studies on the efficiency of sporting performance, the work of Terrien & Andreff (2020) and Klobučník et al. (2019) is the most relevant. Terrien & Andreff (2020) compared 36 European football leagues between 2010 and 2015 with the so-called Data Envelopment Analysis (DEA) method. In order to produce a more competitive league, they suggested considering the following four aspects: (1) the uncertainty of outcome, (2) financial stability, (3) maximizing the number of talented footballers, and (4) increasing competitiveness at a supranational level. Klobučník et al. (2019) conducted a league comparison and (in six leagues) a club-level comparison between

2007 and 2017. According to their results, the efficiency of Hungarian football in terms of sporting performance is the weakest within the CEE region.

Examining nine leagues only, we cannot apply the methods of DEA, cluster or regression analysis, therefore we have built our own efficiency indicator and benchmark-type comparisons. However, the cited studies have still been helpful in determining both the logical process of our examination and the range of data to be collected. A club-level comparison was not possible due to the lack of data, as the clubs in the region only publish financial reports in their own language and business register.

We measure efficiency based on the clubs' resources and international sporting performance. We compare Hungarian results to those of other CEE countries with a similar position in terms of their economic performance and the quality of their leagues. Secondly, we examine whether differences in efficiency can be explained by overly generous public funding that leads to SBC. We also give an indirect estimate of the share of public funds in their budget. Furthermore, in order to illustrate its unique nature, we present some striking examples demonstrating the 'soft' aspect of Hungarian football.

We have collected data from nine CEE countries, whose common trait is that there used to be a socialist regime, and except for one all are now all European Union members (Serbia is officially a candidate for membership). They are the following in alphabetical order: Bulgaria, Croatia, the Czech Republic, Hungary, Poland, Romania, Serbia, Slovakia, and Slovenia.

We have collected data (Table 6.1) of the clubs' business income, consumer interest in them, and their revenue from players' transfers; our efficiency indicator is based on these values. A club can rely on income (András, 2004; UEFA, 2019) either from its consumers (including on-site and media consumers, sponsors, merchandising, and media income) or from its youth training and disposal (for more details of transfer strategy, see: Szabados, 2003; András & Havran, 2015). Our efficiency indicator shows the price of gaining one UEFA league point in million euros.

Table 6.1   *Description and source of data for the nine leagues examined*

Data	Data description	Investigated period	Data source
Sporting success	UEFA-coefficients by leagues; Ranking and average coefficient of the best three clubs	2010–2019	uefa.com
Spectator numbers		2010–2019	transfermarkt.de
Social media interest	Numbers of followers of the federation and the three most successful clubs	31 October 2019	Facebook Instagram Twitter
Google trends search results	Google searches about the nine examined countries (ratio to each other)	2010–2019	https://trends.google.com
Revenue distribution of the leagues	Based on UEFA reports: ticket, sponsorship, TV rights, UEFA remuneration, transfers, and other revenues	2015–2018	UEFA 2016, 2017, 2019, 2020
Number of clubs in the leagues	To calculate revenue per club	2010–2019	uefa.com

Source: Edited by the authors.[2]

Our sample includes ten clubs in Croatia (16 before 2012 and 12 in 2013) and Slovenia, 12 clubs in Hungary (16 before 2016) and Slovakia, 14 clubs in Romania (18 before 2016) and Bulgaria (10 to 16 teams), and 16 clubs in the Czech Republic, Poland, and Serbia.

RESEARCH PROCESS AND FINDINGS

The Efficiency of Sporting Performance of Leagues in the CEE Region

An internationally accepted indicator of sporting performance of individual leagues and the clubs playing in them is the so-called UEFA coefficient (UEFA Club Coefficient, 2020) calculated on the basis of achievements in international cups. This is counted by UEFA itself. These data show the efficiency of individual leagues and clubs five years into the past, which can be significant in the draw of the following years' cups. The point is, therefore, that the higher the UEFA coefficient indicator of a league, the better results of the clubs in five preceding years, and the more competitive it is internationally.

Between 2010 and 2019, there was typically a slight improvement of the international success of the region's clubs. A considerable drop is noticeable in Romania (the average change of cumulated UEFA points was -9.6%) and a smaller one in Bulgaria (-2.5%), but the Romanian league started from a relatively high basis. The change in the UEFA points of the rest of the nations was between 0% and 9%. The number of points collected is the best indicator of success (Figure 6.1). Regarding international sports results between 2010 and 2019, the Czech Republic stands out in the region, with Romania as the runner-up, and Croatia's achievement may also be considered good. Hungary and Slovenia started from the lowest basis, with Slovenia currently doing better. Hungarian clubs have slightly improved over the past ten years, but they are still at the bottom of the list with regards to UEFA points. Clearly, Hungary has been unable to catch up, while some of the other leagues some show improvement. It is typical of the region that due to occasional great successes the five-year collection of points can be biased, but cumulative data for the past ten years provide enough support to balance these out.

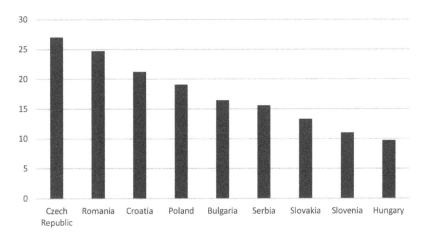

Figure 6.1   Average UEFA points in CEE between 2010 and 2019

Measuring business (market) efficiency
According to contemporary research (for example Frick, 2007; Garcia-del-Barrio & Szymanski, 2009), European football clubs tend to prioritize sporting performance over financial performance, and because of this they do not target paying dividends and high business performance; thus, they aim to produce a financial outcome of around breakeven. Incomes provide the budget which clubs can use to cover their costs and make developments, mostly signing and paying players. Football clubs have three major options to increase their market income (András, 2003).

I. Identifying and comparing incomes based on consumer numbers

I.1. On-site spectators: income from ticket sales basically verifies local interest and the presence of local fans. The changes in the average numbers of local spectators in the region's first division leagues between 2009 and 2018 is shown in Table 6.2. The number of spectators in the Polish league is exceptional, which is partly due to the country's larger population. The average number of spectators of 9,000 means a considerable advantage over other clubs in the region. The Czech league with over 5,000 spectators is second. In the other leagues, the number of spectators is below 4,000; weakest in this respect are the Slovenian and the Croatian leagues with less than 2,000. Concerning the general annual change, the region shows stagnation: only the Polish (5.99%), the Slovenian (6.02%), and the Croatian (3.34%) figures have been increasing, while the Romanian, Bulgarian, and Serbian leagues show a decrease of about 4%, and in the other countries there is stagnation.

Table 6.2   Average spectator numbers in CEE football leagues from 2009–2010 to 2018–2019

Country/ season	2009/ 2010	2010/ 2011	2011/ 2012	2012/ 2013	2013/ 2014	2014/ 2015	2015/ 2016	2016/ 2017	2017/ 2018	2018/ 2019	CAGR
Poland	5394	8646	8804	8418	8482	8350	9151	9682	9490	9106	5.99%
Czech Republic	4948	4493	4729	4836	5071	4726	5081	4895	5547	5552	1.29%
Romania	4967	5010	5305	5317	3901	3875	3264	2613	3334	3528	-3.73%
Hungary	3363	2960	3899	2948	2995	2513	2648	2707	2907	3314	-0.16%
Croatia	2033	1987	2191	2412	3176	2804	2451	2780	2948	2732	3.34%
Slovakia	2487	2311	2184	2124	2202	1982	2435	1975	2161	2264	-1.04%
Serbia	3143	2451	4053	3532	5104	6900	2735	2413	2097	2148	-4.14%
Bulgaria	2756	1864	2737	3749	2778	2839	2147	1734	1739	1911	-3.99%
Slovenia	859	1199	1374	891	899	1072	1538	1371	1205	1454	6.02%

Source: Edited by the authors based on transfermarkt.de.

I.2. Sponsors: in most cases, the goal is to reach consumers by sponsorship contracts, occasionally there is business synergy (a long-term strategic goal) behind the contract (for more on the synergy strategy, see Szabados, 2003 and András & Havran, 2015).

I.3. Television broadcasting rights: based on the market, interest in broadcasting a sporting event comes partly from the possibility of reaching large numbers of consumers.

I.4. Merchandising: income from such products is generated by on-site and media consumers (UEFA records this type of income among commercial profits along with sponsorship. Therefore, we do not discuss it separately).

In connection with income types I.2., I.3., and 1.4., a club can claim that instead of on-site spectators, they base their income on followers using television and online platforms. The number of television followers is not available or not comparable, but online interest can be indirectly estimated.

I.5. Consumers through the media: to estimate media interest in leagues, we have overviewed data on social media and Google trends.

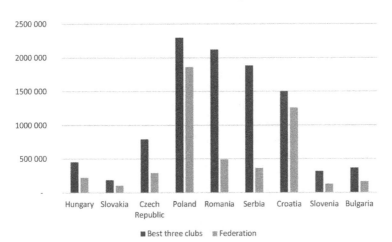

Source: Edited by the authors based on Facebook (2019), Instagram (2019), and Twitter (2019).

Figure 6.2   *Social media followers of national federations and of the three most successful clubs in CEE countries*

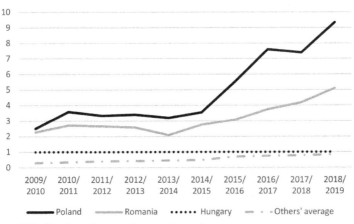

Source: Edited by the authors based on trends.google.com.

Figure 6.3   *Google searches for Hungarian football in a regional comparison from 2009–2010 to 2018–2019*

Figure 6.2 shows that in Poland, Romania, Serbia, and Croatia the most successful clubs have an outstanding group of social media followers, and so do the leagues in Poland and Croatia. If we look at the issue in proportion to population, Poland fits with the regional average, while the Croatian and Serbian leagues stand out in terms of popularity. Proportionately to population, only Bulgaria falls behind Hungary in the number of club followers, and only Slovakia does so with respect to its league followers.

The proportion of Google searches (Figure 6.3) is on an increasing curve everywhere within the region compared to Hungary; interest in the Polish and the Czech league stands out (Figure 6.3 shows the ratios compared to Hungary which is presented with a value of 1). Based on social media and Google searches, it seems that, similar to on-site interest, interest shown via the media is also very low in the case of Hungarian football. Hungarian media consumers' interest is among the lowest in the region. This suggests that there are no so-called 'hidden reserves', i.e., there is no latent demand for Hungarian football.

II. Revenue for sport professional success

Incomes available by national and international performance do not directly depend on the number of consumers. However, for success, significant revenues are necessary. Money from international federations (UEFA revenue for cup success, and FIFA transfers based on players' achievement) counts as market revenue. Revenues for success in international European cups may considerably influence clubs' annual economic performance, therefore we examine these data separately. These forms of income are significant if clubs can get into the so-called 'group stage', which is a genuine challenge to most regional clubs. Success revenue from national leagues also needs to be backed up by local consumer numbers. In other words, if a club cannot prove that it has its regular consumers, it may be rightly assumed that a significant proportion of the league's revenues comes from public funding (jointly marketed broadcasting rights to state television). In any case, we have paid special attention to income from international revenues, which we view as basically market revenue. However, as we can see in Figure 6.1, during the period examined, UEFA points collected by Hungarian clubs were the lowest in the region. This is closely connected to the revenues UEFA paid to Hungary, which therefore is the smallest amount in the region.

III. Players' market performance

Transfer fees from selling players constitute a form of revenue independent of consumer numbers. On the one hand, this revenue is due to the fact that a club possesses a quality youth training system, on the other, to its ability to make profits from buying and cleverly selling players' licences in the players' market. For the former, a well-constructed academy system capable of raising talents, for the latter some kind of players-market-related know-how (contacts, data analysis, widespread observation system, etc.) may constitute a given club's basic skill, enabling its competitive advantage. In the region, we can identify clubs and leagues that owe most of their revenue to their positive balance in the transfer market. As players' market transactions are basically public and traceable, income from this field is easy to identify. According to regional studies, it appears that the value of Hungarian player sales (András & Havran, 2016) and the number of players sold to stronger leagues in the country is among the lowest in the region (Havran, 2017). Young Hungarian players do not devote sufficient time and energy to their own development, although they are aware that, in order to be able to sign abroad, they should (Havran & András, 2018). Independent international audit reports about Hungarian academies also show that the quality of training and players' individual development fall behind international standards (MLSZ, 2014, 2016, 2019).

IV. Other revenue – the role of the state?
UEFA reports use one more category very distinct from the above, namely 'other revenue'. Both in UEFA reports and clubs' national accounting reports, significant amounts appear in this revenue category with no specific justification. Behind them, there is no consumer or other market incentive, as they basically reflect direct or indirect public funding. Our study will show specific cases.

Creating and Calculating the Efficiency Indicator

On p. 139 above, we described how sport professional efficiency can be measured, and the discussion on p. 140 showed the way individual sources of revenue can be estimated. In this chapter, we calculate the efficiency of leagues as a proportion of UEFA points gained in a given year and the resources at their disposal. UEFA has so far provided comparable data for four seasons (2014/2015 to 2017/2018), and we compare points allocated after international successes. As UEFA reports for years 2015, 2016, 2017, and 2018 contain the distribution of regional income, it is possible to examine the management of finances based on a four-year average (Figure 6.4). Overall, it appears that for achieving international success, it is necessary to gradually increase the budget: while in 2015 €15.8 million, in 2018 already €24.5 million 'was needed' to gain one UEFA league point (naturally, this finding includes data on the significantly rising Hungarian incomes).

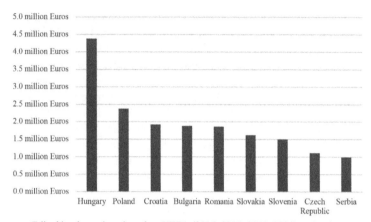

Source: Edited by the authors based on UEFA (2016, 2017, 2019, 2020) and uefa.com.

Figure 6.4   Four years' average international club efficiency (average club revenue in million Euros per one UEFA-point) between 2015 and 2018

The findings show that, in order to gain one UEFA point, Hungarian clubs have the highest demand for resources. In view of the four-year average, the amount is three times higher than that of other leagues, which indicates a huge waste of resources. Based on these calculations, the second highest (the Polish league) seems approximately twice as successful, while the Czech and Serbian clubs are four times as successful as the Hungarian clubs.

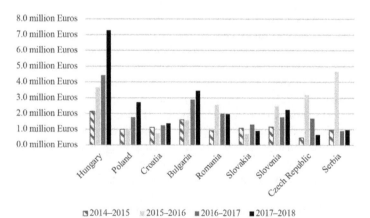

■2014–2015 ▨2015–2016 ■2016-2017 ■2017–2018

Source: Edited by the authors based on UEFA (2016, 2017, 2019, 2020) and uefa.com.

Figure 6.5   Yearly "cost" (in million Euros) of one UEFA-point (international success) between 2015 and 2018

It is clear that if a club from a smaller league gets into the group stage of the Champions League, the UEFA revenue awarded for this appears as an outstanding value (examples can be seen in the case of the Bulgarian, Slovenian, and Serbian clubs). Looking at Hungarian figures, the significant annual increase is especially disquieting (Figure 6.5).

During the period investigated, the annual average inflation rate varied between 0.77% and 1.9% in the nine countries. Therefore, this should not have had a considerable effect, and is not included in our calculation.

Estimating the Presence of Public Funding

According to our hypothesis, the operation of Hungarian clubs is less efficient due to the excessively easily available public funding at their disposal. Because of this, we have examined the extent to which this fact is behind each revenue type. Table 6.3 shows the average of league revenue in the four-year period between 2015 and 2018 grouped according to type of revenue. The three dominant leagues are highlighted for every revenue type. In the region, the total revenue of the Polish league is outstanding, but Croatian, Hungarian, and Czech clubs also have high incomes. Croatian clubs' completely market-based revenues from selling players and UEFA success revenue are worth emphasizing, as well as the sponsored support of Polish clubs with a large consumer base.

Table 6.3   *Four years' average revenue of CEE leagues between 2015 and 2018, data in million euros*

	Hungary	Slovakia	Czech Republic	Poland	Romania	Serbia	Croatia	Slovenia	Bulgaria
Television	**9.64**	0.51	5.41	**29.77**	**24.76**	1.45	1.59	0.51	2.48
UEFA	5.40	4.79	**15.13**	**14.87**	10.22	13.27	**19.04**	7.75	12.57
Tickets	2.09	2.22	**5.81**	**17.43**	3.83	2.97	**3.91**	1.40	2.06
Sponsorship	**33.29**	19.39	**33.89**	**50.22**	10.49	10.68	12.62	6.31	12.65
Transfers	9.04	13.07	**26.56**	22.12	19.65	**29.07**	**54.56**	10.10	9.87
Other	**37.08**	6.20	9.01	**15.01**	**15.56**	4.27	7.85	3.58	11.50
Total	96.54	46.18	95.81	149.41	84.50	61.70	99.56	29.64	51.12

Note: The three highest values in each revenue line are shown in bold type.
Source: UEFA (2016, 2017, 2019, 2020).

Hungarian clubs' other revenues (38%) and sponsorship revenues (34%) are considerable. If we examine the revenues from these different markets, we detect anomalies that the market-based logic cannot explain.

In Hungary, television income is significantly above the regional average. Since UEFA reports have Hungarian clubs' TV income as zero, our own estimate is based on the amount in the contract between the Hungarian league and Hungarian television (MTVA, 2019). Sponsorship income is also significantly above average. Transfer revenue and income from ticket sales is below average. This is reflected on the league level, but if we view outcome per club (we know there may be huge differences between clubs, but there is no regional database on this), differences are even more striking because since 2016 in Hungary there have been as few as 12 clubs in the top tier of the league, with TV and other revenues divided between them. UEFA income is also considerably below average. Overall, the number of on-site and media consumers is very low. Consequently, ticket sales revenue is also low, but sponsorship and television income are among the highest although there is no consumer base.

The transfer market could generate an independent source of market revenue, enabling stable operation even without larger numbers of spectators, but this market is also weak. The relation between ticket sales and sponsorship income is disproportionate, as sponsorship revenue should be based on consumer numbers (see Figure 6.7). However, as can be seen in Figure 6.6, sponsorship in Hungary is not connected to consumer interest, the ratio of sponsorship and ticket revenues amounting to four times (18.62) the regional average (4.58 per league annually) in the 2015 to 2018 period.

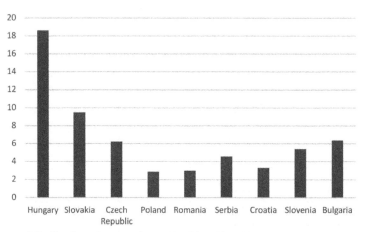

Source: Edited by the authors based on UEFA (2016, 2017, 2019, 2020).

Figure 6.6   *Ratio of sponsorship and ticket revenue in CEE leagues (four-year average between 2015 and 2018)*

The Hungarian figures also stand out in in a comparison of sponsorship revenue and spectator numbers. Taking the nine countries together, the correlation coefficient for the four years is 0.77, while it is 0.91 for Hungary, i.e., the eight other countries' figures demonstrate the link between the two variables that is not there for Hungary. Table 6.4 shows the comparison of the nine countries by main characteristics.

Table 6.4   Comparison of CEE football leagues by main variables

	Hungary	Slovakia	Czech Republic	Poland	Romania	Serbia	Croatia	Slovenia	Bulgaria
Sport success	-	-	++	+	++	0	++	-	0
Spectators	0	-	+	++	+	0	0	--	-
Consumers through media	-	-	0	++	+	+	+	-	-
Transfer revenues	-	-	+	0	0	+	++	-	-
Other revenues	++	--	-	0	0	--	-	--	0
M euros/point (efficiency)	--	+	++	0	+	++	+	+	+

Notes: ++ outstandingly above average; + Above average; 0 Average; - Below average; --
Outstandingly below average.
Source: Edited by the authors.

It appears that eight of the nine countries have similar efficiency and signs of market operation, but Hungary presents different ratios. The presence of SBCs in the other CEE football leagues should be verified with deeper analysis. It can be seen from Table 6.4 that Polish, Czech, and Romanian football clubs have more consumers, and Serbian and Croatian clubs have developed, thanks to transfer revenues. Slovenian, Bulgarian, and Slovakian football clubs reach modest revenues according to their sporting success and efficiency. From the data and examples above, it transpires that in Hungarian football public funding is excessive compared to market revenue. Moreover, rather than growing efficiency, there are contradictory processes. In the following, we illustrate the presence of the SBC syndrome through a few examples.

Kornai (1986) suggests examining five aspects, i.e., soft prices, soft taxes, soft subsidies, soft loans, and soft investments to verify an SBC. In professional football these are complemented (Storm & Nielsen, 2017) with a sixth aspect, i.e., soft accounting. A typical example of *soft prices* is a football club renting the stadium from the local government at below market price. In Hungary, national television channels paying a higher price for broadcasting rights (see above) is another example. *Soft taxes* are tax benefits and special regulations regarding football clubs. In Hungary, law on reduced personal taxation (EKHO, 2020) enables athletes to have significant tax benefits on a considerable proportion of their salaries, which has been increasing in recent years. EKHO, i.e., a sim-plified contribution to public revenues, basically provides artists, musicians, journalists, and specified other groups of intellectuals with tax benefits up to a maximum amount of their annual income. Since 2010, the maximum amount applied to athletes has been gradually increasing (Figure 6.7).

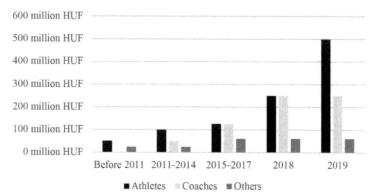

Source: Hungarian Law of Taxation (2005/CXX), edited by the authors.

Figure 6.7   Changing of upper limit of simplified contribution to public revenues in case of athletes, coaches and in some intellectuals (data in HUF million)

The annual growth in this maximum level reflects the fact that there was a real demand from athletes for this. This means that several athletes reach this income level in Hungary. In September 2017 the state introduced another benefit just for athletes, i.e., exempting the football club that employs them from paying taxes, resulting in the athlete having to pay only a 15% tax rate (NAV, 2019). Consequently, in 2019, footballers playing in the Hungarian league with a €1.5 million annual income enjoy a tax benefit of about one million euros. On the one hand, this measure simplifies the signing of foreign players; on the other hand, it makes it difficult for young Hungarian players to play locally. High net wages generally pose an obstacle for young players signing abroad, as this way they are offered little opportunity to play in the relatively weak Hungarian league, where there are numerous better foreign players.

Soft subsidies are resources provided by state companies or companies close to the state. An example in Hungary is the strong presence of construction companies as sponsors. These companies operate mostly with state contracts. According to the UEFA 2020 financial report (UEFA, 2020, p. 44), construction companies contribute 5% of sponsorship revenues in Europe. Therefore, this industry is not regarded as a significant sponsor. Companies operating in construction are typically characterized by business-to-business (or rather business-to-government) work. Furthermore, the disproportion between sponsorship revenue and number of consumers presented above is a further indication of the presence of soft subsidies.

From 2011 any firm in Hungary can reduce its corporate tax if it donates to a sports club (TAO, 2020a). Sports clubs can spend the money primarily on building their infrastructure and developing their youth training system (European Commission, 2020). This is a good example of *soft investment* because with minimal or no resources of their own, clubs would not be able to create financially sustainable infrastructure. What is more, from 2017, clubs can spend the state subsidy from corporate tax on maintaining the facilities they have created with state money (TAO, 2020b).

Almost every club is closely related to politicians (state capitalism). Softness is more typical of football clubs where politicians are given leadership. In the summer of 2020, the club Debrecen, previously participating in the Champions League, fell to the second league and the local government bought the private owner out of the club ownership and now provides a large budget to the football club.

CONCLUSIONS

In this chapter we have examined the interpretation of the SBC syndrome in professional football and its CEE situation through state presence and its consequences in Hungary. It has been found that, regarding sport professional efficiency in the region, Hungary was at the bottom of the list in the period between 2009 and 2019. Hungarian clubs' revenues increased significantly during the 2010s, mainly from sponsorship and other revenues. However, the low level of consumer interest is striking compared to the size of revenue, which is allegedly market-based. Hungary has one of the best funded leagues; nonetheless, it demonstrates one of the weakest sport professional performances. Based on the efficiency indicator, it can be seen that with the same amount of resources Hungarian clubs achieve much less success than their regional competitors. This can be explained by the current level of public funding and the continuous reliance on bailout, causing a soft budget constraint and inefficient operation.

When reconsidering Kornai's (2014) SBC theory, with frivolous spending, reduced cost sensitivity, and state connections coming to the front, it is obvious that the three effects together damage the organization's efficiency. On the one hand, clubs with state connections and backed by companies that work for the state are at an advantage, while clubs with local traditions, youth training, a more serious consumer base, and expertise are at a disadvantage. Invested capital presupposes a different kind of knowledge and expertise, whose development may be slower, thus producing success later and to a lesser extent. This might imply a loss of efficiency regarding the whole of Hungarian football. This phenomenon is likely to have morally destructive effects as well because society and the broader football community may consider it unfair and dishonourable (Kornai, 2014).

In several other leagues in the CEE region, clubs have, to a much larger extent, learnt to acquire market resources and to spend the resources at their disposal in an effective way. They are forced to constantly innovate, learn from better-developed leagues, develop youth training, and operate in a future-oriented, strategic manner. The clubs of these leagues, which operate with smaller but harder budgets, are much more effective with regards to sport professional performance – not only relatively but also in absolute terms.

Our finding is that the existing consumer interest does not justify the present level of broadcasting, sponsorship, and other revenues, which are mostly considered forms of public funding. The results clearly show that the clubs are not efficient and not innovative in comparison: instead of concentrating on youth training and developing local talent, they sign foreign players and pay them high salaries in the hope of short-term success. In parallel, young players get only a short time on the field, but because their wages are higher than their market value, they stay in the local leagues and may lose the motivation to improve and build a career abroad. Business-related goals are targeted only to a limited extent; motivation is reduced both in the sport profession and management. Furthermore, giving public funding based on unique decisions does not help the clubs with the largest consumer base or the best youth training. These types of funding tend to go to clubs important to the decision-makers with resources at their disposal (state capitalism). Decisions are not made on a professional/business basis, thus limiting their own development. Without players signing for stronger leagues, no knowledge is brought back from abroad in the long run in the form of coaches, managers, and players. We have examined the leagues from the league perspective, and it is possible that the existence and degree of softness the Hungarian clubs face vary from club to club.

We do not claim that a Hungarian club could compete on a market basis with the main clubs of the Champions League, but with the resources described they should achieve at least the level of other clubs in the region (group stage). In the long run, the resources invested in football should be reflected in performance. Nevertheless, success is lacking even in the comparison with regional competitors. The soft budget constraint syndrome appears to be an appropriate explanation because – in the time period examined – clubs have been able to rely on significant public funding even though producing minimal results, not being accountable for any requirements and not relying on an increasing consumer base nor gaining most of their revenue from trading players. This is a serious drawback to the national team as well. Since players do not transfer to stronger leagues, excessive public funding poured into club football – contrary to the original goal – may cause the national team's long-term inefficiency. In June 2020, the Hungarian national team was 52nd in the FIFA ranking, overtaking only Bulgaria and Slovenia in the region (FIFA, 2020). As a result of systemic state support and control over Hungarian football clubs, football clubs seem to have returned to the original, socialist concept of SBC. The main difference is that there are no international results anymore.

For future research, it would be interesting to include additional countries, thus conducting a more detailed, even club-level, analysis as well as describing the Eastern European characteristics of the SBC syndrome using qualitative methods on specific case studies. This could result in a better understanding of the different implications of SBC for Western European and Eastern European football.

NOTES

1. The Croatian national team, for example, reached the finals of the World Cup Championship in 2018, and the Croatian Luka Modrić received the Golden Ball award in 2018.
2. We thank the following students of the Sport Economics Master Program of the Corvinus University of Budapest for their assistance in data collection: Tamás Döme, Péter Gacs, and Dávid Határ.

REFERENCES

Altukov, S., Morozov, B., Li, H., & Nauright, J. (2020). Roman Abramovich and his principles of management. *Sport in Society*, 23(9), 1–14.
András, K. (2003). Business elements in sport, on the example of football. Doctoral thesis. Budapest: BKÁE. Phd.lib.uni-corvinus.hu/150/2/riszt_krisztina_en.pdf (accessed 25 January 2020).
András, K. (2004). A hivatásos sport piacai (Markets of professional sport). *Vezetéstudomány*, XXXV, 40–57.
András, K., & Havran, Z. (2015). New business strategies of football clubs. *APSTRACT-Applied Studies in Agribusiness and Commerce*, 9(1–2), 67–74.
András, K., & Havran, Z. (2016). Examination of Central and Eastern European Professional Football Clubs' Sport Success, Financial Position and Business Strategy in International Environment. In *Competitiveness of CEE Economies and Businesses* (pp. 197–210). Springer International Publishing. https://doi: 10.1007/978-3-319-39654-5_10.
András, K., Havran, Zs., & Jandó, Z. (2012): Sportvállalatok külpiacra lépése – Elméleti alapok (Sport companies entering foreign markets – theoretical basics). TM 17. Working Paper; Business Economics Institute, Corvinus University of Budapest. http://edok.lib.uni-corvinus.hu/381/ (accessed 25 January 2020).
Andreff, W. (2015). Governance of Professional Team Sports Clubs: Agency Problems and Soft Budget Constraints. In *Disequilibrium Sports Economics* (pp. 175–228). Edward Elgar Publishing.

Andreff, W. (2018). Financial and sporting performance in French football Ligue 1: Influence on the players' market. *International Journal of Financial Studies*, 6(4), 91.

Brasher, K. (1986). Traditional versus commercial values in sport: The case of tennis. In *The Politics of Sport*, 198–215.

Bremmer, I. (2014). The new rules of globalization. *Harvard Business Review*. https://hbr.org/2014/01/the-new-rules-of-globalization (accessed 25 January 2020).

Buhaş, D. S., Herman, G. V., Paul, F. D., & Stance, L. (2017). Football and economy before and after communism in Romania. *GeoSport for Society*, 6(1), 30–39.

Chikán, A. (2017). Vállalatgazdaságtan (Business Economics). VTOA, Budapest.

D'Andrea, A., & Masciandaro, D. (2016). Financial Fair Play in European Football: Economics and Political Economy – A Review Essay. BAFFI CAREFIN Centre Research Paper No. 2016-15.

Douma, S., & Schreuder, H. (1991). *Economic Approaches to Organizations*. Prentice Hall.

EKHO (2020). Hungarian Law of Taxation (2005/CXX) about simplified contribution to public revenues. https://net.jogtar.hu/jogszabaly?docid=a0500120.tv (accessed 25 July 2020).

European Commission (2020). State aid: Commission clears Hungarian sport support scheme. https://ec.europa.eu/commission/presscorner/detail/en/IP_11_1322 (accessed 27 July 2020).

Franck, E. P. (2014). Financial Fair Play in European club football – What is it all about? University of Zurich, Department of Business Administration, UZH Business Working Paper (328). https://papers.ssrn.com/sol3/papers.cfm?abstract_id =2284615 (accessed 25 January 2020).

Frick, B. (2007). The football players' labor market: Empirical evidence from the major European leagues. *Scottish Journal of Political Economy*, 54(3), 422–446.

Friedman, M., & Friedman, R. (1998). *Választhatsz szabadon*, Akadémiai Kiadó, Budapest.

Garcia-del-Barrio, P., & Szymanski, S. (2009). Goal! Profit maximization versus win maximization in soccer. *Review of Industrial Organization*, 34(1), 45–68.

Girginov, V., & Sandanski, I. (2008). Understanding the changing nature of sports organisations in transforming societies. *Sport Management Review*, 11(1), 21–50. https://doi:10.1016/S1441-3523(08)70102-5.

Havran, Z. (2017). The Significance of Buying and Development of Players in Professional Football. The Characteristics of the Central-Eastern-European and Hungarian Players Market. Doctoral dissertation, Corvinus University of Budapest. http://phd.lib.uni-corvinus.hu/978/ (accessed 25 January 2020).

Havran, Z., & András, K. (2014). Regional export efficiency in the market of football players. *Theory Methodology Practice (TMP)*, 10(2), 3–15.

Havran, Z., & András, K. (2018). A hivatásos és hivatásos pályára készülő labdarúgók fejlesztésének és karriertámogatásának magyarországi vizsgálata (Analyis of how professional footballers and those preparing for the profession are developed and assisted with their career). *Vezetéstudomány-Budapest Management Review*, 49(9), 70–80.

Hodges, A., & Stubbs, P. (2013). The paradoxes of politicisation: Football supporters in Croatia. In A. Schwell et al. (Eds), *New Ethnographies of Football in Europe: People, Passions, Politics* (pp. 55–74). Palgrave Macmillan.

Klobučník, M., Plešivčák, M., & Vrábeľ, M. (2019). Football clubs' sports performance in the context of their market value and GDP in the European Union regions. *Bulletin of Geography. Socio-economic Series*, 45(45), 59–74.

Kornai, J. (1986). The soft budget constraint. *Kyklos*, 39, 3–30.

Kornai, J. (2014). Bevezetés A puha költségvetési korlát című kötethez (Introduction to the The Soft Budget Constraint volume). *Közgazdasági szemle*, 61(7–8), 845–897.

Kornai, J., & Matits, Á. (1987). A vállalatok nyereségének bürokratikus újraelosztása (The bureaucratic redistribution of firms' profits). Közgazdasági és Jogi K. Budapest.

Kornai, J., Maskin, E., & Roland, G. (2003). Understanding the soft budget constraint. *Journal of Economic Literature*, 41(4), 1095–1136.

Lembo, C. (2011). Fifa transfers regulations and UEFA player eligibility rules: Major changes in European football and the negative effect on minors. *Emory International Law Review*, 25, 539.

Lenartowicz, M., & Karwacki, A. (2005). An overview of social conflicts in the history of polish club football. *European Journal for Sport and Society*, 2(2), 97–107. http://dx.doi.org/10.1080/16138171.2005.11687771.

Meyer, K., & Peng, M. W. (2016). *International Business*. Cengage Learning.

MLSZ (2014). Összefoglaló jelentés a Double Pass akadémiai auditjáról (Summary Report of the Double Pass Academic Audit). https://szovetseg.mlsz.hu/hir/osszefoglalo-jelentes-a-double-pass-akademiai-auditjarol (accessed 25 January 2020).

MLSZ (2016). Double Pass Hungary Globális Jelentés (Double Pass Hungary Global Report). https://www.mlsz.hu/wp-content/uploads/2016/06/DP_glob%C3%A1lis-jelent%C3%A9s.pdf (accessed 25 January 2020).

MLSZ (2019). Double Pass Hungary Globális Jelentés (Double Pass Hungary Global Report). https://szovetseg.mlsz.hu/hir/ismet-ertekelte-az-utanpotlasmuhelyeket-a-double-pass (accessed 25 January 2020).

MTVA (2019). Contracts of Hungarian National Television above 5 million HUF. http://mtva.hu/wp-content/uploads/sites/17/2020/02/2019_oktober_MTVA_5-millio-feletti-szerzodesek_egyseges-szerkezetben_2_resz.pdf (accessed 25 January 2020).

NAV (2019). Az egyszerűsített közteherviselési hozzájárulás alapvető szabályai (Basic rules for the simplified contribution to public revenues). https://www.nav.gov.hu/data/cms488673/07_Az_egyszer_sitett_kozteherviselesi_hozzajarulas_alapvet__szabalyai_20190731.pdf (accessed 25 January 2020).

Procházka, D. (2012). Financial conditions and transparency of the Czech professional football clubs. *Prague Economic Papers*, 21(4), 504–521.

Rohde, M., & Breuer, C. (2016). The financial impact of (foreign) private investors on team investments and profits in professional football: Empirical evidence from the premier league. *Applied Economics and Finance*, 3(2), 243–255.

Roşca, V. I. (2017). The Europeanisation of Romanian football: What do UEFA country coefficients reveal? *Management & Marketing. Challenges for the Knowledge Society*, 12(4), 652–673.

Sárközy, T. et al. (2000). A magyar sportjog alapjai (Basics of Hungarian sports law). HVG-ORAC Lap- és Könyvkiadó, Budapest.

Smith, A. (1992). *Nemzetek gazdagsága (The Wealth of Nations)*. E gazdagság természetének és okainak vizsgálata. Közgazdasági és Jogi Könyvkiadó Budapest.

Storm, R. K. (2012). The need for regulating professional soccer in Europe: A soft budget constraint approach argument. *Sport, Business and Management: An International Journal* 2(1), 21–38. http://dx.doi.org/10.1108/20426781211207647.

Storm, R. K., & Nielsen, K. (2012). Soft budget constraints in professional football. *European Sport Management Quarterly*, 12(2), 183–201.

Storm, R. K., & Nielsen, K. (2017). Profit maximization, win optimization and soft budget constraints in professional team sports. http://eprints.bbk.ac.uk/18426/3/18426.pdf (accessed 25 January 2020).

Szabados, G. (2003). Labdarúgóklubok stratégiái. (Strategies of football clubs). *Vezetéstudomány*, XXXIV. évf. 2003, 09, 32–43.

Szymanski, S. (2014). On the ball: European soccer's success can be credited, in part, to the liberalization of the players' market. But what will the future bring? *Finance & Development*, 51(1), 26–28.

TAO (2020a). 1996/LXXXI. Act on Corporate Tax and Dividend Tax of Hungary-22/C. § Tax relief for support for spectator team sports.

TAO (2020b). 2018/LXXXII. Act of Hungary – amending certain tax acts in relation to EU obligations and certain acts on tax administration.

Terrien, M., & Andreff, W. (2020). Organisational efficiency of national football leagues in Europe. *European Sport Management Quarterly*, 20(2), 205–224.

UEFA (2016). The European Club Footballing Landscape. Club Licensing Benchmarking Report Financial Year 2015. https://www.uefa.com/insideuefa/protecting-the-game/club-licensing/ (accessed 25 January 2020).

UEFA (2017). The European Club Footballing Landscape, Club Licensing Benchmarking Report Financial Year 2016. https://www.uefa.com/MultimediaFiles/Download/OfficialDocument/uefaorg/Clublicensing/02/53/00/22/2530022_DOWNLOAD.pdf (accessed 25 January 2020).

UEFA (2019). The European Club Footballing Landscape, Club Licensing Benchmarking Report Financial Year 2017. https://www.uefa.com/MultimediaFiles/Download/OfficialDocument/uefaorg/Clublicensing/02/59/40/27/2594027_DOWNLOAD.pdf (accessed 25 January 2020).

UEFA (2020). The European Club Footballing Landscape, Club Licensing Benchmarking Report Financial Year 2018. https://www.footballbenchmark.com/documents/files/UEFA%20Club%20Licensing%20Benchmarking%20report_2020_FY%202018.pdf (accessed 25 January 2020).

UEFA Club Coefficient (2020). https://www.uefa.com/memberassociations/uefarankings/club/#/yr/2020 (accessed 25 January 2020).

Vincze, G., Fügedi, B., Dancs, H., & Bognár, J. (2008). The effect of the 1989–1990 political transition in Hungary on the development and training of football talent. *Kinesiology*, 40(1), 50–60.

Online Sources for Database

- www.facebook.com
- www.instagram.com
- www.transfermarkt.de
- www.trends.google.com
- www.twitter.com
- www.uefa.com

7. Is there evidence of softness in the budget constraint in football? Some evidence from English clubs

Stefan Szymanski

INTRODUCTION

The financial problems of football clubs in Europe have attracted a great deal of attention. UEFA (2012) reported that 56% of clubs playing in the top divisions in Europe failed to meet at least one of the following criteria in 2010:

- no negative equity (negative equity means that the value of liabilities exceeds the value of assets, and therefore the business is bankrupt);
- no overdue payables (overdue payables means that the club is late making payments on its debts);
- has been certified by its auditors as a going concern (if a business is not a going concern, then without the injection of new capital it will be forced into bankruptcy).

This statistic related simply to the top divisions. For divisions below the top tier, the situation is generally far worse. It is not an exaggeration to say that at any point in time over the last decade a majority of professional football clubs could not credibly certify to being able to repay debts without external support. Moreover, as Szymanski (2015) elaborates, this problem is far from new. Insolvency has dogged professional football clubs since the 19th century.

The question is: why? The soft budget constraint theory is advocated by Andreff (2007, 2018) and Storm & Nielsen (2012) – henceforth ASN. Andreff (2007) explains it thus: there is 'managerial lax financial behaviour', arising because 'shareholders behave as non-profit-seeking investors' and because there exists an 'arms race among football clubs eager to enroll the most efficient players'.[1] Storm & Nielsen (2012) describe it as a 'syndrome' which manifests itself thus:

> soft subsidies are given by 'sugar daddy' owners in the form of additional cash and capital in cases of looming insolvency ... Many league football clubs routinely fail to pay taxes and the tax authorities have often little incentive to enforce payments through the legal system. Furthermore, when clubs enter administration and are reconstructed tax arrears are almost always among the debt obligations that are not being met. Banks, local governments and other stakeholders often provide clubs with soft credit. When football clubs fail to meet their credit obligations to banks credit contracts are often renegotiated, repayment schedules are extended, and the debt burden reduced. Local government support may similarly take the form of loans without expectation or enforcement of repayment.

The essence of this theory is that there is no penalty for the clubs when they breach their financial obligations. Of course, clubs are fictional persons, while it is the real persons making decisions who are responsible, and the theory of the soft budget constraint applies to these decisions. This chapter provides evidence as to whether there are penalties for the real people who are responsible for the decisions that lead to financial failure. Using data from professional English clubs, I show that there a very high probability that managers, in the football sense (coaches) and in the fiduciary sense (company directors), are in fact quite likely to face a penalty in terms of losing their jobs. This is a challenge for the explanatory power of the soft budget constraint theory. I propose an alternative explanation for financial failure which fits the data well.

THEORY

(a) The Soft Budget Constraint in General

The concept of the soft budget constraint was first articulated by Kornai (1979, 1980, 1986). He was addressing a problem of the Soviet-era planned economies, whereby state-owned enterprises failed to meet plan targets. This typically arose because the enterprises were unable to produce their quota of goods with the inputs supplied, and hence were in deficit. Kornai observed that, rather than these enterprises being closed down, as is typically the case with capitalist businesses whose liabilities exceed their assets, the planned enterprises were usually allowed to write off any deficit and continue operating, usually going on to fail to meet the next plan's targets as well.

The concept of bankruptcy itself had little meaning in this context. For a person or business to be bankrupt, they must have the capacity to (a) own assets and (b) take on liabilities (obligations which in turn represent assets to another party). Firms in the planned economy system lacked both capacities since all enterprises belonged to the state, and most forms of private ownership in the production system simply were not permitted.[2] As the owner of an enterprise, the state could choose to keep it open or close it, supply it with additional inputs, and alter its targets. Kornai's insight was that managers had little incentive to meet targets without an incentive constraint such as bankruptcy. In the capitalist system, the assets and liabilities of the firm are vested in the owners, who appoint managers to run the business on their behalf. In the event that liabilities exceed assets, creditors can sue for the closure of the business and proceed with the forced sale of assets with a view to recovering as much of the liabilities owed to them as possible. As a result, not only do the owners (shareholders) see their business liquidated, but the managers typically lose their jobs as well. This is commonly deemed a powerful motivation to retain solvency.

ASN argue that this constraint is largely absent for the owners and managers of football clubs. While football clubs are mostly organized on a capitalist basis, and therefore bankruptcy is in theory possible, they argue that it does not impose a constraint in practice. There are two different arguments at work here.

First, they argue that if bankruptcy is threatened, then either the owners will put in more money, or creditors such as the banks and tax authorities will not insist on being paid, writing off liabilities. Thus, clubs live on the verge of bankruptcy, but never actually go bankrupt (e.g., Storm & Nielsen, 2012, p. 194). It is certainly the case that football clubs often receive injections of capital, often to prevent bankruptcy from occurring. That is because a football club generates value other than financial profits. Clubs have value to the community, and association with a club can bring prestige not typically to be found in the ownership of other capitalist enterprises. But it's not clear that this is the same as a soft budget constraint. Injections of capital usually come with additional conditions, and often require the dilution of ownership of existing shareholders and replacement of managers. It is seldom costless to the owners and management team. Moreover, there are many other examples from other businesses in a capitalist system where financial distress does not lead to bankruptcy but some kind of 'bailout', which we do not automatically label as a soft budget constraint. This is because those injecting the capital often perceive a benefit to themselves from assuming an interest in the business. The fact is that the threat of bankruptcy is ever present in capitalist system and football clubs are not immune.

Second, if the club does enter bankruptcy proceedings, it will be bailed out and re-launched under new ownership. Thus, ASN observe that clubs are never 'liquidated', meaning that the enterprise disappears entirely. They do not address in detail the meaning of liquidation in this context, but they appear to mean that the club would cease to exist in any form. In reality, there are several ways in which a bankrupt club can be revived. These include:

- Making a deal with creditors to write off some debt so that the company is once again a going concern.
- Selling the assets of the club to a new owner, with old debts either written off by creditors or assumed by the new owner (usually some combination of the two).
- Closure of the club and the establishment of a new club with a similar name to play at the old stadium.
- Full liquidation – all assets sold off – and a new club with a similar name created in a new location near to the old one.
- Full liquidation and no revival of a club in the vicinity.

Of these five, all but the last one are quite common. One reading of ASN is that they think the fifth option is the only one which implies that there is a hard budget constraint. It would appear that they consider the other four to represent instances of a soft budget constraint, although presumably in ascending degrees of hardness.[3]

Normally, however, of these five, all but the first case are usually considered to be examples of a *hard* budget constraint. In the first case, it's not clear that the owners lose anything, and the existing managers may keep their jobs. Yet even in such cases, part of the negotiation may involve the requirement of the owners to accept additional liabilities (e.g., by mortgaging some of their private property as security for creditors) or the replacement of key personnel. But in the other four cases, the owners lose ownership of the club, and typically walk away with nothing, while the new owners typically bring in new management.

Sometimes there may be a gap of some years before the club is revived.[4] But few towns that have a professional football team ever lose it permanently. This is not because of the soft budget constraint, but because the club represents the community. If one ownership group fails and is unable to continue due to bankruptcy, then a new one is formed by members of the community to revive the club. The 'social capital' of a football club is generally its guarantor of survival.

As pointed out above, it is not easy to assess this general formulation of the soft budget constraint argument, given Kornai's original theory applied to a planned economy without private property, while football clubs operate in a capitalist system where bankruptcy is a real threat. Not least, a real threat to the clubs themselves, among which instances of bankruptcy are common. A specific model, with applications to a capitalist environment, is illuminating.

(b) A Theoretical Model of the Soft Budget Constraint

Kornai, Maskin & Roland (2003) described the general case where a budget constrained (BC) organization faces a hard budget constraint 'as long as it does not receive support from other organizations to cover its deficit and is obliged to reduce or cease its activity if the deficit persists', while 'the soft budget constraint phenomenon occurs if one or more supporting organizations (S-organizations) are ready to cover all or part of the deficit' (p. 1097). In their review they are careful to say that no single model can capture the entire soft budget constraint phenomenon, but they point to the work of Dewatripont & Maskin (1995) and the problem of commitment as central to the discussion.

A key insight of this work is that the soft budget constraint problem concerns incentives for individuals. Thus, if the BC organization is a football club, it is the owners who will seek a bailout if required from the S-organization – which could be a bank or another investor. The question then becomes: why is the S-organization unwilling to refuse a bailout? They describe the following model. Suppose that a principal (the S-organization, e.g., a bank or some other creditor) funds an agent (BC, the club) to fund a project (e.g., acquire players), which with some probability p is an effortless success, but with probability 1 - p is less successful. In this case, with some (unobservable) effort on the part of the agent, the project can still be a success, but otherwise the best option is to liquidate the project and obtain a zero return. However, with a bailout, the project can still generate a small return, even if the agent makes no effort. What Dewatripont & Maskin show is that when the project gets the less successful draw (with probability 1 - p) the equilibrium is for the project to be refinanced while the agent makes no effort, rather than the agent making an effort and turning the project into a success, even though the payoff to this outcome is higher. This can be illustrated using the decision tree in Figure 7.1.

At date 0 the principal makes a decision to invest, after which the project is revealed as either type 1 (with probability α), in which case no effort is required of the agent and a return R_q is generated for the principal and B_q for the agent, or the project is revealed as the inferior type 2 (with probability 1 - α). The agent now makes an unobservable decision at date 1 about *whether* to supply effort (e_h), in which case the project still returns R_q for the principal and B_q for the agent, *or* to do nothing (e_l), in which case the returns are zero for both principal and agent.

If the principal can commit never to review the investment, then as long as supplying effort is not too costly, the agent naturally chooses to supply effort in type 2 situations. If however, in the light of zero effort supply by the agent, the principal can at time 2 make a further investment which rescues the project and achieves a return (R_s, B_s), which is greater than zero, then there exist plausible equilibria where this is exactly what happens.

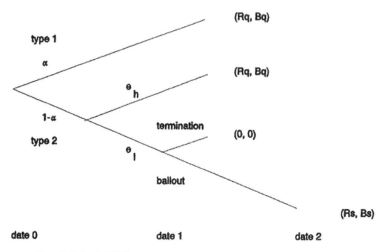

Source: Qian & Roland (1998).

Figure 7.1   Commitment and the soft budget constraint

The outcomes depend on the payoffs assumed, but it is easy to generate examples where (a) the outcome (R_s, B_s) is worse than the outcome (R_q, B_q) and yet, because the principal cannot commit to not going down this path, this is the equilibrium. Thus, for example, when the principal can commit never to invest at date 2 (which implies a hard budget constraint), the agent will choose e_h in type 2 cases if $R_q + B_q > e_h - e_l$. But if the principal cannot commit to keeping a date 2 investment off the table (which can be interpreted as a bailout, reflecting a soft budget constraint), then if we assume $R_s + B_s - e_l > R_q + B_q - e_h$ then $e_h - e_l > R_q + B_q - (R_s + B_s)$. Assume that $B_s = (1+x) B_q$ and $R_s = \frac{1}{2}$, then both (a) e_l is preferred if $e_h - e_l > R_q - xB_q$ and (b) this is inefficient if $R_q + B_q > e_h - e_l > R_q - xB_q$. One example of such a case is $R_q = 1, B_q = 1, e_h = 1, e_l = 0$ and $x > 0$.[5]

The important intuition that emerges from the modeling is that the real problem here is the inability to pre-commit. The principal would prefer ex ante not to have the option for a bailout to keep the agent honest but cannot do so. Of course, this is precisely the sort of pre-commitment that we expect to see in the capitalist system from hard-hearted bankers and the like. The argument is that this works for regular businesses but not for football clubs.

An important corollary of this analysis is that the agent maintains a financial relationship throughout the process. There is no firing of managers, there is no insolvency of football clubs, and there is no liquidation of companies that own football clubs.

EVIDENCE ABOUT COMPANY DIRECTORS AND MANAGERS (COACHES) OF INSOLVENT FOOTBALL CLUBS

In the previous section it was argued that a key feature of the model of the soft budget constraint is that when faced with a shortfall, the relationship between the principal/creditors and the agent/club representatives is unbroken. In England, we have detailed records of 67 club insolvencies involving legal proceedings between 1982 and 2010. It is relatively simple to identify the manager (coach) of the club. In the data described below we also have information on the identity of the club directors who manage the business of the club. In the soft budget constraint narrative of ASN, these are the individuals most likely to be accused of reckless spending, allegedly in the knowledge that they will be bailed out in the event of failure.

Table 7.1 lists 45 club insolvencies between 1983 and 2010. This is not the complete list, given that there were 67 insolvencies in this period, but these are the ones for which we were able to identify the directors one year before insolvency and within two years after insolvency. The data is taken from Companies House, whose website provides (free of charge) statutory information on limited liability companies for the public.[6] The financial statements of football clubs (all of which are owned by limited liability companies) must list the names of the company directors. Note, however, that when a company becomes insolvent, it may not post accounts, since once the business is insolvent the reporting framework changes. Moreover, in many cases, the old 'limited liability' company is liquidated, and ownership of the football club passes to a new limited liability company. Thus, the data in Table 7.1 refer only to cases where there is no more than a one-year gap between the financial statement immediately before the insolvency and the first financial statement registered after the insolvency. Thus, of the 22 cases not listed below, the most likely outcome was that all of the club directors before the insolvency were no longer club directors after the insolvency.

The data in Table 7.1 are summarized in Table 7.2. Typically, the board of directors consisted of five to six members before insolvency, while the post-insolvency club had around eight directors. On average, the new board included fewer than two survivors from the old board. On average 33% of directors survived the insolvency. In a small number of cases (six, or 13%) all of the directors survived, while in one-third of cases (15) none of the directors survived insolvency as directors.

If we assumed that in the remaining 22 cases none of the directors survived, then the average rate of survivorship would fall to 23%.

Table 7.1   *Board changes surrounding insolvency dates, 1983–2010*

Club	Season ending	Number of members of old board	Number of members of new board	Number of survivors
Bristol City	1983	9	9	1
Hereford United	1983	7	9	6
Hull City	1983	7	8	1
Wolverhampton Wanderers	1984	5	9	0
Bradford City	1985	4	6	0
Charlton Athletic	1985	7	9	0
Derby County	1985	7	9	6
Wolverhampton Wanderers	1986	6	7	0
Middlesbrough	1987	7	9	1
Swansea City	1987	8	7	1
Halifax Town	1988	11	7	0
Rotherham United	1988	5	7	2
Tranmere Rovers	1988	9	9	4
Aldershot	1990	4	4	0
Halifax Town	1990	4	8	3
Northampton Town	1993	9	9	5
Doncaster Rovers	1994	5	7	0
Barnet	1995	6	7	1
Hartlepool United	1995	3	6	3
Exeter City	1996	6	8	1
Gillingham	1996	7	8	2
Darlington	1998	4	7	2
Millwall	1998	6	9	2
Luton Town	2000	4	9	3
Oxford United	2000	3	6	3
Portsmouth	2000	5	7	1
Crystal Palace	2001	1	6	0
Swindon Town	2001	5	8	5
Rotherham United	2002	4	6	2
Bradford City	2003	4	8	4
Bury	2003	3	8	0
Carlisle United	2003	8	9	2
Lincoln City	2003	7	8	2
Swindon Town	2003	5	7	4

Club	Season ending	Number of members of old board	Number of members of new board	Number of survivors
York City	2003	4	11	0
Barnsley	2004	7	6	0
Ipswich Town	2004	6	9	5
Leicester City	2004	3	9	0
Port Vale	2004	4	9	0
Swansea City	2004	6	9	6
Darlington	2005	6	3	0
Derby County	2005	3	9	0
Cambridge United	2006	6	8	1
Leeds United	2008	5	6	2
Darlington	2010	3	5	3

Table 7.2   Summary data for club directors

Number of cases	45
Average number of members of old board	5.5
Average number of members of new board	7.6
Average number of survivors	1.9
Average percentage of survivors	34%
Number of cases with no survivors	15 (33%)
Number of cases with 100% survivors	6 (13%)

The manager (head coach) of a football club is almost never a member of the board of directors. Thus, while the manager is the most prominent executive in any club, his powers are limited. However, managers are often blamed for the alleged profligacy of a club, and therefore for causing a club to fall into financial distress. The implications for the manager of financial distress are very different depending on whether he retains his job. ASN imply that the manager will likely retain his job in the event of insolvency. Table 7.3 provides some data on what actually happens.

Table 7.3 lists 65 club insolvencies together with the manager in place in the first league game played after the date of insolvency event. At the insolvency date, the manager will have been in office for a number of games (which can be zero, if newly appointed), and will remain in place for a number of games until the employment spell ends (which could also be zero). Table 7.3 lists the number of games in the job at insolvency, the total tenure, the number of games remaining in the employment spell after the insolvency event, and this value expressed as a percentage of the total games in the entire employment spell.

Table 7.3   *Managerial (head coach) turnover around the date of insolvency*

Team	Year	Manager	Tenure at insolvency	Total tenure	Tenure remaining at insolvency	% of tenure at insolvency
Bristol City	1982	Bobby Houghton	54	54	0	100%
Millwall	1997	Jimmy Nicholl	42	42	0	100%
Hull	1982	Mike Smith	91	92	1	99%
Crystal Palace	2010	Neil Warnock	112	114	2	98%
Barnsley	2002	Nigel Spackman	31	33	2	98%
Hartlepool	1995	John McPhail	30	34	4	94%
Newport County	1987	Jimmy Mullen	26	31	5	88%
Luton	2008	Kevin Blackwell	26	31	5	84%
Gillingham	1995	Mike Flanagan	65	71	6	84%
Hereford	1982	Frank Lord	114	121	7	92%
Derby	1984	Peter Taylor	55	62	7	94%
Portsmouth	2010	Avram Grant	15	23	8	89%
Chesterfield	2002	Nicky Law	59	70	11	65%
Wolverhampton	1986	Bill McGarry	1	12	11	84%
Tranmore	1987	Ronnie Moore	1	12	11	8%
Darlington	2009	Dave Penney	109	121	12	8%
Swindon	2000	Jimmy Quinn	68	80	12	90%
Swansea	1986	John Bond	36	48	12	85%
Oxford	2000	Malcolm Shotton	70	83	13	75%
Oldham	2004	Iain Dowie	51	67	16	84%
Bournemouth	2008	Kevin Bond	66	83	17	76%
Barnet	1994	Gary Phillips	28	46	18	80%
York	2003	Terry Dolan	134	154	20	61%
Rotherham	1987	Norman Hunter	87	112	25	87%
Bradford	2004	Bryan Robson	1	27	26	78%
Exeter	1995	Terry Cooper	39	66	27	4%
Leeds	2008	Dennis Wise	34	61	27	59%
Halifax	1999	Kieran O'Regan	11	39	28	56%

Team	Year	Manager	Tenure at insolvency	Total tenure	Tenure remaining at insolvency	% of tenure at insolvency
Chester	1999	Kevin Ratcliffe	157	190	33	28%
Rotherham	2007	Alan Knill	26	59	33	83%
Portsmouth	1999	Alan Ball	52	87	35	44%
Leicester	2003	Micky Adams	20	58	38	60%
Swansea	2003	Brian Flynn	32	73	41	34%
Northampton	1993	Phil Chard	7	48	41	44%
Southampton	2010	Alan Pardew	1	44	43	15%
Stockport	2010	Gary Ablett	1	44	43	2%
Carlisle	2003	Roddy Collins	1	50	49	2%
Port Vale	2003	Brian Horton	179	231	52	2%
Crystal Palace	1999	Steve Coppell	14	66	52	77%
Luton	1999	Lennie Lawrence	153	208	55	21%
Rotherham	2008	Mark Robins	53	110	57	74%
Hull	2001	Billy Russell	34	92	58	48%
Doncaster	1993	Steve Beaglehole	29	90	61	37%
Bradford	2003	Nicky Law	20	83	63	32%
Notts County	2003	Bill Dearden	22	92	70	24%
Aldershot	1990	Len Walker	186	257	71	24%
Bury	2002	Andy Preece	113	187	74	72%
Derby	2004	George Burley	24	99	75	60%
Wolverhampton	1983	Graham Hawkins	1	76	75	24%
Wrexham	2005	Denis Smith	151	245	94	1%
Darlington	2004	David Hodgson	11	134	123	62%
Halifax	1987	Billy Ayre	2	146	144	8%
Swindon	2002	Andy King	24	173	149	1%
Ipswich	2003	Joe Royle	17	170	153	14%
Bradford	1984	Trevor Cherry	31	186	155	10%
Darlington	1997	David Hodgson	29	184	155	17%
Bournemouth	1997	Mel Machin	118	274	156	16%
Middlesborough	1987	Bruce Rioch	15	176	161	43%

Team	Year	Manager	Tenure at insolvency	Total tenure	Tenure remaining at insolvency	% of tenure at insolvency
Huddersfield	2004	Peter Jackson	1	174	173	9%
Luton	2004	Mike Newell	1	176	175	1%
Lincoln	2003	Keith Alexander	1	184	183	1%
Rotherham	2001	Ronnie Moore	152	352	200	43%
Queens Park Rangers	2001	Ian Holloway	7	229	222	3%
Charlton	1984	Lennie Lawrence	48	357	309	13%

Some care is required in interpreting the data. An insolvency event as described here is a matter of legal record, the registration of certain declarations to a court. However, the financial state of a club is likely to be well known before the event. Hence there are ten managers in place at the first game after the insolvency event, for whom this was their first game as manager. Logically, the previous manager was fired just before the insolvency event. If we add to this the two managers whose tenure ended with the first game after the insolvency event, then it is apparent that 20% of managers were fired between the last game before the insolvency event and the first game after the insolvency event. Taking a range between five games before and five games after (typically clubs play around five league games per month), 17 managers lost their job (26%).

This needs to be taken in the context of the average job tenure in football. Between 1983 and 2010, there were a total of 112,954 games played and 1,402 manager turnovers (these could be dismissals, resignations, or retirements), or an average of one turnover every 80 games. If turnover was random, then this would amount to a 1.2% probability each game. In reality, the turnover of managers around the insolvency period occurred at a much higher rate than that.

Thus, we can conclude that the assumption of a continuing relationship after insolvency as implied by the commitment version of the soft budget constraint story is not well supported by the data. Company directors have a higher than 50% probability of losing their job, and managers have a probability of losing their job around the insolvency event that is not far short of 50%. Taken together, it seems almost inevitable that any individual holding one of these positions at the date of insolvency is at risk of losing their jobs. This suggests the following amendment to the commitment model.

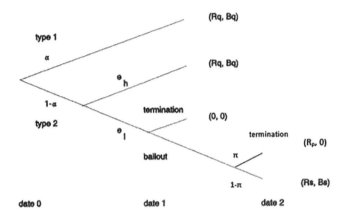

Figure 7.2   Commitment and the soft budget constraint (adjusted)

In this example an extra node is added at date 2, which allows the project to survive with some probability (π) – the business is bailed out – but the agent is dismissed (termination). Alternatively, with probability $1 - \pi$ the business is bailed out and the agent is retained. In the case of dismissal the agent gets a payoff of zero (although reputational effects might plausibly make this payoff less than zero), and the principal gets a payoff R_p where $0 < R_p \leq R_s$. Thus, the payoff of the principal may be lower than it would have been with the current agent. However, ex ante the agent may be unsure about whether this is the case. Note that if the agent were certain that $R_p < R_s$, then he would not make any effort, knowing that in the event that the project is revealed to be inferior type 2, then if the agent supplies low effort he will still not be dismissed, but if it is possible that $R_p = R_s$, then dismissal is not irrational. In the example given above, as $\pi -> 1$ the payoff to high effort relative to low effort increases. With a high enough probability of dismissal, the soft budget constraint commitment problem disappears. Given the dismissal rates for directors and managers in the cases of insolvency identified above, it seems this is not the primary cause of insolvency, in English football at least.

AN ALTERNATIVE EXPLANATION

In a series of papers, Szymanski (2017), Scelles et al. (2018) and Szymanski & Weimar (2019) offer an alternative explanation of persistent insolvency. The papers deal with insolvency in English, French and German football, respectively, and show that although the regulatory frameworks in each country are quite different, the experience of insolvency is quite similar, as is shown in Table 7.4.

Table 7.4   Football club insolvencies in England, France and Germany by tier, 1992–2014

Tier	1	2	3	4	5	1-3	1-5
Germany	0	2	28	53	23	40	106
England	2	18	24	29	24	44	97
France	3	9	28	N/A	N/A	40	N/A

The common feature of all of these league systems, and most other professional football league systems, is the institution of promotion and relegation. Table 7.4 demonstrates that insolvency is very rare in the top division, but extremely common in the lower divisions. Relegation creates financial distress because revenues fall sharply, while contractual commitments make it hard to reduce costs as quickly. Players can be traded, but following relegation, buyers are aware that the seller is under financial pressure and therefore are likely to offer below-market prices. Moreover, clubs that trade all of their best players risk collapsing in a spiral that leads to second relegation, a rare but not that unusual occurrence, which adds yet further to the financial stress.

Szymanski (2017) shows that insolvency is most likely when clubs underperform relative to expectations. Thus, given the investment in players by a team, there is an expectation of performance, in terms of both league standing and revenues conditional on that league standing. This relationship is remarkably stable. However, if teams underperform over a number of years, financial failure becomes increasingly likely. This underperformance is associated with random shocks – i.e., they are not predictable. One shock is unlikely to lead to financial failure, but a series of negative shocks make financial failure increasingly probable.

The relationship between insolvency and underperformance is illustrated in Figure 7.3. This shows the league position of clubs in the years before and after insolvency events. In the five seasons leading up to an insolvency event, the average league rank of the insolvent clubs falls from around 48th to around 63rd. (In England the top division has 20 clubs and the next three divisions in the hierarchy have 24 each, so that this change represents a fall from near the top of the third tier to the vicinity of the relegation of the third tier.) On average, a team that drops 15 ranks is likely to be relegated.

Unlike the soft budget constraint account, this theory can be supported by direct evidence. Econometric estimates of the likelihood of insolvency in England, France and Germany all confirm that the negative adverse shocks are correlated with insolvency.[7] This explanation fits the data and does not rely on the soft budget constraint theory.

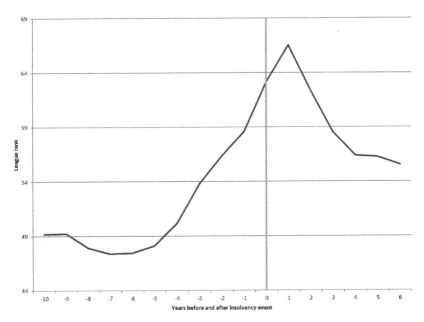

Figure 7.3   *Average league ranking of insolvent clubs in English football*

CONCLUSION

This chapter has examined the soft budget constraint theory of financial failure in football using data from the English football leagues. The soft budget constraint theory rests on the assumption that even if the club fails, the employees of the club will retain their jobs. Using data on membership of the board of directors and the club manager (head coach), it is shown that there is in fact a high probability of dismissal (higher for directors than for managers). This undermines the theory of the soft budget constraint. An alternative theory, developed in a recent series of papers (Szymanski, 2017; Scelles et al., 2018; and Szymanski & Weimar, 2019) is shown to fit the data more plausibly. This theory is based not on a failure of governance but on the riskiness inherent in the system of promotion and relegation. This theory has been tested against the data and been shown to fit. The challenge for advocates of the soft budget constraint theory is to develop an empirical test. For the moment, the soft budget constraint theory is no more than an untested assertion.

NOTES

1. Andreff (2007, p. 657).
2. States varied in terms of their recognition of private property. Individuals could own property as citizens, but the 'means of production' were socialized, with the exception of small farm plots. See, e.g., Ioffe (1982).
3. For example, Andreff (2018) on French clubs: 'in fact, among the 25 professional and amateur clubs (in the top seven divisions) that have actually been liquidated between 1978 and 2017, only one really vanished: Calais, which was liquidated in 2017, has not (yet?) re-created an amateur team of adult football'.
4. One of the most famous examples in English football is Accrington Stanley, an old mill town in Lancashire whose football club was founded in 1891, was forced to resign from the Football League in 1962 due to financial problems and was liquidated in 1966. The new club was not formed until 1968, and after many years operating in the lower leagues, it returned to the Football League in 2006.
5. An important part of this argument is that the benefit to the agent is not tradeable, otherwise the agent could sell his benefit to the principal. Thus, it should be thought of as something inalienable such as a reputation.
6. https://beta.companieshouse.gov.uk/.
7. Andreff (2018) falsely claims that demand shocks do not account for the French data (Scelles et al., 2018) because attendance demand did not always fall prior to insolvency. The econometric analysis in Scelles et al. (2018) identifies the negative demand shocks directly (Table 6, p. 15). These are statistically significant in a regression on insolvencies and hence, contrary to Andreff, support the theory.

REFERENCES

Andreff, W. (2007). French football: A financial crisis rooted in weak governance. *Journal of Sports Economics*, 8(6), 652–661.
Andreff, W. (2018). Financial and sporting performance in French football Ligue 1: Influence on the players' market. *International Journal of Financial Studies*, 6(4), 91.
Dewatripont, M., & Maskin, E. (1995). Credit and efficiency in centralized and decentralized economies. *The Review of Economic Studies*, 62(4), 541–555.
Ioffe, O. S. (1982). Law and economy in the USSR. *Harvard Law Review*, 1591–1625.
Kornai, J. (1979). Resource-constrained versus demand-constrained systems. *Econometrica*, 47(4), 801–819.
Kornai, J. (1980). *Economics of Shortage*. Amsterdam: North-Holland.
Kornai, J. (1986). The soft budget constraint. *Kyklos*, 39(1), 3–30.
Kornai, J., Maskin, E., & Roland, G. (2003). Understanding the soft budget constraint. *Journal of Economic Literature*, 41(4), 1095–1136.
Qian Y., & Roland, G. (1998). Federalism and the soft budget constraint. *American Economic Review*, 88(5), 1142–1162.
Scelles, N., Szymanski, S., & Dermit-Richard, N. (2018). Insolvency in French soccer: The case of payment failure. *Journal of Sports Economics*, 19(5), 603–624.
Storm, R. K., & Nielsen, K. (2012). Soft budget constraints in professional football. *European Sport Management Quarterly*, 12(2), 183–201.
Szymanski, S. (2015). *Money and football: A Soccernomics Guide: Why Chievo Verona, Unterhaching, and Scunthorpe United Will Never Win the Champions*

League, Why Manchester City, Roma, and Paris St. Germain Can, and Why Real Madrid, Bayern Munich, and Manchester United Cannot Be Stopped (International edition). Nation Books.

Szymanski, S. (2017). Entry into exit: Insolvency in English professional football. *Scottish Journal of Political Economy*, 64(4), 419–444.

Szymanski, S., & Weimar, D. (2019). Insolvencies in professional football: A German Sonderweg. *International Journal of Sport Finance*, 14(4), 54–88.

UEFA (2012). Club Licensing Benchmarking Report. https://www.uefa.com/MultimediaFiles/Download/Tech/uefaorg/General/02/09/18/26/2091826_DOWNLOAD.pdf.

8. Limits of softness in professional team sport clubs

Klaus Nielsen, Christian Gjersing Nielsen and Rasmus K. Storm

INTRODUCTION

European professional team sports provide ample evidence of the existence of soft budget constraints (SBCs). Originally, the SBC, as identified and explained by János Kornai, related to (state-owned) firms in socialist and post-socialist economies. However, similar phenomena are far from uncommon in capitalist economies, and the peculiar economics of professional team sport clubs (PTSCs) can be understood through the lens of the SBC theory. Many PTSCs experience persistent deficits and debts, but they are almost always rescued by sugar daddies, supporters, local governments or creditors in ways akin to the mechanisms of SBC.

In recent years, the application of the SBC framework to PTSCs has been growing exponentially. The usefulness of the framework in explaining both financial distress and the survival mechanisms of PTSCs is well established. It is arguably important to provide further evidence of the phenomenon of SBC in the context of PTSCs, including its application to new empirical contexts as it is done in the other contributions to this book. It is also crucial to study further the societal mechanisms behind the softness of budget constraints and to identify varying degrees of softness in different contexts. However, it is paramount to identify the limits of softness as well. When is softness not soft enough? Why do some PTSCs go bust even if conditions of softness prevail?

No theoretical approach can explain all phenomena in a field. To advance the SBC approach, it is important to test its limits and overall explanatory power. In particular, it is the application of the SBC approach in capitalist economies that necessities awareness of the limits of softness. In socialist economies, the existence of SBCs may to a large extent be without limits, at least for state enterprises, as the phenomenon of bankruptcy of such enterprises did not exist. However, this cannot be transferred directly to companies in capitalist economies, including PTSCs.

There are many examples of insolvencies as well as liquidation of professional football clubs. Most cases involves lower-league clubs, but there are also several examples of top-tier clubs experiencing that their budget constraints are not soft enough. There are also several cases of insolvencies and liquidation in other team sports, typically in the team sports with the second or third largest following and revenue base in the countries in question.

This chapter analyses cases where PTSCs have failed financially without being rescued. Its focus is on clubs where favourable conditions of softness prevail, while this is still not soft enough to ensure survival. The aim is to conclude under what conditions there are limits to softness in European professional team sports. The chapter includes a brief overview of football clubs that have failed despite extensive softness, with a focus on the Big Five European leagues as well as Scotland and Denmark. Further, we conduct two case studies of (former) well-established professional team sports clubs that faced limits of softness and (thus) did not manage to survive a financial crisis. One of these cases is well known: Glasgow Rangers being one of the two mighty football clubs in Scotland. The club is an integral part of a societal context that provides it with almost the highest imaginable degree of softness, but it collapsed even so. The other case is a team handball club in Denmark: Gudme-Oure-Gudbjerg (GOG). This case is in many respects at the opposite end of the scale compared to Glasgow Rangers. It is not a football club but represents one of the other team sports that, like football, take advantage of and struggle with SBCs, although at a much lower economic level. It is small and based in a thinly populated local community. However, it has been very successful in the Danish, and to some extent also the European, handball context, and similar to Glasgow Rangers, it thrived for a long time on SBCs but then experienced limits of softness that eventually led to its collapse. Both cases represent top-level clubs with strong societal support and a rich history of sporting success, thus predicting their failures to be – according to the theory – highly improbable. Yet they both faced a situation where the environmental conditions in the end were not soft enough to rescue them. This choice of contrasting cases represents what is termed 'maximum variation' in the case study research literature (Seawright & Gerring, 2008). They are analysed with the same theoretical framework; it shows variety in terms of the size of some variables but also similarity with respect to some of the mechanisms of SBCs. In combination with the overview of failed top football clubs, the two cases are used to develop general conclusions about the conditions where budget constraints are very soft but not soft enough.

The chapter is structured as follows. First, we present the overall empirical and theoretical context. Second, we provide an overview of insolvencies in European football with a focus on top-tier clubs in selected countries. Third and fourth, we analyse, first, the Glasgow Rangers case, and second, the GOG case. The final section provides general conclusions about the limits to soft-ness in European PTSCs.

FINANCIAL DISTRESS, SOFT BUDGET CONSTRAINTS AND INSOLVENCY PROCEEDINGS

The financial situation in European professional team sports has been exam-ined extensively in the last decades. Evidence and explanations are provided by academic studies (e.g., Lago et al., 2006), various reports (e.g., Beech et al., 2010) and investigative journalism (e.g., Conn, 2004). The 2010 UEFA club licensing benchmarking report (UEFA, 2010) showed that more than half of the top-division clubs in Europe reported losses. More than a quarter of the clubs reported significant losses, spending 120% or more of income on player wages. Since then, the situation has improved significantly. The 2018 financial year was the second consecutive year of overall profitability for European top-division club football, as detailed in the 2020 UEFA club licensing bench-marking report (UEFA, 2020) following a decade of continuous aggregate losses. Further, net assets increased from less than €2bn to more than €9bn in the space of a decade. This is a significant turnaround considering the €5bn of accumulated losses in just three years at the turn of the decade before UEFA's Financial Fair Play (FFP) regulations were introduced at the outset of the 2011–2012 football season. In combination with the improved regulation by national football associations and UEFA's licensing rules, the FFP regulations are likely to have had a major impact on the overall financial situation of European club football (Franck, 2018), although some of the evidence is mixed (Ahtiainen & Jarva, 2020).[1]

However, the increased profitability is concentrated in the 'Big Five' leagues (England, France, Germany, Italy and Spain) and particularly in the big clubs in the five most wealthy leagues. The improvement of the situation for the other clubs in the top division in these countries has been modest, while the clubs in the lower tiers are still in a financially precarious situation. In middle-income leagues (the top 20 leagues apart from the 'Big Five') 48% of clubs were loss-making, and in lower-income leagues (i.e., outside of the top 20 leagues), more than half of the clubs (54%) recorded losses in 2018 (UEFA, 2020, p. 113). Apart from the top clubs in the top leagues, most European clubs still experience significant financial pressure resulting in (often large) deficits and frequent cases of insolvency. Their survival often depends on benefactors and bailouts. This is particularly so among clubs in the second or third tiers of the national league systems.

Explanations of the financial crisis of PTSCs differ. A popular theory under-stands it as a result of win maximizing (rather than profit maximizing) club behaviour (i.e., Kesenne, 1996). Szymanski (2010) and others stress the impact of institutional factors such as the open European league system with promo-tion/relegation. Andreff (2007, 2014, 2015), Franck (2014, 2018) and Storm & Nielsen (2012, 2015) have pioneered an alternative explanation. They argue that the application of Kornai's SBC approach to the context of European professional team sports can improve the understanding of the mechanisms behind clubs' finances, the abnormally high survival rate, club finances and the need for and effect of financial fair play.

We refer to the introduction of this book for a more detailed presentation of the SBC approach. In this context we will merely stress that, from an empirical point of view, the budget restrictions of a football club vary from (perfect) hard, over almost hard to soft and extremely soft depending on the context the organization in question faces. It is not clear from the literature how to operationalize this continuum, but it can be used as a theoretical heuristic tool to understand specific cases. It is helpful to distinguish five conditions of hardness (Kornai et al., 2003; Maskin, 1999) in the assessment of the degree of hardness/softness of the environment of a given case. They are as follows: H1: exogenous prices (where the organization is a price taker of in- and outputs); H2: hard taxes (where the organization cannot obtain exemptions from tax rules or legislation); H3: hard subsidies (where direct or indirect public sub-sidies are not provided for the organization); H4: no credit (where no credit from other organizations – for example other firms or banks – can be obtained to help the organization); and H5: no external investment (where there is no injection of external capital for running the organization (expect for its founda-tion)). Storm & Nielsen (2015) add another condition of hardness (H6: no soft accounting practices) where no 'creative' accounting practices can be applied to help the distressed organization from collapsing – a phenomenon which is found in both in the American and European context.

Corresponding to the conditions for hardness, the softening of budget constraints can be divided into six types: S1: soft pricing (e.g., when a public stadium and/or training facility is made available to football clubs at below market fees and when governments or city councils buy naming rights to stadia at above market prices); S2: soft taxation (e.g., tax exemptions, non-payment of taxes and non-enforcement or amnesty of tax liabilities); S3: soft subsidies (e.g., provided by governments or rich 'glory seekers' to reduce deficits and pay off debts to keep clubs running); S4: soft credits (e.g., acceptance of overdrafts, unpaid bills and non-enforcement of repayment arrangements with routine postponement and rescheduling of debt); S5: soft investments (e.g., when the government or other sponsors pay for a part, or perhaps all, of the costs when clubs build new stadia or other revenue-boosting infrastructure); and S6: soft accounting (e.g., discretionary and flexible accounting praxis).

If all conditions of hardness are in place, an ideal-type situation of 'perfect hardness' exercises its coercion. 'Perfect hardness' establishes a theoretical (bi)pole for analytical understanding. Such a situation is seldom found in practice. In particular, 'hardness' in relation to credit and investment (H4 and H5) are practically non-existing conditions in modern economies. These conditions presume a very limited role of the financial system, and hardness in these respects would not only coerce organizations to be effective in a static sense, but would also limit risk-taking and innovation, and generally impede dynamic efficiency. 'Perfect softness', on the other hand, can be said to characterize a situation where the growth of the organization has no link to its financial performance, or when the firm keeps surviving '... even when investment entails grave losses ...' (Kornai, 1979, p. 807). This would be the case if all conditions of hardness are softened to various degrees but usually only one or a few of the H-conditions of hardness need to be softened to secure the survival of a given organization.

Under conditions of softness, ex ante *expectations* of ex post rescue in case of financial crisis start to develop within PTSCs. This will impact on behavioural patterns of their management. The impact varies according to the specific context. Under some conditions the budget constraints are softer than in other contexts. This is the case when clubs are powerful vehicles for strengthening local (and possibly also social, political and religious) identity. It is also the case when there are significant employment and broader economic impacts of a club going under. Similarly, strong social capital (i.e., supportive networks, for example between club chairman, CEO of bank and mayor) have a softening impact on the budget constraints.

While there is a high survival rate among football clubs, it is also evident that there are limits to softness in the context of European football and in PTSCs in general. There are theoretical reasons as well as empirical evidence for that. Kornai's SBC theory was originally developed to understand phenomena such as widespread shortages in centrally planned economies where the capabilities of the state for rescuing companies are in principle unlimited. In democratic market economies, on the other hand, there are both constitutional limitations of state power as well as limits to tax-financed softening imposed by democratic decision making. Further, there is actual empirical evidence that sometimes football clubs are not rescued in case of financial problems. The aim of this study is to examine clubs that could have expected bailouts in case of financial distress because they were perceived to be too big or too important to fail but ended up facing a hard budget constraint and folded anyway.

When this happens, the first step is administration, that is initiation of insolvency proceedings.[2] The legal insolvency rules and regulations are slightly different across Europe. However, the basic steps of the process are similar in all European countries. The first step is the initiation of insolvency proceedings. This can be triggered by any creditor or the company itself in case of the event of insolvency. Insolvency is a term for the situation when an individual or a company can no longer meet their financial obligations to lenders as debts become due. It is likely that many football clubs regularly experience insolvency without entering administration, although clear evidence is hard to find. In this stage, the clubs are rescued either by creditors coming up with more financial support, or because no creditor is willing to trigger administration. Sometimes it is in the interest of the club itself to file for administration. This is the case if a dire financial situation is expected to only get worse. It may also be caused by expectations of a favourable outcome of the administration process.

When a club enters administration, it loses its right to govern its own business, which is taken over by an appointed administrator. In principle, administration works to protect companies from their creditors. The administrator has the task to restructure the business so that it can be re-established as a going concern. This involves renegotiation of its relationship with its creditors through a Company Voluntary Agreement (CVA), including the writing-down of debts to a presumably sustainable level. A CVA is a legally binding agreement with the company's creditors to allow a proportion of its debts to be paid back over time. Most of the creditors (in the UK minimum 75%, by value of their claims) need to support the proposal. Once a proposal for a CVA has been approved, all unsecured creditors are bound by the arrangement. The company can carry on trading as usual, and often the directors remain in control.

It is a case of SBC if a football club uses the administration process as a means to clear its debts and then carry on afterwards, leaving behind the creditors receiving only a small share of their claims. However, there are sanctions involved which makes the administration route an unattractive solution to financial distress for the clubs. Some sanctions are specific for football clubs and other PTSCs. In a football context, the regulators of the game impose sporting penalties on clubs entering administration. The penalty includes points deduction, which often ends with relegation of the club at the end of the season. In some cases, the penalty involves forced relegation to lower tiers in the league systems, but in other cases regulatory ambiguity is used to minimize the sanction by taking the financial self-interest of other clubs into account.

Another specific football business rule impacts on the insolvency proceedings in the context of football. The 'Football Creditors Rule' means that clubs and players must be paid in full ahead of all other creditors if a league club enters insolvency. This leaves less money for other creditors and reduces the incentive for creditor initiation of insolvency proceedings in the first place. It also reduces their incentives for rejecting a CVA proposal as it will leave them with very little after the compensation of football creditors, whereas a CVA allowing the club to continue at least involves the possibility of higher future payments.

This may be part of the reason why administration seldom ends with the liquidation of football clubs. The insolvency proceedings almost always end with an agreement with creditors and a writing-down of the debts. In cases with no such agreement, the club is liquidated, which means that the business is brought to an end, with its assets being distributed to the claimants based on the priority of their claims. When the assets include property, they are converted into cash or cash equivalents by selling them on the open market. When a football club owns property in the form of a stadium or training grounds, there are often no alternative economic ways of using the assets, so the purchasers typically intend to use them for their original purpose. The lack of alternatives reduces demand and accordingly the price. This creates opportunities for a new club to rise as a phoenix club from the ashes of the old one. The physical assets of the old club can be bought for a small amount by a new entity with such a strong resemblance to the old one that fans, supporters and the general public cannot spot the difference. It may seem as if even liquidation may offer ways out of financial distress that allow football clubs to continue.

There are of course agency issues that provide strong disincentives for entering the administration and liquidation path of survival. The executive management of football clubs will most often try to avoid these alternatives. However, the specific characteristics of the football business create soft budget constraints that even in these extreme situations tilt the process in favour of continuation of the football club as a going concern in one form or another.

INSOLVENCY AND BANKRUPTCY IN EUROPEAN FOOTBALL

The primary impacts of SBCs on PTSCs appear before the stage of insolvency proceedings. In situations of financial distress, the softness of budget constraints is reflected in actions by rescuers who mobilize one or more of the softness conditions S1–S6. Deficits are covered, new capital is injected, credit terms are relaxed, subsidies or favourable pricing of deals are provided by local or national governments, taxes are not paid and/or deficits are disguised by creative accounting. This happens before situations of insolvency arise. The presence of SBCs may also have the effect that insolvency proceedings are not initiated in situations of actual insolvency. The tax authorities may choose not to initiate the required legal steps, creditors may choose to wait and owners and clubs may choose to muddle through, hoping for better days. This happens in other industries as well, but the environment around PTSCs makes such instances of SBCs more common in this context than elsewhere.

When clubs enter administration, they experience limits of softness, although SBCs may also influence the process after insolvency proceedings are initiated. They impact the possibility and the character of a deal with creditors to write off some debt so that the company is once again a going concern. This also impacts on the possibility of a sale of the assets of the club to a new owner where old debts are either written off by creditors or assumed by the new owner. It is more questionable whether this is a case of SBCs, as argued by Szymanski in his contribution to this volume, as the behavioural context is no doubt different than the one assumed to foster SBCs. This is not a situation of rescue which impacts on the behaviour of owners and managers in a way that softens budget constraints. However, new owners may have motives which are different from profits, such as ownership as consumption and/or a vehicle for higher profits in other lines of business. This induces future softness, and fans and the attached community may provide pressure for this solution. In other words, the environmental conditions and alternative owner motives may project softness of future budget constraints.

The other possible outcomes of insolvency proceedings are: closure of the club and the establishment of a new club with a similar name to play at the old stadium; full liquidation with all assets sold off and a new club with a similar name created and full liquidation and no revival of a club. All three alternatives definitely represent situations where the softness of budget constraints is not soft enough. Such cases show the limits of softness.

Insolvencies of PSCTs leading to the initiation of insolvency procedures with administration as the first step are not an unusual phenomenon. This section provides a brief overview of studies and major cases of clubs entering administration in the Big Five European leagues as well as Scotland and Denmark. The data document that it is very seldom that top-division clubs experience insolvency that leads to insolvency procedures, whereas this happens frequently in the second tier and in clubs in lower tiers. The data also show that it is very seldom that insolvency proceedings end with liquidation of the assets of the club. In the vast majority of cases, a deal is made with creditors to write off some debt so that the company can continue trading. In other cases, new owners take over the debt of the insolvent clubs.

England

Szymanski (2012, 2017) provides evidence of insolvencies of English football clubs in the top four tiers. The evidence shows that there were 67 club insolvencies involving legal proceedings between 1982 and 2010. All cases involve clubs participating in the second, third and fourth tiers of English football. Thirteen clubs experienced insolvency more than once over this period. All the professional football clubs that became insolvent still survive. 'Either new investors acquired the club and injected capital, or, in a small number of cases, the business was liquidated but the club was resurrected, and the new legal entity took over the stadium' (Szymanski, 2017, pp. 422–423).

In the top division of English football, only one club (Portsmouth Football Club) has ever formally entered insolvency proceedings. During the period

2010–2013, the club was put into administration twice. Large persistent deficits led to an accumulated debt of £135m, out of which £37m was owed to HMRC (the British tax authority). The second administration was preceded by a transfer of ownership, adding to a long chain of such transfers over a short period. The new owner was a Russian businessman. Soon after, a Europe-wide arrest warrant for alleged asset stripping of a Lithuanian bank was issued for the owner. The club was saved from liquidation in 2013 after being bought out by a fan-owned trust. At that time the club had twice suffered rounds of points deduction and three consecutive relegations.

Previously, Leeds United has experienced a similar fate. Similar to what happened to Portsmouth FC, the club over-invested after an initial spell of sporting success, and the subsequent fall was steep. The club entered into administration in 2007 but was saved after a deal of debt write-off and the entrance of a new owner. The process of sporting decline resembled the subsequent experience of Portsmouth FC, including points deduction and fire sales of players.

Regulation by the English Football Association (licensing, 'fit and proper' owner tests, etc.) has been strengthened in recent years. This is likely to have improved the situation. However, there have been many recent cases of administration in the lower leagues. A prominent example is Bolton Wanderers (2019). Another is Bury FC – a rare case of full liquidation that has not happened since 1992 when Maidstone United FC was forced out of the Football League and ceased to exist. At the time of writing, Bury FC still exists as an empty shell. In May 2021 the administrators put up the stadium for sale. The liquidation happened despite strong community and political support for the club. A group of fans formed a new club, Bury AFC, which has been permitted to enter the English football pyramid in its tenth tier, seven tiers down from Bury FC's League One status in 2019/2020. Bury had experienced continuous financial distress since 2001. A collapsed TV deal and perhaps the high density of league clubs in the Manchester area with a consequent smaller catchment area contributed to the collapse of the club.

Italy

Italian football has had its fair share of scandals including match fixing, illegal betting and mafia involvement. Bankruptcies also happen frequently. As in England bankruptcy is more common for clubs in the lower tiers than for the clubs in the top division (Serie A). A recent example is the chaotic start to the 2018/2019 season after three Serie B clubs (Avellino, Bari and Cesena) went bankrupt. Different from English football, the (local and national) government occasionally provides major subsidies to clubs in financial distress. An example is the '*Salvo Calcio*' decree introduced by the Italian parliament in 2002 (Storm & Nielsen, 2012, p. 194). The rescue of S.S. Lazio is another example. The club has been in almost permanent crisis. In 2005, it reached an agreement with the Italian tax authorities to pay an extraordinary €140m tax liability over an extended period of 23 years. The club has also suffered from financial irregularities involving owners, such as the scandal involving the club owner and his multinational food products company Cirio in 2002. Generally, it seems to be muddling through in a state of constant actual insolvency and staying in the race for buying top players in spite of relatively low revenues (The Laziali, 2020).

Despite the generally supportive institutional environment, there are examples of insolvency and liquidation of Italian top-division clubs. In most cases, liquidation is avoided, and the club is allowed to continue as a going concern. In other cases, a club with a similar name is reinstated in its prior league position very quickly. Prominent examples are Parma, Fiorentina and Perugia.

Parma was put into administration in 2004 and soon after was liquidated following the collapse of its parent company Parmalat. A re-formed club was allowed to stay in Serie A. However, financial troubles led to a succession of ownership changes and the club's eventual bankruptcy in March 2015, with total liabilities of €218m, including €63m unpaid salaries. A re-formed club was allowed to enter the fourth tier of Italian football. After successive promotions, it re-entered Serie A in the 2018/2019 season.

Fiorentina has for years over-invested in trying to achieve Italian and European success. Its sporting ambitions were fulfilled but the consequence was rapidly increasing debts, reaching €32m in 2002. The club was unable to raise sufficient funds to pay the players' wages so it went into administration in June 2002, resulting in its liquidation. A newly formed successor club started in the fourth tier in the 2001/2002 season (Serie C2) but it was already back in Serie A in the 2003/2004 season. The club skipped Serie C1 and was admitted into Serie B, which was only made possible by the Italian Football Federation's decision to increase the number of teams in Serie B from 20 to 24 and promote Fiorentina for 'sports merits'.

Perugia is an example of a major club which has not regained its prior status after liquidation. It folded in 2005 and was re-founded the same year under a new name, before dissolving once again in 2010, taking on its current name. Since then, it has played in the lower leagues. Although Perugia is a provincial club with a rather small market size, the club experienced a decade of extraordinary sporting success in the 10–15 years before its financial collapse. The architect was an eccentric entrepreneur who took over the presidency of the club in 1991. The club's sporting success was shadowed by a period of financial scandals, controversial signings and allegations of bribery, in addition to the accumulation of an unsustainable debt burden. In the end, nobody was willing to take over the club following its insolvency (Attwood, 2019).

Spain

Many Spanish football clubs were in deep financial trouble in the late 2000s and early 2010s (Bosca et al., 2008). In 2011, half of the clubs in the top two divisions entered insolvency proceedings (Minder, 2011). In 2012, the total debts of the clubs in La Liga were an astonishing £3bn (Gibson, 2010). Government subsidies and beneficial tax arrangements prevented mass-scale bankruptcies. Spanish football suffers from lack of solidarity and a huge financial divide between the two giants, Real Madrid and FC Barcelona, and the rest. For instance, there is no joint sale of television rights in Spain, which means that the two top clubs earn up to 100 times as much from this source than other La Liga clubs. Many clubs are constantly on the brink of collapse but are able to survive by means of soft taxation, soft credit and soft pricing (beneficial property deals).

In Spain, the tax authorities appear to be less prone to trigger insolvency proceedings and more willing to accept voluntary agreements to bring clubs out of administration than in most other countries. However, more important has been the tax scheme which has benefited football clubs that formally operate as non-profit entities. The scheme has been challenged by the European Commission as a case of violating EU state aid rules. For years, the regulators have been trying to stop highly successful commercial clubs such as Real Madrid and FC Barcelona from free riding on the back of taxpayers. The rulings by the European Commission against four La Liga clubs (CA Osasuna and Athletic Bilbao in addition to the two top clubs) were upheld in a decision by the European Court of Justice in March 2021.

The coronavirus pandemic initiated a new major financial crisis for Spanish football clubs following the suspension of La Liga in April 2020. Many clubs experienced major financial distress after the loss of broadcasters' revenue and matchday income. This time, the Spanish football association (RFEF) engineered a rescue package in the form a bailout plan of €500m to help the first and second division clubs financially. The money was raised after talks with several banks that were willing to offer a line of credit worth this total amount. The plan included flexibility of repaying the amount over a six-year period.

However, despite generous tax arrangements and soft credit several clubs have been put into administration, including clubs in the top tier. The most recent example is Malaga FC, which entered insolvency proceedings in 2020 resulting in the club putting its entire player squad up for sale. Remarkably, Real Madrid and FC Barcelona often not only record the largest revenues by far, but also the largest deficits. FC Barcelona recorded a staggering annual loss of €100m for 2019/2020 and a debt pile of more than €1bn. This is extreme even by the lofty standards of Spanish football, and the subsequent development will test the widespread assumption that successful FC Barcelona representing Catalan identity will never go bust even in the case of the most extreme softness.

Germany and France

German and French football clubs are generally perceived as better run than their counterparts in England, Italy and Spain. However, Szymanski & Weimar (2019) show that Germany is in fact little different from the rest of Europe, at least insofar as the financial instability of football clubs is concerned. Data from official insolvency procedures document 88 cases of insolvency of German football clubs in the period 1981–2017. The authors identify 21 cases where clubs that once played in one or both of the top tiers have become insolvent after relegation to a lower tier. Moreover, this includes examples of formerly prominent clubs, for example KFC Uerdingen (previously Bayer 05 Uerdingen), which went through insolvency proceedings in 2005. In 2003, VfB Leipzig, a former German champion, went bankrupt and was dissolved. Recently, another former Bundesliga club has gone bankrupt. In the 1990s, SG Wattenscheid 09 played for four seasons in the top division, but financial difficulties forced it to file for bankruptcy during the 2019/2020 season, resulting in relegation to the Oberliga Westfalen (the fifth tier of the German football league system) for the 2020/2021 season.

Scelles et al. (2018) examine insolvency in the top three divisions in French soccer. They identify 79 cases of insolvency in the period 1970–2014. Between 2009 and 2014, the clubs of Grenoble, Strasbourg, Gueugnon, Besançon, Sedan, Le Mans, Rouen and Vannes went bankrupt (ibid.). Additionally, Dermit-Richard & François, in their contribution to this volume, have identified four more bankruptcies since: Arles-Avignon (2014), Evian-Thonon Gaillard (2016), Istres (2017) and Bastia (2018). Examples of insolvency in the top division are rare. However, in December 2020, French football suffered a huge blow when a €3bn deal with a media company collapsed. This has major financial impacts on French league clubs. It is expected that several top-division clubs may not survive as a consequence.

Scotland

Scotland has the most famous – and infamous – case of financial collapse of a top football club: Glasgow Rangers. This case has peculiar characteristics and will be presented and discussed in a subsequent section of this chapter. In terms of the institutional environment around insolvency and liquidation, Scotland is not much different from England, and as in England, there are many examples of Scottish clubs entering insolvency procedures. However, compared to England there are far more examples in Scotland of clubs in the top division entering administration. Livingston FC entered administration twice, in 2004 and 2009. The club narrowly escaped from liquidation through the emergence of new owners. Two other recent cases from the Scottish Premier League are Heart of Midlothian FC and Dunfermline FC. Both clubs entered administration in 2013, and both were taken over by fan groups after debt reduction by means of CVAs. However, prior to the collapse of Glasgow Rangers, the end result has been liquidation and relocation of clubs in only three cases in the last half-century: Meadowbank Thistle (1995), Airdriedonians/Clydebank (2002) and Gretna FC (2008) (SPL Stats, 2012).

In this context, the case of Gretna FC is of special interest. Gretna is a highly unlikely place for a top football club, with a population of only 3,000. The club won promotion in three successive seasons, was runner-up in the Scottish FA Cup, qualified for the UEFA Cup and reached the Scottish Premier League in the 2007/2008 seasons. However, in 2008 the club was placed in administration. The financial status of the club was beyond repair. It was soon liquidated and ceased to exist. The supporters formed a new club playing in a league sitting in the sixth tier of the Scottish Football League system. The quick progress of the previous years was enabled through generous financial support from a maverick English businessman, Brooks Mileson. The equally spectacular demise followed the owner's sudden withdrawal of financial support in April 2008 and his death half a year later.

Denmark

In Denmark, there are at least six cases of bankruptcy of clubs in the top three tiers: Boldklubben Frem (1993 and 2010), Lyngby FC (2001), FC Nordjylland (2004), Køge (2009), FC Amager (2009) and FC Fyn (2013). Some of these cases (FC Nordjylland, FC Amager, FC Fyn). represent mergers going wrong, resulting in a return to the prior situation. The cases show that fan support may suffer from mergers as it is difficult to transfer a sense of identity and attachment to one club onto a merger with other clubs. Boldklubben Frem is located in a working-class area of Copenhagen and plays in a worn-out stadium. Its revenue streams do not match its aspirations linked to former greatness, and competition from other clubs in the capital has made it difficult for the club to survive. The most interesting case is perhaps Lyngby FC. The club had played in the top division since 1980 with much success (two championships and three cups) when it went bankrupt in 2001. It failed to mobilize enough local political support. The location of the club in an area with a large proportion of relatively old and well-off citizens and a sub-standard stadium made it difficult to generate substantial fan support. Further, the main owner of the club at the time was suspected of being involved in dubious financial activities which reduced the incentives among potential supporters for keeping the club afloat.

Summing Up

There are very few examples of top clubs in Europe that ceased to exist. Examples include KSV Waregem (Belgium) and FC Amsterdam (Netherlands) which both disappeared following mergers with other clubs. However, this is more common in countries without a long footballing history. Examples include the Los Angeles Aztecs in the USA and Dalian Shide and Jiangsu FC in China. All three clubs won national championships and folded soon after. In all cases the owners had little tolerance for lack of short-term profitability and fan culture was not entrenched.

Most cases of administration lead to a CVA, writing off debt. Such cases are incidents of SBC when this is intentional and/or initiated with the expectation of a positive outcome. However, as documented by Szymanski in his contribution to this volume this may have adverse impacts for management so it may not have the same behavioural consequences as other SBC cases.

THE CASE OF GLASGOW RANGERS – THE FALL OF A SPENDTHRIFT GIANT DESPITE UNIQUE SOFTNESS

One of the few cases of a large club being liquidated is almost the most unlikely case that you can imagine. Glasgow Rangers is a club with an extremely strong identity and high societal support. The emotional attachment of fans is unique as the club is linked to strongly entrenched religious, political and societal identities. It was also very successful in terms of sporting outcomes, having been successful in European competitions and having won the Scottish championship 55 times, which is a world record for domestic league championships. Even so, the club entered insolvency procedures in February 2012, and it was liquidated a few months later. The collapse of Glasgow Rangers (titled 'Rangers' in the following) shows (a) the extreme softness of budget constraints which made it possible for Rangers to hang on for long in spite of gross financial mismanagement, but also (b) that there are limits to softness. Even in such a club the budget constraints may not be soft enough. It is the purpose of the following case study to identify the context, the conditions and the actions that led to this outcome.

The Rangers case study[3] starts with a discussion of the role of the club in Scottish society. This is followed by a presentation of the events that led the club into financial administration, the unsuccessful attempts at agreeing a write-off of debt with creditors and the subsequent developments that led the phoenix club to start from the bottom in the fourth tier of the Scottish Football League system. The concluding section identifies the crucial factors behind the liquidation and the subsequent sporting demotion.

The Identity of Rangers

Glasgow Rangers was formed in 1872 and has been a dominant force in Scottish football ever since the start of the Scottish Football League in 1890. Rangers and another Glasgow club, Celtic FC, together have won 106 of the championships since then. Early on, Rangers and Celtic co-existed on relatively friendly terms. However, soon the two clubs became embroiled on opposing sides of the strong division lines in Scottish society, which the two clubs both represented and strengthened. Irish immigration to Scotland in the early 20th century created tensions. Celtic became the club linked to Ireland and the Irish diaspora in Scotland. Rangers, on the other hand, became the British/ Scottish establishment club. The tensions and mutual animosity between the clubs increased as a result of the political violence and upheaval during the Irish War of Independence (1912–1921). The subsequent tensions in Northern Ireland spilled over into the footballing rivalry in Glasgow. While the fans and the management of Celtic strongly supported the Irish Republican cause, Rangers became staunchly Unionist/Loyalist. Some Rangers fans have even openly applauded successful violent acts by paramilitary Protestant groups in Northern Ireland, with placards in the stands. The fact that the division was not only political but also religious entrenched the conflict even further. Rangers were openly Protestant and anti-Catholic. In 1918, the management of Rangers decided that they would not employ Catholic players. This ban was maintained for more than 70 years. The club rivalry was also enhanced by social and party political affiliations. The predominantly Irish fanbase of Celtic had relatively low average incomes and the vast majority voted Labour, whereas most fans of Rangers were better off, and the club had close links to the Conservative Party. Both clubs can be seen as thriving on the bitter and divisive segregation of Scottish society. The social and political differences between the fanbase of the clubs further contributed to the strong embeddedness of the two clubs on each side of the religious fault lines of Scottish society, linked to different loyalties in relation to 'the Irish question'. In the last decades, the tensions have been reduced. However, our case study club still has huge support based on a uniquely strong identity which made it highly unlikely that the club would not be rescued in case of financial distress.

The Path to Administration

During the 1990s and 2000s, Rangers regularly posted huge financial losses and accumulated an enormous debt, partly visible and partly hidden. A change of ownership in 1988 signalled a radical change in club strategy. The idea was to borrow for success through the acquisition of expensive star players. Transfer fee costs and the player wage budget increased substantially. This happened at a time when football clubs' revenues were boosted by the development of a multitude of new television opportunities and the associated increase in sponsorship. Debt financing was meant to ensure that Rangers would take advantage of the increase of new revenue sources through total dominance in the domestic league and European success. Although Rangers achieved sustained domestic success, success in European tournaments proved elusive. Despite significant growth in match attendance, sponsorships and other revenues, the overspending continued. In the period 1991–1996 alone, Rangers spent more than £30m on transfer fees. This was more than any other club in Britain which is remarkable considering the much higher revenues of English Premier League clubs. Further, extravagant wages were paid to international superstars to entice them to Glasgow (O'Donnell, 2019, p. 230), and debts grew to unseen levels. In the 1990s, the debt fluctuated between £20m and £40m (O'Donnell, 2019, p. 249). In 2003, the official figures showed a deficit of £30m and a total debt of £66m.

This was enabled by generous lenders, primarily banks (HBOS, and until 2001, Bank of Scotland, which then became part of HBOS) that provided the club with almost unlimited credit prior to the financial crisis of 2008/2009. This was partly an extreme result of the predominance of excessive lending in the pre-crisis period, and partly an effect of the perception of the club as one of the big Scottish institutions. Another reason was seemingly the social capital of the Rangers owner who had a 'bonhomie' relationship with the banks' directors. However, the banks were not completely happy with Rangers' overspending. In 1999, the main provider of bank loans, the Bank of Scotland, had tried to restrict Rangers' excessive spending through the acquisition of a 7% stake in the club that was meant as a 'security', i.e., a 'floating charge' on the club's income and assets, which would become a fixed charge in case of the event of insolvency.

The club attempted to raise additional capital. In 1996, the ENIC Group invested £40m in Rangers for a 20% share in the club which David Murray (the owner) bought back for £8.7m eight years later. Much less successful was an attempt in 2004 to raise funds from existing shareholders to reduce the club's debt. Only a little more than £1m was raised. However, the unsuccessful attempt to inject capital from others than the owner resulted in the injection of new capital (£50m) by the underwriter, which was the owner's mother company. The club was still effectively insolvent. The owner was merely moving vast amounts of money around his companies, borrowing money with one hand, and paying off Rangers' liabilities with the other. However, the banks were reassured by the consequent improvement of Rangers' balance sheets, which encouraged them to continue to bankroll Rangers. HBOS provided Rangers with a further £15m overdraft facility and agreed to restructure its remaining debt.

The taxpayers contributed a major although involuntary part in keeping the spendthrift money-losing club in business, which is what became decisive in the end. Part of this was open non-payment of taxes. Another part was the result of deliberate tax avoidance. Most important was the use of the so-called Employment Benefit Trust (EBT) scheme. The scheme worked as follows. The player received a normal wage supplemented by a loan. The employer paid money into an offshore trust, and, in addition to the fully disclosed salary, a player or any other employee would then be able to take a loan from their individual sub-trust and use it as a normal salary. The loans were supposed to be paid back after ten years, but the player could then apply for indefinite deferment, until he eventually died, at which point the amount could be written off against inheritance tax. Because the payments were technically loans, they were not subject to income tax and national insurance contributions, and the arrangement was attractive to both parties, although not for the tax authorities. The scheme is a legal form of tax avoidance and has been used in many companies. However, Rangers' application of the scheme was special in one important sense. It was accompanied by hidden side letters which explicitly guaranteed to the players that the money from the sub-trusts was actually (untaxed) additional payment that was never intended to be repaid, rather than loans. The problem was that if it could be proved that this was the case, the 'loan' would be disguised remuneration and taxable, which is why the side letters were kept secret. The EBT scheme was used by Rangers between 2001 and 2010. It helped Rangers continue to apply its loan-based acquisition of star talent.

Rangers had also applied another tax avoidance scheme, a Discounted Option Scheme (DOS), in connection with the purchase of two foreign star players. This was a form of tax planning that was popular at the time among bankers trying to avoid paying tax on their bonuses. The beneficiaries of the scheme were offered options of shares in an offshore 'money-box' company from where they could extract cash as a dividend. They could then avoid tax on the dividend if they did not bring their earnings to the UK. The tax authorities had deemed the scheme unlawful. This so-called 'wee tax case' added up to a £2.5m tax liability, which was recognized by the club but remained unpaid.

Much worse for the club was the aftermath of a raid on its offices in July 2007 by the City of London Police. The raid was meant to resolve issues in relation to under-the-table transfer payments in football. However, as an unexpected side-effect the raid uncovered a 'smoking gun' in the form of evidence of the actual use of EBTs, including side letters. The tax bill for the illegal application of the scheme added up to potentially £49m, including interest and penalties.

The threat of insolvency was imminent and something the Rangers chairman had to address on a daily basis. The fragility of the situation was addressed in

a statement by the club's chairman (O'Donnell, 2019, p. 275). He expressed
the belief that there was no danger of insolvency because the value of the
club's assets (players, stadium and training ground) was higher than the debt
figure. However, this was an obvious case of soft accounting with dubious
valuation of assets. Further, it ignored the ticking time bomb of the tax bill
connected to the use of the EBT scheme.

When the international banking crisis hit the economy in 2008, the severity
of situation soon became evident. In September, two days after the collapse of
the investment bank Lehmann Brothers, Rangers' bankers HBOS experienced
a liquidity crisis similar to the one earlier in the year that led to a run on the
Northern Rock bank and its subsequent transfer to public ownership. In the
case of HBOS, the government facilitated an effective takeover by another
bank, Lloyds TSB. As a result, Rangers lost its ability to independently govern
its business.

The takeover effectively ended the indulgent relationship between the
owner of Rangers and the directors of its main lender. Lloyds started to initiate
cutbacks with an embargo on signings and a potential fire sale of players.
However, they were unable to impose austerity. Only two players left in the
transfer window. Further, the expensive lifestyle of the club continued. Players
stayed at the same super expensive hotels and a pre-season trip to Australia the
following summer went ahead.

Despite the obvious overspending, the attempts by the bank to impose
restrictions were met with strong opposition from the fans. In October 2009,
the manager Walter Smith claimed that that Lloyds was effectively running
the club, which provoked furious fan groups to threaten an organized boycott
of the bank, and the bank's representative on the board was victimized as the
'enemy within'. There was seemingly no recognition of any limits to the softness of budget constraints among the supporters of the club.

In April 2010, it emerged that the financial situation of Rangers was even
worse than previously thought when HMRC (HM Revenue and Customs)
made clear the enormous tax bills following the club's use of the controversial EBT and DOS tax avoidance schemes. HMRC demanded an amount of
roughly £49m – on top of the debt to Lloyds (£30m). The claim was disputed
by Rangers, which argued that it was a case of legal tax avoidance. This started
a long march through tribunals and courts, ending with a final decision in the
Supreme Court in 2017 in favour of HMRC.

Still, the supporters of the club did not seem to realize the serious state and
the potential disastrous consequences of the club's financial troubles. Neither
was there any recognition that the trouble was self-inflicted. Most media
reports applauded the seemingly benevolent owner, which further ignited the
illusions and the furious backlash among the fans. It was through social media
rather than the established media that the detailed evidence of the scandal

was communicated (O'Donnell, 2019, pp. 311–312). Most traditional media seemed to be as seduced by David Murray as the friendly bankers whom he was able to convince to lend him the vast sums of money.

David Murray had felt the heat for some time. He had been trying in vain to sell the club since 2006. With the crippling debt burden and the potential tax bill, he took the club off the market. Many expected that he would use the ultimate softness card, i.e., entering the club into administration to clear its debt and then pick up the assets at a bargain price. However, surprisingly he was able to offload the club to a new owner, Craig Whyte, who bought the controlling interest in the club for a sum of £1 in May 2011. Part of the deal was a pledge from the new owner that he would clear the bank debt, settle the 'wee tax case' with HMRC and invest money into the playing squad and the stadium. The new owner had claimed to be a billionaire, but it soon became evident that his past should have been better scrutinized before the transfer of ownership went ahead.

The new owner fulfilled the pledge to pay off the Lloyds debt. However, he was far from a billionaire and did so by borrowing £26.7m from the firm Ticketus. The collateral for the loan was future season ticket sales, so in effect the transaction kicked the can down the road by restricting the future income of Rangers with the borrowed amount plus interest. After taking control of Rangers, Whyte took a step that further worsened its relationship with the tax authorities. He failed to remit the pay-as-you-earn (PAYE) tax, VAT and national insurance (NI) contributions to HMRC, which he used instead to pay day-to-day overheads. The liabilities of the 'wee tax case' were not met. There was huge pressure on Whyte to invest in the club. Expectations were raised high among the fans after media reports about his presumed 'off the radar' wealth. He announced his intention to make £25m available to the manager over a five-year period. However, there is no evidence of any investment from the new owner into the club during his brief spell as owner.

It emerged that Craig Whyte had previously been banned as a company director for seven years. Subsequently, the Scottish Football Association (SFA) investigated the purchase of the club and concluded that Whyte was not a 'fit and proper' owner. In June 2012, Strathclyde Police started an investigation into the purchase of the club and its subsequent financial management. In 2013, Ticketus successfully sued Craig Whyte for damages. The year after, he was arrested in connection with alleged fraud carried out during the purchase of Rangers and was banned from being a company director for 15 years. In 2015, he was declared personally bankrupt for non-payment of damages awarded to Ticketus.

Administration and Liquidation

On 14 February 2012, Rangers officially entered into administration, triggered by a successful petition by HMRC. It emerged that the club's total debts could be £134m. The tax liabilities were by far the biggest share. It consisted mainly of the accumulated unpaid taxes because of the EBT scheme, which was disputed by Rangers. Other considerable parts were the taxes owed by the 'wee tax case' and the lack of payment of PAYE, VAT and NI contributions initiated by Whyte which alone added up to £9m. Interest and penalties further increased the owed amount. In addition to tax liabilities, the club owed £26.7m to Ticketus. Further, there were debts to other football clubs and a multitude of other creditors, including The Scottish Ambulance Service, Strathclyde Police, Glasgow City Council as well as taxi firms, catering companies, face painters, local garages and fans with debenture seats at Ibrox, the club's stadium.

Whyte was allowed by the Court of Session to appoint his preferred administrators, Duff and Phelps, a firm that had advised and assisted him with the takeover of the club less than a year earlier. The firm was later criticized for treating the club with velvet gloves during administration. They did not proceed with the sale of players or other assets and allowed the club to carry on in attempting to sign a new striker while in administration. The administrators were criticized for giving too much priority to enabling Rangers to continue as a going concern rather than taking care of the interests of the creditors.

The administrators engineered a purchase of the club by a consortium led by the businessman Charles Green. The stated objective of the new owners was to exit administration via a CVA. Charles Green offered the creditors a total of £8.5m, a fraction of the total debt, with liquidation as the alternative. In addition, in the case of liquidation, a binding agreement with Green was put in place about transfer of the business and assets of the club, including the stadium, to a new company Sevco, owned by the consortium. The sum for this transfer was a modest £5.5m, including £1.5m for the Ibrox stadium and the Murray Park training ground. This is only a tiny fraction of the club's self-evaluation of the value of these assets at £119m in 2005, in an earlier attempt to fight off insolvency by overstating their value. There has seldom been a more transparent example of soft accounting.

The attempt to agree upon a CVA collapsed in June 2012. The death blow was dealt by HMRC, which voted against the agreement. HMRC had been offered £1.9m, a meagre amount which contributed to the decision to reject the deal. Further, the decision was in line with its policy of not voting for a CVA in cases where a company has a history of non-compliance with regard to tax obligations, which arguably was the case with Rangers. O'Donnell (2019, p. 330) concludes,

> There was simply no motivation on the part of HMRC to agree a settlement which may have incentivized other companies, including other football clubs, to disregard their financial responsibilities and obligations in the hope that they might ultimately be able to barter with the agency a few pence of a pound of what they were owed, once liquidation was looming.

The proceedings have not been finalized at the time of writing this chapter, but it appears unlikely that HMRC will end up with a higher amount than offered in the CVA. However, this was seemingly of less importance to HMRC than the implied deterrence of future offenders, or otherwise expressed, the effectual hardening of the budget constraint.

However, HMRC chose not to challenge Sevco's stripped-down purchase of the club's assets despite the option of covering part of the tax liabilities from a sale of the assets at the market price. HMRC abstained from forcing a selling-off of the stadium and the training ground and explained in a statement that 'the intention is not to wipe Rangers off the face of the map'. Although it is difficult to use physical assets such as Ibrox and Murray Park for other purposes, a sale of those assets could arguably have covered a much higher part of the tax liabilities of the club than any alternative outcomes of the liquidation. However, the tax authorities chose to preclude this possibility, which can be seen as an additional softening of the budget constraint in the sense that it contributes an important precondition for the success of a phoenix club.

Following the rejection of the CVA, the sale of the business and assets of Rangers to Sevco Scotland Ltd proceeded as agreed. An accountancy firm, BDO, was appointed as liquidators. The liquidators later sued Duff and Phelps with a claim of £56.8m for failing to pursue the interests of the creditors by engineering a sub-value sale of the physical assets and for failing to sell high-profile players. BDO are believed to have had Ibrox valued on the open market at £25m, before Sevco ended up buying the assets of the club for £5.5m in June 2012. This follows a multitude of other legal cases in the aftermath of the collapse of Rangers. For instance, Duff and Phelps had earlier agreed a £25m settlement for being made responsible for a 'malicious prosecution in connection with the collapsed club fraud case'.

An attempt to engineer a supporter buyout of the Sevco consortium was rejected, which led to calls for supporters not to renew their season tickets in order to starve the new owners of funds and force them out. This was effectual even if it did not achieve its ultimate aim. Only 250 season tickets had been sold in early July. As a result, Royal Bank of Scotland declined to provide

Rangers with the corporate banking facilities it needed. Further, the primary sponsor Tennent decided to remain but renegotiated a substantially smaller deal.

The independent inquiry of the Scottish Football Association (SFA) into the purchase of the club concluded that the club had brought 'the game into disrepute' for becoming insolvent and imposed a year-long transfer embargo and fines totalling £160,000. This decision provoked anger among the Rangers owner and the fans. In vain, the club used all the formal options of appeal. Representatives of the club accused the SFA panel who made the decision of wanting to kill Rangers and attempted to intimidate the members of the panel through abusive and threatening communications.

The Sporting Aftermath

The name of the liquidated club was 'The Rangers Football Club plc'. Sevco changed its name to 'The Rangers Football Club Ltd'. This was a subtle change which was meant to enable a seamless re-emergence of the club as if nothing had happened. It was seen as crucial to ensure that the history of the club was not broken, and in spite of attempts by Celtic fans and others to deny the new company the right to represent a continuation of the old Rangers, this is what has gradually been accepted.

Sevco had hoped and perhaps expected that the Scottish Premier League would allow the new Rangers entity to take the place of the old Rangers, allowing it to play in the SPL in the 2012/2013 season. There is an obvious economic rationale for such an expectation. The economic and sporting dominance of Rangers and Celtic in Scottish football is overwhelming (Morrow, 2015, pp. 330–333). The two clubs generate about 70% of the SPL turnover. Further, other SPL clubs have high attendances from their home matches with the two top clubs. Sixty-five per cent of the average audience in the 2010/2011 season was from the so-called Old Firm derbies between Rangers and Celtic. Twenty-eight per cent of the attendance was from other matches involving either Rangers and Celtic, whereas only 6% of the audience attended matches in which neither Rangers nor was Celtic involved. Accordingly, the other SPL clubs had a clear economic interest in keeping Rangers on board. If they punished the club beyond the traditional means of points deduction, they would bring substantial economic damage on themselves.

However, the SPL decided against an automatic re-entry in spite of the economic self-interest of its members. This forced the new Rangers to apply for direct entry into the SFL (Scottish Football League) First Division (the second tier of Scottish football). This would have brought substantially extra revenues to the First Division clubs. However, they also decided to neglect economic self-interest and decided instead to let the club re-enter the league system in its fourth tier (the Third Division). The re-entry was preconditioned by a year-long transfer embargo and payment of all outstanding fines and football-related debts. After three promotions in four years, Rangers re-entered the SPL for the 2016/2017 season. In the 2020/2021 season, the club won the Scottish championship after nine years of uninterrupted Celtic dominance.

Summary

The Rangers story is an extreme case of tension and contradictions between sporting and financial logic (Morrow, 2015). Often, the financial logic takes precedence over the sporting logic, but sometimes it is obviously the other way round. The strategy of debt-financed growth in a period of increasing revenue streams was not without an economic/financial rationale. At least, this was so in the beginning. However, the continuation of overspending was rather a case of predominance of sporting logic. The decision to relegate Rangers to the fourth tier was obviously a case of sporting logic trumping financial logic. The sporting logic was mostly carried by the fans and supporters. The supporters of the other SPL clubs had discussed the topic for months on social media, and a consensus around a resounding 'no' to the option of the new company taking the place of the liquidated Rangers had emerged with such strength that it would be difficult for the clubs to allow this to happen. The outcome is seen by some as an example of other clubs taking revenge on a club which had for a long time had out-competed them by illegal means. It can also be seen as a fan-led decision giving priority to sporting integrity instead of economic concerns.

The Rangers case provides ample evidence of the existence of soft budget constraints. All the six types of SBC outlined at the beginning of this chapter can be identified in this case. Other unique types of softness can be identified as well. The most important types of softness that allowed the club to overspend in such spectacular fashion for so long were soft taxation and soft credit. Soft taxation took many forms, from open non-payment of taxes to hidden fraudulent transactions. Limits to soft taxation proved in the end to be the undoing of the club. The tax authorities decided to take the legal route of triggering insolvency procedures, and later to force liquidation by rejecting the suggested CVA, rather than accepting the non-payment of taxes. Soft credit was provided by the banks all way through until the limits of credit under the conditions of the credit crunch curtailed borrowing and debts.

The non-payment of bills to a number of small creditors can perhaps be seen as non-voluntary loans – i.e., soft credit – or soft subsidies to the club. The sale of the liquidated club's assets to Sevco at a heavily discounted price is an example of soft pricing that made it possible for the phoenix club to continue as Rangers with as little disturbance as possible. Further, there were many examples of soft accounting. The widely different valuation of the club's physical assets dependent on the purpose of the valuation is testament to the extreme flexibility of this measure. It appears that the club regularly used soft accounting as a means to disguise actual insolvency, fend off the creditors and fool business partners, fans, the media and the general public.

The Rangers case also provides evidence of forms of softness which are not included in the typology of softness (S1–S6) presented earlier in this chapter. This typology does not take into account the possibility of additional softness in the process of administration and liquidation. Rangers experienced softness during the process of administration as a result of the administrators' actions, although these actions did not end with an agreement that would allow the club to clear its debt burden before proceeding with its business, as is the common outcome when football clubs enter administration. Further, after liquidation, the new company was provided with opportunities to proceed in the footsteps of the old company without too much disruption, if it had not been for the punishment meted out by the football authorities which did not allow the club to re-emerge in one of the top leagues soon after. Of course, these forms of softness beyond the initiation of insolvency procedures, and even beyond the burial of the old club, are different from the other forms of softness in the sense that the behavioural implications are different. The management of football clubs does not deliberately use the possibility of soft liquidation procedures to limit the disturbances experienced in the transfer from the old to the new club. It is also evident that in most cases the clubs will fend off administration by all means available. However, this is not necessarily so in other cases. As Szymanski shows in his contribution to this book, many CEOs and managers often survive insolvency procedures ending in CVAs, and the mere possibility of survival may provide an incentive to the club management to use administration as a means to clear the business of its debts. In other cases, the pressure from other stakeholders for taking advantage of soft administration may force the management to choose voluntary administration in spite of its own narrow self-interest.

THE CASE OF GOG – OVERSPENDING, CREDIT CRUNCH AND COLLAPSE OF A SMALL-TOWN CHAMPION

The Danish team handball club GOG went bankrupt in 2010 and was, like Rangers, demoted. Like Rangers, the club quickly recovered under new legal entities, returning to the top tier within a few years and won the Danish championship in 2021/22. Yet, the clubs have little else in common. Glasgow has over 600,000 inhabitants, and Rangers has average 50,000 spectators at home, while GOG – enclosed by farmland in the small village of Gudme with under 900 inhabitants – averages 1,780 spectators for its home matches (2021/22). The difference in size is further manifested in their respective debt burdens. While GOG had total debt obligations of €3m when declared bankrupt, Rangers had accumulated £134m/€156m in debt upon its liquidation (2019 prices).

GOG is a textbook case[4] of a club which is the rallying point of a minuscule society. Despite its location and modest catchment area, it has been one of the most successful handball clubs in Danish history. The club was founded in 1973 and became a dominating force in Danish team handball from the mid-1980s until its bankruptcy in 2010. From 1987–2010, the men's side won seven championships and had just two finishes outside the top three, while the women's side had 11 top-three finishes from 1987–2003, including four championships. Internationally, team handball is considered a niche sport. However, it enjoys significant media attention in Denmark, where it is the second most popular sport (Hedal, 2006). Its popularity has been influenced by the success of the national teams. Throughout the mid-1990s and early 2000s, the women's national team became one of the most dominant teams in the international team handball scene, winning three European Championships (1994, 1996, 2002), one World Championship (1997) and three Olympic Championships (1996, 2000, 2004). The men's national team won their first medal in recent history at the European Championships in 2002 and their first gold medal at the European Championship in 2008 and again in 2012 and won the Olympics in 2016 and the World Championship in 2019 and 2021. Despite handball's popularity, it remains a small business. In 2018/2019 the average turnover in the men's top tier amounted to just above €2m (Alfast Nielsen & Storm, 2020). In comparison, the average turnover in football's top tier was approximately €24m, including non-football related activities (C.G. Nielsen et al., 2020).

While no public records exist of GOG's financial information prior to 1999, Nielsen writes that revenue amounted to approximately €0.4m in 1987 (E. Nielsen, 2017, p. 79). First-team players were compensated with €26 (2021 prices) for each point, with a win equalling two points and a draw one point, €13 in travel allowance if they had to take the ferry, and an additional €644 if they won the championship (p. 58). During the 1990s, team handball gradually became more professionalized. As resources for the purchase of players in team handball were limited – with the Bosman ruling not in effect until 1995 – the importance of a strong talent development system was pronounced, and GOG excelled in this discipline. The club even reached the men's Cup Winners Cup Final in 1995 while primarily fielding local talent. To date, GOG is, without parallel, the most successful Danish club measured by youth team performances. However, as the commercialization of team handball increased in the late 1990s and 2000s, so did competition for talent, and it became increasingly more difficult to hold onto local talent without offering players competitive economic compensation. In the early 2000s, several resourceful football clubs entered the handball market, threatening the establishment, which responded by increasing their costs in the arms race for talent. League revenues (and costs) increased steadily until 2008, but in the aftermath of the financial crisis, in just one year, from 2009 to 2010, revenues declined by 32%, sending many clubs to the verge of bankruptcy, and while most clubs were rescued, GOG was declared bankrupt on 26 January 2010. It was ultimately the negative shock to the Danish handball economy in the aftermath of the financial crises that led to GOG's bankruptcy. Yet, it was also the culmination of a debt that had grown out of proportion and was hidden by unsustainable accounting practices.

A Balanced Start

In 1999/2000, GOG A/S was established as a limited liability company running the men's and women's first-tier squads on the licence of the amateur club. The club played in a municipally owned arena run by a quasi-public self-governing institution, Fonden Gudmehallerne.[5] GOG was relatively well-run during its first years as a professional entity and managed to balance income – with over two-thirds of revenue coming from sponsorship deals – and costs, resulting in modest (accounting) profits. Further, the club successfully ran a commercial newspaper and a graphic production subsidiary. At the same time, debt was kept at a manageable level. GOG strengthened its capital base in its first financial year as a professional entity (1999/2000), raising €410,000 (2021 prices) in net revenues by issuing Class B shares. This amount, however, was less than expected, and was therefore considered a minor disappointment (BT, 2000).

The Acquisition of the Arena

GOG was located in Gudme Municipality[6] with a population of less than 6,500, and throughout the period GOG found itself on a commercial tightrope between being locally anchored and increasing its market size. Being a club in the countryside has both strengths and weaknesses. In a small community, the club is typically the beacon of the local area, which can strengthen the proximity and local attachment to the club (Nielsen et al., 2019), but it can also be commercially limiting due to the modest customer base. In GOG it was primarily larger national brands located outside of Gudme that were the main drivers of sponsorship revenue (Nielsen, 2017, p. 80), which is why the club considered moving its home matches to the larger market of Svendborg[7] and Denmark's third-largest city, Odense,[8] as the only feasible solutions.

To keep GOG in Gudme, the municipality began working towards selling the arena to the club in an attractive deal (Abildtrup, 2002). In 2003, the club acquired it at a bargain price through a newly founded subsidiary, Gudmehallerne A/S. GOG acquired a 22% stake in Gudmehallerne A/S, including all Class A shares with full rights to all future dividends as well as majority voting rights (74%) for €174,000 (2021 prices). Fonden Gudmehallerne injected its total equity of €0.7m, including a loan of €77,000, for 78% of the (Class B) shares in exchange for one board representative (of four) and 'the right to use the facilities at a reasonable price' (Sandgaard, 2012). While the loan – which has never been paid back – is an example of *soft credit*, the injection of equity was de facto a subsidy to GOG, and hence a *soft investment*. This was underpinned shortly after when the arena was revalued within the first year of the takeover.

'Fair Value' as a Soft Accounting Tool

Acquiring the arena through a subsidiary was the starting point of a vicious debt cycle which allowed GOG to (increasingly) engage in creative accounting. The club treated the arena as an investment property, where revaluation is recognized on the income statement using the fair value model. Hence, appreciation of the property boosts (accounting) profits, while depreciation reduces them. Although 'fair value' should be based on the maximum use of observable data and minimal use of non-observable data (PwC, 2020, pp. 45–50), in practice the estimates can often be arbitrary and discretionary. Hence, if a business can convince the auditor that the estimates are generally in the accurate range, it can give them wiggle room to 'adjust' profits. The lack of transparency regarding the revaluation process makes it difficult to ratify with certainty whether appreciations are a result of creative accounting. It can be even more challenging to evaluate the fair value of a sports arena, having characteristics of a local monopoly, with no directly comparable market. Despite this, the revaluations of the arena were highly conspicuous, and a board member elected in November 2009 – with insight in the accounting practices applied before his inauguration – argues that the revaluations were an 'income regulator' for GOG A/S with the purpose of concealing the true state of affairs (Interview, 1 July 2020).

In March 2003, Gudmehallerne A/S acquired the arena for €1.9m (2021 prices), while real estate appraisers valued it at €2.1m in October the same year. Despite this, management chose to revalue it at €2.6m within the same financial year. It was decided that the added equity only applied to the Class A shares, all owned by GOG. This manoeuvre increased the 'value' of its stake nearly threefold, which turned a large deficit of nearly €0.5m into a marginal profit. Remarkably, the board declared with no further comments that the result was satisfying and that it was the fifth year in a row that GOG A/S had managed to show a profit (GOG A/S, 2004). Despite a decline in operational profits – and a 73% decline in 2004/2005 (Gudmehallerne A/S, 2005) – the arena was appreciated twice during the next four years. When the operational profits of Gudmehallerne A/S increased to new highs in 2008/2009 it was once again revalued by €0.4m (2021 prices). However, in 2009/2010 – the year GOG was declared bankrupt – the arena was depreciated by approximately €0.5m after a new board, with a new managing director, had taken control of the new business entity (reconstruction), GOG 2010 A/S. After the bankruptcy, GOG 2010 A/S and Fonden Gudmehallerne negotiated a reduction in the bank's receivables in exchange for sponsorships, and acquired the Class A shares for the same nominal amount as the bankrupted entity had done in 2003 (Sandgaard, 2012).

An Attempt to Increase Market Size

Although the 'fair value' method allowed GOG to artificially boost accounting profits, it was nothing more than a pretence which postponed the problems. A year later (2004/2005), it became apparent that the club was in serious difficulties. Its equity had dropped dangerously low, and the Danish Handball Association had further decided to strengthen the capital requirements, with effect from 2008. As a response, GOG resolved to raise capital by once again issuing shares. This brought in approximately €0.5m (2021 prices) in net revenues, which allowed the club to stay afloat (GOG Svendborg TGI A/S, 2006). Although the club had succeeded in bringing in *external investments* in both 2000 and again in 2006, the actual economic resources invested were modest, indicating a lack of (economic) support for the club.

GOG found itself in a difficult situation with the funding of two elite clubs (men's and women's). The Danish women's league was considered the best in the world at the time, which manifested itself in European dominance, with Slagelse FH and Viborg HK winning six of seven Champions League titles from 2004–2010. Although no public information exists of the allocation between the men's and women's sides, former managing director Arne Buch estimated that, in 2006, the payroll was split 55–45 in favour of the women (Nielsen, 2017, p. 88). However, while the men's side enjoyed immense sporting success, winning the championship in 2003/2004, securing third place in 2004/2005 and finishing runners-up in 2005/2006, the women played for secondary positions. Despite attempts to hide this fact in the annual reports, there was a clear imbalance between revenues and costs, and GOG had to increase incoming cashflow to keep up with – and preferably surpass – the top clubs in spending power. To do so, the club initiated an official strategy to become 'the team handball club of Funen'[9] by relocating an increasing number of matches to Svendborg and Odense. As a part of this strategy, GOG acquired the small newly promoted neighbouring club Tved G&I, located on the fringe

of Svendborg. To increase its appeal to citizens, potential sponsors and investors in Svendborg, the club changed its name to GOG Svendborg TGI. The
ambitions were higher than ever: the men's side should now become a serious
competitor at the international level, while the women's team should return
to the top of the Danish league and qualify for a European final within five
years (GOG Svendborg TGI A/S, 2006, p. 5). Further, a construction plan for a
3,000-capacity multi-arena in Svendborg was released. However, GOG exper-
imented with relocating some of its matches to an arena in Svendborg with
little success, and the new arena never materialized (Nielsen, 2017, p. 220).
In 2007/2008 GOG relocated all but one of the women's home matches to
Odense, yet despite a massive increase in the average attendance, from 867 to
1,951, it did not become an apparent commercial success, and further the move
met resistance at the grassroots level (Nielsen, 2017, p. 89).

Increased Competition and Growth Slowing

The 2006/2007 season became an apparent sporting success for the men's side,
who won the Danish championship with a parade of world-class talent, including Mikkel Hansen (later three-times 'World Player of the Year') and Niklas
Landin (later two-times 'World Player of the Year'). The revenue growth, in
handball was on the rise and in just three years – from 2004/2005 to 2006/2007
– GOG had increased its sponsorship revenues by 44%, while simultaneously
increasing its debt.

Following the championship, many of the best players left the club, and due
to the massive revenue growth it had become increasingly expensive to hire
players on new contracts. Further, the dominance of the established clubs was
challenged by Parken Sport Entertainment A/S – the conglomerate behind the
football club FC Copenhagen – under the brand FCK Handball, founded in
2004. In 2007/2008, the team won its first championship, defeating GOG in
the final. Despite an impressive display in the Champions League, including
two draws against the later winners from Ciudad Real, GOG's position as
a permanent top-three club was now threatened.

GOG had experienced a 229% growth in sponsorship revenue from
the establishment of the professional organization in 1999 to 2007, but in
2007/2008 sponsorship revenue remained stagnant. While sponsorship contracts were mostly seasonal, player contracts were up to three years in length,
and as a reaction to the increased competition for talent, clubs often signed
contracts with players up to one and a half years in advance (Interview, 1
July 2020). Many clubs came under pressure when sponsorship revenues
did not rise as projected, as they were still obligated to pay their players
on longer-term contracts. In 2007/2008, GOG reported a loss of €0.4m. In
one year, the club had increased its short-term debt by 43%, from €1.4m to
€2.0m, while debt-to-equity doubled from 1.6 to 3.2. In the annual report,

management wrote the following: 'A positive development is expected in the financial year of 2008/09. With increasing revenue and a very tight cost control it is the expectation that the net result will be positive' (GOG Svendborg TGI A/S, 2008, p. 5). The expectations can seem naive – as indeed they were – considering that the annual report was released during the financial crises in November 2008. Yet, at the time the prevailing belief was that the Danish entertainment sector was immune to the general turmoil that hit the rest of the economy. Additionally, Denmark had just won the European Men's Handball Championship in January 2008, which was believed to have a positive economic effect on the domestic league.

Spending Frenzy

Despite the optimism and focus on tight cost control expressed in the annual report, GOG's sponsorship revenues dropped by 21% in 2008/2009, while staff costs increased by 10%. In 2008, three board members – who later resigned voluntarily as a consequence of how the club was run (Dyssel & Grube, 2010) – warned the management as well as the rest of the board that the club was heading towards bankruptcy (Nielsen, 2017, p. 283). However, this had little effect on the club's spending habits. Most spectacular – and controversial – was the signing in mid-2008 of the Danish international Kasper Nielsen, who became the highest-paid player in the Danish league (Kjer, 2008). The player later played a leading role in GOG's bankruptcy and was proclaimed as the villain by some. Allegedly, the board had agreed unanimously that Kasper Nielsen was too expensive, but 11 days later Arne Buch had signed him regardless (Nielsen, 2017, p. 224). Also allegedly, Arne Buch had contacted some of the board members personally after the meeting and convinced them to accept the deal (Interview, 1 July 2020). Remarkably, none of the board members resigned on this occasion.

Weighed down by the financial crises, it became apparent that some of the sponsors could not live up to their responsibilities, while the bank further hardened the credit constraint, tightening the terms of the club's overdraft facility (Ertmann, 2009). The club had to reduce its payroll heavily and/or attract larger investors to avoid bankruptcy. In April 2009, GOG managed to negotiate a four-month temporary 20% pay cut with all 50 employees in the organization (Holbech, 2009a). Until this point GOG had maintained full autonomy, holding 80% of the voting rights, but when its existence came under threat, it was decided that the club had to sell off its Class A shares in mid-2009. The club was able to raise approximately €0.5m from new investors, which was the minimum requirement for the club to be able to continue its operations (Herning Folkeblad, 2009), but still not nearly enough to avoid bankruptcy. Once again, GOG had struggled to bring in larger sums of capital in problematic times.

To raise further capital and cut costs, the contractual rights of the women's side were transferred to a new company and sold off in a deal bringing in approximately €0.5m, while GOG kept a minority stake (Nielsen, 2017, p. 226). Yet, the club's financial situation was so critical that it could not get the financial statement approved and signed by an auditor, which was a requirement for transferring the first-tier licence. GOG therefore applied for a dispensation from the rules due to extraordinary circumstances, arguing that the divestment would be crucial to avoid bankruptcy, which the committee allowed (Mitchell, 2009) – an example of *soft regulation*. In mid-2009, the German club Melsungen contacted GOG offering to take Kasper Nielsen on loan, paying approximately two-thirds of his yearly salary. Despite the economic turmoil and the threat of bankruptcy, GOG declined the offer as, according to Arne Buch, it was considered 'way too unattractive as it did not even cover his salary in GOG' (Jyllands-Posten, 2009). Arne Buch – who had been employed by the club since 1987 – was fired in October 2009. He later explained the reasoning behind the increased risk-taking:

> The Danish national team had won the European Championship in January 2008, which we believed would result in a boom in the men's handball league, similar to what happened to women's handball in the 1990s. We simply had to be willing to put the money on the line. As champions in 2007 and runners-up in 2008, we were in a favourable position when the boom would strike.[10] (Nielsen, 2017, p. 90)

The gamble, however, did not pay off, and for the first time since 2000, the men's side finished outside the top three, in fourth place.

The Bankruptcy

In November 2009, when a newly elected board presented the 2008/2009 annual report applying the 'going concern' principle (GOG Svendborg TGI A/S, 2009), a record high deficit of €1m (2021 prices) was reported, in spite of a further €0.4m appreciation of the arena. The debt was higher than ever, equity was negative and the 'staff costs-to-turnover ratio' was now over 100%. Many of the new investors felt that they had been tricked into investing in GOG by the old management due to untransparent accounting methods. In this regard, the new managing director accused the old board and executive directors of applying unsustainable accounting practices, implying the use of *soft accounting* (Holbech, 2009b). In June 2010, the total debt was assessed to more than €3m (2019 prices) by the curator, including €0.74m owed to the tax authorities, while assets were valued at only €0.25m (Dyssel, 2010).

According to the board members, at one point GOG had not been paying its taxes for 12 months, but the local tax authorities had not raised claims against the club (Interview, 1 July 2020). This was a case of *soft taxation*. According to a later board member, 'GOG did everything in their power to postpone all their debt and show a "balanced" income statement. However, it only resulted in inflated numbers, but did not bring liquidity. It was not illegal, but definitely creative' (Interview, 1 July 2020). Further, its subsidiary Gudmehallerne A/S had taken a €0.3m loan with the arena as guarantee. The funds had then been re-channelled into the club with capital from selling the Class A shares as guarantee (ibid.).

At an extraordinary general meeting in the days before Christmas, the new management and board of directors launched a rescue plan that involved the injection of fresh capital into a new business entity and then transferring the first-tier licence to the new entity (Lindholt, 2009). However, it required that the players accepted a temporary reduction in their salaries, while claims from banks and tax authorities were up for negotiation as well. On 5 January, they had still not found a solution, and the club was forced into administration, being deducted two points (Bech, 2010). The negotiations with players proceeded while multiple GOG players – including Kasper Nielsen – were participating at the European Men's Handball Championship in January. Yet, on 26 January, GOG was declared bankrupt in court by the clubs' supervising attorney. The negotiations between the club and Kasper Nielsen had collapsed, and the supervising attorney decided – on behalf of the board – to declare the club bankrupt: 'We negotiated until 10–15 minutes before the hearing today, but a few key elements – including issues regarding a single player (Kasper Nielsen's salary reduction) – were unsolvable' (Holbech, 2010). According to Kasper Nielsen, he had already signed a deal accepting a pay cut a few days earlier, but later said that the club wanted him to accept a new deal, which he had accepted by e-mail, though without signing the agreement (Nielsen, 2017, p. 271). In the news, it appeared as if it was the missing signature that was the problem (Ritzau, 2010). However, according to one of the board members, it was a disagreement about the contract length – a private treaty agreement of two further years that was not stated in the official contract – which was the straw that broke the camel's back and ultimately led to the decision to liquidate the club (Interview, 1 July 2020).

Why Softness was Not Enough

GOG's bankruptcy was, however, an outcome of multiple factors. First, the club accumulated too much debt, which it tried to conceal by applying various accounting tricks. Second, while the club was able to increase its spending, as the sponsorship revenue kept rising, the financial crises led to the collapse of the house of cards. The financial pressure and need for rationalization among the sponsors had devastating consequences for GOG, which also suffered from the stricter lending terms. Third, although GOG had some political backing, it was not so pronounced that it had significant influence on the club's survival. In 2007/2008 – after Gudme became a part of the Svendborg Municipality – the municipality signed a sponsorship deal (approximately €60,000 yearly) with GOG. A citizen filed a complaint in 2008 claiming that the deal was illegal. However, Svendborg Municipality was able to demonstrate that it received a more than fair return from GOG (Jakobsen, 2008). The state administration, monitoring public sponsorships, decided that the deal was fully legal and hence could not be considered a (*soft*) subsidy (Holst, 2017). However, while GOG was the local focal point in Gudme Municipality, Svendborg Municipality was more detached from the club. This is underpinned in a report from 2008 – initiated by Svendborg Municipality – concluding that remarkably few associated GOG with Svendborg Municipality (Corcom, 2008). Fourth, GOG never really succeeded in attracting large investors when issuing shares. This may be due to the limited market size and the lack of potential investors – in the form of businesses and high net worth individuals – in the immediate area, together with the fact that handball does not enjoy the same status as football.

Further, after the club was declared bankrupt, Kasper Nielsen wondered aloud whether the board actually preferred the club to go bankrupt (Nielsen, 2017, p. 271). Although the statement is conspiratorial, from a theoretical perspective it is not inconceivable that bankruptcy was the preferred outcome, as the problems kept piling up. Taking the overwhelming debt, the difficult business environment and GOG's relatively poor history of raising capital into consideration, it is likely that the temporary salary reduction would simply postpone bankruptcy or force the club to lower its longer-term sporting ambitions. Despite demotion to the third tier, getting rid of all debt seemed more favourable from a longer-term perspective.

Szymanski discusses the impacts on the management of bankruptcy in his contribution to this volume. In the case of GOG, the impacts were limited. In 2009, board membership had been reduced from nine to three. The three members of the new board were all reconstituted as three of the seven members of the board – and one of them as chairman – of the new business entity. Although this development could not have been predicted with absolute certainty, it is unlikely that the possibility of adverse consequences for management had significantly modifying effects on a preference for writing off debts in the insolvency situation.

CONCLUSION – WHEN ARE SOFT BUDGET CONSTRAINTS NOT SOFT ENOUGH?

The examples of insolvency and liquidation included in this chapter show the softness of budget constraints experienced by these clubs in the process leading up to insolvency and liquidation. There is evidence of widespread existence of all six types of softness. Possibly, another form of softness can be added. Soft regulation is explicitly mentioned in the GOG case, but it is actually quite common that the implementation of the rules and regulations of the football associations is less than strict, which can be seen as another type of softness. This type of softness may occur when clubs experience financial distress while still being going concerns. However, as the Rangers case shows, it may also prevail when a club undergoes insolvency proceedings or is even in the process of liquidation.

Beech et al. (2010) identify five types of insolvency in English football clubs, which include clubs that have failed to cope with relegation; failed to pay monies due to the government; seen 'soft debts' become 'hard debts'; lost the ownership of their stadium; or have become 'repeat offenders'. Most of the cases of insolvency identified in the chapter fall within one or more of these five types, but there are other causes as well, as evidenced by the cases summarized in this chapter. In this concluding section, we will contribute to answering the question 'when is softness not soft enough?' by summarizing the causes for insolvency – and liquidation – in the cases covered by this chapter.

It is likely that many PTSCs survive long periods of insolvency. The most immediate cause for the collapse of PTSCs is hardly insolvency in itself, but rather *too much* accumulated debt. Debt repayment can be postponed, repayment terms can be renegotiated and new loans can be taken up, but at some point the indebtedness is simply too much. One of the creditors, or the club itself, then initiates the insolvency proceedings and the house of cards collapses. However, it is difficult, if not impossible, to define when much is too much. This depends on the status of the club, its support and the preferences of the creditors. It also depends on the way the club perceives its overall situation. It may misread the situation and believe that there is still some wiggle room left when the creditors initiate insolvency procedures.

The structure of the debt is also important. Most often, it seems to be a petition from the tax authorities that initiates insolvency procedures. As shown by the Rangers case, it may also be the tax authorities that decline to sign a CVA, thereby triggering liquidation of the club's assets. It is more difficult for a local bank or other creditors with a physical presence in local communities to be directly instrumental in forcing a club out of existence, but national tax authorities are less prone to local pressure. Other creditors may also be more inclined than the tax authorities to accept a CVA with only very small pay-outs rather than forcing liquidation, because of expectations of only modest rewards from liquidation. Such expectations may not be as important for the tax authorities, which may prefer liquidation because of its longer-term effect as a deterrent to other clubs. Further, the football creditors rule acts as a disincentive for triggering insolvency proceedings for non-football creditors, as the remaining amounts may be rather low once the football creditors have been paid. However, this may be a less important concern for the tax authorities than for other creditors. Nonetheless, in many of the insolvency cases covered in this chapter, the insolvent clubs seem to have miscalculated the importance of the structure of the debt. Often repayment or restructuring of bank debts is given priority over payment of unpaid taxes even when debts to the tax authorities are higher than other debts.

The behaviour of the tax authorities towards PTSCs is not only dependent on the size of the debts and the intended deterrence effect. It seems to harden the resolve of the tax man if the troubled club has a record of repeated non-compliance with tax rules. This is even more so in cases of fraudulent behaviour by the club. In the Rangers case, the use of aggressive tax avoidance schemes may itself have had this effect, but the hidden side letters most definitely did. Of course, political interests may also interfere with the decision making in some contexts. This is more predominant in some countries than in others. There are cases in Spain and Italy where political interference or political pressure has influenced how tax authorities behave in situations of actual insolvency.

Although it is often the size of the tax liabilities that prove decisive, it may well be debts to other creditors such as bank debts that are the cause for the collapse of clubs. This is the case when 'soft loans' become 'hard loans', which happened in the Rangers case when the previous lenders became part of Lloyds Bank. Such changes may also result in the breakdown of supportive social networks between club owners, club chairmen, bank directors and others.

Ownership of clubs is often of crucial importance for the survival of clubs in financial distress. Existing or new owners may prevent insolvency and the initiation of insolvency proceedings through injection of new cash. New owners may step in when existing owners are unable or unwilling to go on to support the club financially. This may also happen as part of the insolvency proceedings. However, sometimes the accumulated debts are so high that new owners cannot be found. In such cases, supporters' trusts may come up with just enough money to take over the club following a CVA. In some unique cases, the owner of a club has been so generous prior to insolvency that a total collapse is unavoidable if the owner suddenly withdraws support, as happened with Gretna FC and Perugia.

Owners of football clubs and other PTSCs are typically wealthy individual entrepreneurs/tycoons, although other forms of ownership exist. Ownership by big corporations is rare but does exist, especially in Italy. This can be a mixed blessing. It guarantees potential access to relatively unlimited funds. However, it also makes the club vulnerable to crises and even the collapse of the supporting company, as shown in the case of Parma. Ownership by fans/supporters is another form of ownership that often emerges as the outcome of insolvency proceedings – a form of 'safety net' that guarantees the continuation of the club, possibly as another legal entity. Here the problem is almost the opposite that of ownership by big corporations. Limited funds may constrain investment in players and sustained ownership by supporters is limited to lower divisions.

The collapse of football clubs is sometimes linked to the characteristics of owners. Eccentric behaviour by an owner may keep the ball rolling for a while but may also lead to a spectacular collapse, as happened in the case of Perugia. Owners may have records of dubious business transactions. Unfortunately, this may not be fully transparent at the point of takeover of the club. The purchase of Rangers by Craig Whyte is one such case. The introduction of checks by the football associations as to whether a prospective owner is a 'fit and proper' owner is an imperfect means to prevent clubs from engaging with dodgy buyers. Sometimes, the mere suspicion of fraudulent behaviour by a club owner may make it more difficult to gain enough support from the local municipality and local banks to fend off crises, as it was the case with Lyngby.

In other cases, insolvency of PTSCs is caused by economic events outside of the control of the clubs. The credit crunch in 2008/2009 had major efforts on many clubs, as did the pandemic in 2020/2021. The collapse of GOG was, to a large extent, an effect of the 2008/2009 financial crisis, mainly via its negative effects on sponsorship revenue. It also contributed to Rangers' crisis, through the negative impact on its main lender banks which ended up as part of a bank with less tolerance towards high club indebtedness. There are also examples of more indirect impacts of financial crises on clubs' finances when declining property prices expose clubs that have diversified into property investment. Other external developments with severe negative impacts on the finances of PTSCs leading to insolvency and administration include the collapse of TV deals such as the ITV Digital deal with the English Football League in 2002 and the French Ligue 1's deal with a media company in 2020.

By far the largest cost item for clubs is player wages. Failure to pay players in time is often a symptom of insolvency (e.g., Parma and Perugia), which may trigger bankruptcy and liquidation. Often, players accept a significant wage reduction to save the clubs. However, in other cases (some) players do not accept this, as happened in the Rangers case. Fire sales of players, and maybe the full squad (e.g., Malaga), may be necessary. In this situation, the market conditions strongly favour buyers with very low transfer fees as a result, as happened in the case of Leeds United. The clubs will only earn a very small sum from the fire sales, which contributes to the collapse of the club.

Pressure from fans/supporters/local communities has major impacts on the finances of clubs. Club owners are expected to invest rather than earn a profit. Sporting success has absolute priority, and there is little tolerance for measures taken to balance the books if it has impacts on the chances of promotion or avoiding relegation. On the other hand, a strong fanbase and support from the local community attracts investors, mobilizes soft credit and other forms of SBC, and helps clubs prosper. However, this is obviously insufficient when clubs fail. The limits of softness depend on the strength of the fanbase and local support. Clubs in municipal areas with a high density of PTSCs are particularly vulnerable, as their fanbase may be more limited and volatile and local community support less entrenched than in areas where clubs have a larger market size and are unchallenged carriers of local identity. When clubs merge there is a risk that the constituent units suffer in terms of fan support as the fans may not transfer their full loyalty to the new entity. This may contribute to the collapse of a merger club.

Relegation is often seen as a major cause for financial difficulties which in some cases end in administration. There are obvious material reasons for this, such as significantly lowered revenue combined with difficulties in reducing the wage bill in the short run. However, other factors impact as well. Perceptions of the status of the clubs contribute to financially unsustainable decisions when relegation to a lower league is seen as an exception that will need to be counteracted quickly.

The collapse of clubs may also be caused by sharpened regulation by the football league association. Generally, the licensing rules and the penalties for entering administration have become stricter over time. This is intended as a preventive measure, but points penalties and relegation to lower divisions may also push some clubs into administration. In other cases, the introduction of more stringent administration of rules regarding approval of club takeovers by new owners has prevented clubs from crucial injections of investment that may have improved their chances of survival, at least in the short run.

The list of possible causes for the collapse of PTSCs despite the widespread existence of soft budget constraints mainly refer to clubs entering insolvency proceedings. In some cases, this ends with the liquidation of the clubs. This may be triggered by a failure to find new owners or too many creditors rejecting the CVAs on offer. Often, the sale of the liquidated assets is unlikely to bring in much cash to pay off creditors, which is an incentive to accept a CVA with even very modest repayment. However, in many cases the tax liabilities constitute a significant share of the debt, which means that a CVA fails if the tax authorities do not accept the agreement, which they may sometimes do to deter other clubs from pursuing growth through high indebtedness.

Another issue is what happens after liquidation. Typically, the club is allowed to continue in another legal form, often playing in and owning the same stadium. The major penalty in such cases is relegation on top of points deduction. The club can be relegated to a division one or more tiers lower in the league system. Even in the case of relatively clear rules, this is, to a large extent, up to the (other) league clubs who may choose to implement the sporting logic embedded in the rules, as happened in the Rangers case. They may alternatively choose to bend the rules following the financial logic, as has happened in other cases such as Fiorentina. Very seldom does it happen that clubs fold without the emergence of a phoenix club. Such exceptional cases occur in countries like China and the USA, where the local embeddedness of clubs is limited, where fan culture is relatively undeveloped and where clubs are allowed to follow a purely financial logic.

This section has provided an overview of reasons for the collapse of PTSCs. Together, this constitutes a preliminary answer to the question of when softness is not soft enough. The answer is preliminary as it is mainly based on two case studies supplemented with a brief overview of major cases of administration and liquidation in seven European countries. The overview is likely to cover some of the main circumstances and contexts that constitute limits of softness. However, more research is needed. This may take the form of testing hypotheses developed from the above overview. It may also take the form of more in-depth case studies. Such future research is important not only to further develop the theoretical approach but also to help provide more empirical clarity and instrumental practical advice.

NOTES

1. See also the chapter by Bertheussen and Solberg in this volume.
2. Bankruptcy and the initiation of insolvency proceedings, or insolvency proce-dures, are synonyms for the same legal process.
3. The fall of the giant club received a lot of media interest, and several books and academic articles studying the events have been published. The following case study is primarily based on two books (see O'Donnell, 2019 and Whyte, 2020) and an academic article by Morrow (2015), supplemented by a website about 'Administration and liquidation of The Rangers Football Club (https://en .wikipedia.org/wiki/Administration_and_liquidation_of_The_Rangers_Football _Club_plc), as well as some of the media sources listed in that website. O'Donnell (2019) has been particularly useful. The book provides a detailed dis-cussion of the history of the club and a thorough analysis of the events leading to its eventual liquidation and the emergence of a phoenix club. It has been accused of a Celtic-leaning bias by supporters of Rangers. However, the detailed analysis of the financial collapse of the club seems to be both very well researched and balanced.

4.   This case study is based on data from the news media, annual accounts and a monograph about the case (Nielsen, 2017). Further evidence originates from interviews with board members.
5.   Fonden Gudmehallerne consisted of six representatives from amateur sports clubs using the facility, including GIG's amateur department.
6.   In 2007, Gudme merged with Svendborg and Egebjerg Kommune due to a structural reform with the purpose of merging municipalities into larger entities.
7.   Svendborg is located approximately 15 km from Gudme and had a population of 28,000 in 2002.
8.   Odense is located approximately 45 km from Gudme and had a population of 145,000 in 2002.
9.   GOG is located on the southern part of the island of Funen which in 2006 had a population of 447,060.
10. Translated from Danish.

REFERENCES

Abildtrup, N. (2002). GOG pressede kommunen. Retrieved 29 June 2020, from https:// fyens.dk/artikel/gog-pressede-kommunen.

Ahtiainen, S., & Jarva, H. (2020). Has UEFA's financial fair play regulation increased football clubs' profitability? *European Sport Management Quarterly*. https://doi .org/10.1080/16184742.2020.1820062.

Alfast Nielsen, M., & Storm, R. K. (2020). Stabil omsætning men tilbagegang i årsresultaterne for dansk håndbold før coronakrisen. Retrieved 9 September 2020, from https:// idan.dk/nyhedsoversigt/nyheder/2020/b332_stabil-omsaetning-men-tilbagegang-i -aarsresultaterne-for-dansk-haandbold-foer-coronakrisen/.

Andreff, W. (2007). French football: a financial crisis rooted in weak governance. *Journal of Sports Economics*, 8(6), 652–61.

Andreff, W. (2014). Building blocks for a disequilibrium model of a disequilibrium model of a European team sports league. *International Journal of Sport Finance*, 9(1), 20–38. Retrieved from https://www.scopus.com/inward/record.uri?eid=2-s2.0 -84894201089&partnerID=40&md5=4c63237c546918eb7d0f003e4d37fcd1.

Andreff, W. (2015). Governance of professional team sport clubs: Agency problem and soft budget constraint. In W. Andreff (Ed.), *Disequilibrium Sport Economics: Competitive Imbalance and Budget Constraints* (pp. 175–223). Cheltenham, UK and Northampton, MA: Edward Elgar Publishing Limited.

Attwood, A. (2019). The madness of Luciano Gaucchi, the owner who took Perugia to Serie A through whatever means necessary. https://thesefootballtimes.co/2019/05/ 20/the-madness-of-luciano-gaucci-the-owner-who-took-perugia-to-serie-a-through -whatever-means-necessary/.

Bech, M. (2010). GOG går i betalingsstandsning. Retrieved 29 June 2020, from https:// politiken.dk/sport/haandbold/art4832942/GOG-går-i-betalingsstandsning.

Beech, J., Horsman, S. J. L., & Magraw, J. (2010). Insolvency events among English football clubs. *International Journal of Sports Marketing & Sponsorship*, 11(3), 236–249.

Bosca, J. E., Liern, V., Martinez, A., & Sala, R. (2008). The Spanish football crisis. *European Sport Management Quarterly*, 8(2), 165–177.

BT (2000). GOG til aktierne. Retrieved 29 June 2020, from https://www.bt.dk/sport/ gog-til-aktierne.

Conn, D. (2004). *The Beautiful Game: Searching for the Heart of Football*. London: Yellow Jersey Press.

Corcom (2008). *Mit Svendborg*. Skævninge. Retrieved from https://lasso.dk/firmaer/ 25927117/corcom-vsren-jrstian-ndrer-selskabsform-og-skifter-navn/Q1ZSLTEtMj U5MjcxMTd8Ni40fDcvNi8yMDE2lDEyOjAwOjAwIEFNfEV0bGl2.

Dyssel, H.-H. (2010). GOG-gæld på over 20 mio. kroner. Retrieved 30 June 2020, from https://fyens.dk/artikel/gog-gæld-på-over-20-mio-kroner.

Dyssel, H.-H., & Grube, O. (2010). Nikkedukker i GOG-bestyrelse. Retrieved 29 June 2020, from https://fyens.dk/artikel/nikkedukker-i-gog-bestyrelse-2010-1-29

Ertmann, B. (2009). GOG har økonomiske problemer. Retrieved 29 June 2020, from https://jyllands-posten.dk/sport/handbold/ECE4085077/GOG-har-økonomiske -problemer/

Franck, E. (2014). Financial Fair Play in Europen club football: What is it all about? *International Journal of Sport Finance*, 9(3), 193–217. https://doi.org/10.2139/ssrn .2284615.

Franck, E. (2018). European club football after 'five treatments' with Financial Fair Play – Time for an Assessment. *International Journal of Financial Studies*, 6(97). https://doi.org/10.3390/ijfs6040097.

Gibson, O. (2010). La Liga debts reach £3bn to leave Spanish game in crisis. *The Guardian*, 19 May.

GOG A/S (2004). *GOG A/S årsrapport for 2003/2004*. Gudme.

GOG Svendborg TGI A/S (2006). *GOG Svendborg TGI A/S årsrapport for 2005/2006*. Gudme.

GOG Svendborg TGI A/S (2008). *GOG Svendborg TGI A/S årsrapport for 2007/2008*. Gudme.

GOG Svendborg TGI A/S (2009). *GOG Svendborg TGI A/S årsrapport for 2008/2009*. Gudme.

Gudmehallerne A/S. (2005). *Gudmehallerne A/S årsrapport for året 2004/2005*. Gudme.

Hedal, M. (2006). *Sport på dansk tv. En analyse af samspillet mellem sport og dansk tv, 1993–2005*. København: Idrættens Analyseinstitut.

Herning Folkeblad (2009). GOG har fundet pengene. Retrieved 29 June 2020, from https://www.herningfolkeblad.dk/artikel/84afc215-164b-4f51-a14a-98b834f9c030/.

Holbech, O. (2009a). Alle i GOG går ned i løn. Retrieved 29 June 2020, from https:// www.tv2fyn.dk/fyn/alle-i-gog-gar-ned-i-lon.

Holbech, O. (2009b). Redningsplan for GOG trækker ud. Retrieved 29 June 2020, from https://www.tv2fyn.dk/fyn/redningsplan-gog-traekker-ud

Holbech, O. (2010). GOG konkurs efter dramatisk forløb. Retrieved 29 June 2020, from https://www.tv2fyn.dk/fyn/gog-konkurs-efter-dramatisk-forlob.

Holst, B. (2017). Tilsyn ikke i tvivl: Kommunale VIP-billetter er lovlige. Retrieved 3 July 2020, from https://www.midtjyllandsavis.dk/artikel/d9eca19f-6eb9-405b-8904 -4e60743ae8af/.

Jakobsen, F. (2008). GOG-sponsoratet er for billigt. Retrieved 3 July 2020, from https://fyens.dk/artikel/gog-sponsoratet-er-for-billigt-2008-3-17.

Jyllands-Posten (2009). GOG afslog millionbeløb. Retrieved 29 June 2020, from https://jyllands-posten.dk/sport/handbold/article4261958.ece/.

Kesenne, S. (1996). League management in professional team sports with win maxi-mizing clubs. *Journal of Sports Economics*, 1, 56–65.

Kjer, M. (2008). Kasper Nielsen er den dyreste. Retrieved 29 June 2020, from https:// sport.tv2.dk/2008-07-31-kasper-nielsen-er-den-dyreste.

Kornai, J. (1979). Resource-constrained versus demand-constrained systems. *Econometrica*, 47, 801–819.

Kornai, J., Maskin, E., & Roland, G. (2003). Understanding the soft budget constraint. *Journal of Economic Literature*, 41(4), 1095–1136. https://doi.org/10.1257/002205103771799999.

Lago, U., Simmons, R., & Szymanski, S. (2006). The financial crisis in European football: An introduction. *Journal of Sports Economic*, 7(3), 3–12.

Lindholt, B. (2009). GOG-aktionærer sagde ja til redningsplan. Retrieved 29 June 2020, from https://fyens.dk/artikel/gog-aktionærer-sagde-ja-til-redningsplan.

Maskin, E. S. (1999). Recent theoretical work on the soft budget constraint. *American Economic Review*, 89(2), 421–425. https://doi.org/10.1257/aer.89.2.421.

Minder, R. (2011). A dark cloud over Spanish football. *New York Times*, 18 April.

Mitchell, J. (2009). Odense klar til Håndboldligaen. Retrieved 29 June 2020, from https://www.bt.dk/haandbold/odense-klar-til-haandboldligaen.

Morrow, S. (2015). Power and logics in Scottish football: The financial collapse of Rangers FC. *Sport, Business and Management: An International Journal*, 5(4), 325–343.

Nielsen, C. G., Pedersen, L. B., & Storm, R. K. (2019). The value of having a first-tier football club in the municipality (even) when tangible benefits are absent. *Sport, Business and Management: An International Journal*. https://doi.org/10.1108/SBM-2018-0055.

Nielsen, E. (2017). *Gudmekongerne – bogen om GOG*. Odense: Turbine.

O'Donnell, S. (2019). *Tangled in Blue. The Rise and Fall of Rangers FC*. Worthing: Pitts Publishing.

PwC (2020). *Regnskabshåndbogen 2020*. Hellerup.

Ritzau (2010). Kasper Nielsen beklager GOG-konkurs. Retrieved 29 June 2020, from https://fyens.dk/artikel/kasper-nielsen-beklager-gog-konkurs-2010-1-26(2).

Sandgaard, F. (2012). Ejendomshistorier Gudmehallerne. Retrieved 29 June 2020, from https://www.svendborghistorie.dk/historier/ejendomshistorier/782-gudmehallerne.

Scelles, N., Szymanski, S., & Dermit-Richard, N. (2018). Insolvency in French soccer. *Journal of Sports Economics*, 19(5), 603–624.

Seawright J., & Gerring, J. (2008). Case selection techniques in case study research: A menu of qualitative and quantitative options. *Political Research Quarterly*, 61(2), 294–308.

SPL Stats (2012). Liquidation and relocation in Scottish football (and how to deal with the history). https://splstats.wordpress.com/2012/06/24/liquidation-and-relocation-in-scottish-football-and-how-to-deal-with-the-history/.

Storm, R. K., & Nielsen, K. (2012). Soft budget constraints in professional football. *European Sport Management Quarterly*, 12(2), 183–201. https://doi.org/10.1080/16184742.2012.670660.

Storm, R. K., & Nielsen, K. (2015). Soft budget constraints in European and US leagues – Similarities and differences. In W. Andreff (Ed.), *Disequilibrium Sport Economics: Competitive Imbalance and Budget Constraints* (pp. 151–171). Cheltenham: Edward Elgar Publishing. https://doi.org/10.4337/9781783479368.00012.

Szymanski, S. (2010). *The Comparative Economics of Sport*. Palgrave Macmillan.

Szymanski, S. (2012). Insolvency in English professional football: Irrational exuberance or negative shocks? North American Association of Sports Economists. *Working Paper Series*, Paper No. 12-02.

Szymanski, S. (2017). Entry into exit: Insolvency in English professional football. *Scottish Journal of Political Economy*, 64(4), 419–444.

Szymanski, S., & Weimar, D. (2019). Insolvencies in professional sports: Evidence from German football. *International Journal of Sport Finance*, 14, 54–68.
The Laziali (2020). Lazio: Financial problems exist. https://thelaziali.com/2020/04/07/lazio-financial-problems-exist/.
UEFA (2010). *The European Club Footballing Landscape.* Club Licensing Benchmarking Report. Financial Year 2008. Nyon: UEFA.
UEFA (2020). *The European Club Footballing Landscape.* Club Licensing Benchmarking Report. Financial Year 2018. Nyon: UEFA.
Whyte, C. (2020). *Into the Bear Pit.* Edinburgh: Arena.

Index